EAT WELL
The YoChee Way

The Easy and Delicious Way to Cut Fat and Calories with Natural YoChee [Yogurt Cheese]

NIKKI & DAVID GOLDBECK

CERES PRESS

Acknowledgments
Our thanks to the following folks for their advice, support and patience: Rudy Schur, Cathy Lewis, Peter Desberg, Meredith Gould, Joan Munkacsi, Katie Jellinghaus, Iris Litt, Sandra Gebbeken, Barry Samuels, Mark Black, Diane Kniss, Boyce Brawley, John-Michael Savocca, Philip Greenberg, Carl Dixon, Mark Fortier, Maryann Palumbo, and Greg Mowrey.

Other books by Nikki & David Goldbeck
The Healthiest Diet in the World
American Wholefoods Cuisine
The Good Breakfast Book
The Smart Kitchen

Printing: 10 9 8 7 6 5 4 3 2
First Edition
Copyright Nikki and David Goldbeck, 2001. All rights reserved.
Cover design by Katie Jellinghaus

Library of Congress Control Number: 2001092186

ISBN: 1-886101-09-4

Ceres Press
PO Box 87
Woodstock, New York 12498
845-679-5573
HealthiestDiet.com
cem620@aol.com

Printed in Canada

❧ Contents ❧

INTRODUCTION

In the thirty years we have been helping people discover healthier ways of eating, YoChee is the closest we have come to finding what one might consider a miracle food. *YoChee* is our new name for what is often called yogurt cheese—an age-old food with an awkward name. We adopted this name because YoChee deserves a more modern and attractive designation. Coincidentally, YoChee evokes the well-known Chinese word *chi*, which means energy.

This under-appreciated food has the ability to overcome many of today's most significant food dilemmas. It is hardly a secret that people love foods with a rich creamy texture. Unfortunately, it is very easy for our diets to become overburdened by these foods, which are invariably high in calories and fat—particularly the troublesome saturated fats. YoChee, however, allows you to actually (forgive us) "have your cake and eat it, too." (No need to take our word for it. Just try the Very Berry Shortcakes on page 282 or the Custardy YoCheesecake on page 289.)

We did not discover or invent YoChee. In fact, it has been eaten for generations in the Middle East, where it goes by many names, including leban, lebanee, labna, chaka or suzma, depending on what country you are in. What we have discovered is that it can be added to the daily diet in many more ways than traditional leban-eaters ever imagined. What we have invented are the 275 recipes and numerous tips we offer here to entice you to make YoChee a regular part of your life.

WHAT IS YOCHEE?

One could say that YoChee is the *essence of yogurt*, or yogurt in concentrated form. This might not sound like a big deal. "I eat already eat yogurt," you might say, "and it's healthy as it is." Indeed, in the last thirty years people have come to appreciate the health and culinary benefits of yogurt. So why bother with a whole book about concentrated yogurt?

Here's why: because with YoChee you will enjoy all of yogurt's qualities, only now they will be even better. The simple act of concentrating yogurt by draining it and removing some of the liquid transforms it into a new food that is more nutritious and much more versatile. By preparing dishes with YoChee, you can achieve the sensual delights of many once-fatty foods and at the same time improve your diet.

A pleasant surprise is that to make YoChee all you have to do is spoon yogurt into a draining device and let gravity do all the work. If you can use a spoon, you can make YoChee.

WHAT IS THE YOCHEE WAY?

Eating The YoChee Way means no more than simply substituting YoChee for high-fat foods like butter, margarine, cream cheese, sour cream and mayonnaise on your table and in cooking. This one step can substantially lower your intake of fat and calories and add valuable protein and calcium to your meals. YoChee is the key to making your diet better right now.

WHO NEEDS YOCHEE?

* Everyone interested in eating healthfully

* Calcium-seekers

* Protein-seekers

* The lactose-intolerant

* Vegetarians

* Meat-eaters (Although there is no meat, poultry or fish in the book, by providing reduced-fat alternatives to commonly eaten foods, meat-eaters have an important tool for lowering overall fat and saturated fat intake.)

FOR NONCOOKS

There will always be a healthy cream cheese-like spread ready to use in your YoChee maker. This is the first thing you can do with YoChee that you can't do with yogurt—spread it. As a matter of fact, many people never use it for any purpose other than as a spread instead of butter, cream cheese and mayonnaise. Think of it, just a few hours after you spoon some yogurt into a draining device, you can start smearing it on a bagel or muffin! In return you will save as much as 40 to 100 calories and 5 to 10 grams of fat per tablespoon (see YoChee's Nutritional Makeup for more details). If you never use YoChee for anything else, this alone will be worth the small effort needed to make it.

Furthermore, with YoChee you can create numerous simple dishes that you thought you could only make with high-fat foods. For example, it excels when it comes to creamy salad dressings, as demonstrated in our Creamy Orange Vinaigrette and Thick & Creamy Blue Cheese Dressings. And it is an ideal replacement for some or all of the mayonnaise in your favorite egg, macaroni, tuna, chicken or fish salads, where it improves the flavor, texture and nutritional value.

YoChee can similarly enhance beans, pasta and grains either during cooking or at the table. You will be amazed by the taste transformation that takes place by simply adding a few spoonfuls of YoChee—what we call YoChee pearls —to stews, chili, soups, rice, macaroni with sauce, even salads.

COOKING THE YOCHEE WAY

When it comes to cooking, YoChee can serve you in ways that might seem impossible. Because it is more heat-tolerant than yogurt—which tends to curdle in hot foods—you can prepare numerous dishes without depending on high-fat ingredients.

Imagine—creamy soups, smooth spreads and NoWorry sauces and dessert toppings that have *no* fat and *no* artificial ingredients. Get ready for OneLESS egg recipes, where YoChee acts as a natural egg extender (and also adds protein and calcium). Enhance your menus with YoChee versions of Onion Dip, Caesar Salad, Black Bean Hummus, Stuffed Portobello Mushrooms, Pasta Alfredo Style, lasagnas, pizzas, Russian Vegetable Pie, Mushroom Risotto, YoChee pestos and more.

Getting people to eat vegetables is an ongoing problem. YoChee makes vegetables more attractive, easily replacing butter and high-fat sauces as a flavoring. Sweet Cream Carrots, Garlic Mashed Potatoes, Beautiful Beets, Broiled Tomatoes and Spicy Orange Coleslaw are just a few of the recipes that are sure to improve everyone's view of these vital foods.

When used in frozen desserts and puddings, YoChee imparts a rich, smooth texture. You are rewarded with sweet treats such as Chocolate Mousse, Tortoni, Fresh Fruit with Raspberry Swirl, and Soft-Serve Banana YoChee that are low in fat and calories and make notable contributions in terms of protein and calcium.

In baking, YoChee produces cakes with a tender crumb—much like sour cream does, but without the all the fat and calories. Indulge in Creamy YoChee Brownies, Fresh Fruit Coffeecake, Skillet Pear Cobbler and the like, and at the same time make a positive contribution to your diet.

Tᴀᴋɪɴɢ Tʜᴇ YᴏCʜᴇᴇ Wᴀʏ ɪꜱ Eᴀꜱʏ

To make things as convenient as possible, *Eat Well The YoChee Way* includes instructions for making YoChee, plus approximately 275 recipes for using it in everything from soup to dessert. The recipes are easy to follow, use readily available ingredients and are designed for new as well as experienced cooks.

Numerous tips, simple suggestions and fast assemblages make YoChee accessible to everyone.

A ⏰ beside the recipe title indicates especially easy choices. In addition, each recipe is accompanied by a nutritional analysis, including calories, protein, fat (both saturated and unsaturated), carbohydrates and calcium.

In time you will discover many original ways to use YoChee. We hope you will share them with others by posting them on our website at YoChee.com or HealthiestDiet.com.

Finally, keep in mind that while YoChee is a very valuable part of a healthy diet, it cannot create good health on its own. This is why we combine YoChee with whole grains, legumes and lots of vegetables and fruit to provide dishes that are full of flavor and exemplary food value.

Join us on The YoChee Way. You'll never look back.

Nikki & David Goldbeck

WHY YOCHEE?

Rich creamy foods are tempting because of their smooth "mouthfeel," or melt-in-your-mouth sensation. As we said earlier, the price of this pleasure usually comes in the form of fat, and often the troublesome saturated kind. YoChee can provide a similar sensual experience, but remarkably it can be low in fat or fat-free, depending on the yogurt it is made from.

YoChee is an excellent source of protein and calcium, two very important nutrients. Therefore, by adding YoChee to more of the foods you eat, you can continue to enjoy the sensual pleasures associated with fatty foods and at the same time actually improve their nutritional value.

Since plain, unflavored yogurt has many similar qualities, you may ask why you should convert it from a soft pudding-like consistency into a thick, spreadable cheese. Our response: For the tiny amount of work involved, there is an enormous return.

* YoChee can take the place of some or all of the mayonnaise, sour cream, cream cheese, whipped cream, solid shortenings, oil or eggs in many familiar dishes. Once this potential is recognized, even unskilled cooks can easily find new applications.

* YoChee is simple to make. There is no cooking, and it takes just seconds of your time. All you need are a few simple utensils and the force of gravity.

* YoChee has a pleasing taste that is less tart than the yogurt it came from.

* YoChee made from low-fat or even nonfat yogurt has the same pleasurable effect on the palate that is generally associated only with high-fat foods.

* YoChee concentrates yogurt's nutrients so that you get more value from an equal volume.

* YoChee tolerates heat well, making it more practical in cooking than yogurt.

YoChee Nutrition

Taste generally comes first in determining a food's acceptance. Because YoChee is so versatile, we have found that taste alone is enough to interest people in it. (When you get to the recipes, you will see what we mean.) Nonetheless, YoChee has more to offer than just good eating. It also has extraordinary health-enhancing qualities.

The principal nutritional elements in YoChee are protein, calcium, potassium and the B vitamins riboflavin and B_{12}. Although there will be some differences in nutritional makeup depending on the brand of yogurt used, comparisons with other foods show-off its outstanding qualities (see YoChee's Nutritional Makeup, page x).

Calcium

½ cup YoChee provides 235mg. calcium.

The calcium contribution of YoChee is impressive—just one-half cup furnishes about 235mg. of calcium. This figure may be even higher if the yogurt your YoChee is made with contains such calcium-boosting ingredients as whey or nonfat dry milk solids.

YoChee provides more calcium than a comparable portion of yogurt, despite the fact that about one-third of the initial calcium is lost to the liquid that drains out. Furthermore, YoChee has much more calcium than the 150mg. found in the same volume of milk, a food that is widely promoted for its calcium value. Low-fat cottage cheese, although similarly low in calories and fat, has just 70mg.

In addition, YoChee offers a far better calcium return than the high-calorie, high-fat foods it easily replaces. For example, cream cheese contains 90mg. of calcium per one-half cup, and as little as 65mg. when it's whipped. The same amount of sour cream, another food that is superfluous when YoChee is available, provides 130mg. of calcium. Whipped fresh heavy cream contributes just 40mg. per half cup, while mayonnaise, which YoChee can once again supplant, offers a mere 20mg .

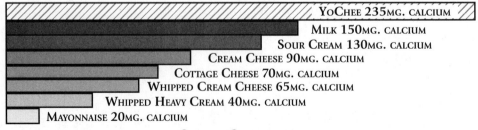

YoChee 235mg. calcium
Milk 150mg. calcium
Sour Cream 130mg. calcium
Cream Cheese 90mg. calcium
Cottage Cheese 70mg. calcium
Whipped Cream Cheese 65mg. calcium
Whipped Heavy Cream 40mg. calcium
Mayonnaise 20mg. calcium

Calcium Comparisons

YoChee's high calcium content can be of great benefit, as this key mineral is deficient in many people's diets. Not only is it important for bone strength in growing children and adults to protect against rickets and the serious bone-weakening condition osteoporosis, it is equally vital in other areas of health.

The United States government recommendations regarding calcium intake are:

Ages 4 to 8 – 800mg. calcium daily
Ages 9 to 18 – 1,300mg. calcium daily
Ages 18 to 50 – 1,000mg. calcium daily
Age 51 thereafter – 1,200mg. calcium daily
Pregnant and nursing women – 1,200mg. calcium daily

Many people do not come close to these goals. According to government surveys, most older women consume as little as 600 to 700mg. of calcium in their daily diet. And fewer than 15 percent of adolescent females and young adult women reach the target for this age group.

In addition to assuring a sound skeleton, calcium keeps the cardiovascular system running smoothly by regulating nerve transmissions, muscle contractions, blood clotting and blood pressure. When dietary intake of calcium is low, blood pressure has a tendency to rise. Thus a diet aimed at controlling blood pressure and preventing its elevation to dangerous levels, a condition known as hypertension, relies on adequate intake of calcium-rich foods.

Research has also shown that yogurt lowers blood cholesterol. This seems to be due in part to the ability of calcium to keep circulating cholesterol from reentering the bloodstream. The bacterial cultures unique to yogurt and YoChee play a role here as well.

Calcium also appears to have cancer-protecting properties. People with diets high in calcium have a lower risk of colorectal cancer, the third-highest cause of cancer deaths among both men and women in the U.S. Once again, the calcium appears to bind with cancer-promoting substances, making them harmless. Since calcium is necessary for cells to mature properly and certain cancers are caused by abnormal cell maturation, this may be another avenue of protection. This cancer-lowering influence is thought to be greater with fermented dairy products such as yogurt and YoChee.

There is a common misconception that calcium-rich foods promote kidney stones. This notion came about because calcium is one of the main components of calcium-oxalate stones, the most common form of kidney stones. In fact, calcium may actually help prevent kidney stones. It does this by coupling with oxalates before

YoChee's Nutritional Makeup

Food *½ cup*	Calories	Fat *grams*	Saturated Fat *grams*
YoChee, nonfat	85	---	---
YoChee, low-fat	100	3	1
YoChee cream, nonfat	95	---	---
Yogurt, nonfat	50	---	---
Yogurt, low-fat	55	1	<1
Cream cheese, block	405	40	25.5
Cream cheese, whipped	279	28	17.5
Sour cream	246	24	15
Whipped heavy cream	206	22	14
Cool Whip™	100	6	6
Mayonnaise	800	90	13.5
Butter	814	92	57.5

Food *½ cup*	Protein *grams*	Carbohydrate *grams*	Calcium *milligrams*
YoChee, nonfat	10.5	10	235
YoChee, low-fat	9	9	225
YoChee cream, nonfat	10	13	250
Yogurt, nonfat	5	8	220
Yogurt, low-fat	4.5	7	195
Cream cheese, block	9	3	90
Cream cheese, whipped	6	2	65
Sour cream	3.5	5	130
Whipped heavy cream	1	2	40
Cool Whip™	0	8	0
Mayonnaise	1.5	1	20
Butter	1	<1	25

Values for YoChee as analyzed at Ameritech laboratories, College Point, NY.

Remaining data from The Food Processor Recipe Analysis Software, ESHA Research.

they have a chance to enter the urinary tract and form stones. Thus, to reduce the risk of kidney stones, foods that have high oxalate levels, such as spinach, nuts, tea, chocolate, beets, rhubarb, strawberries and wheat bran, should be eaten with calcium-containing foods. In addition, consuming small portions of calcium-rich foods with each meal can help trap the oxalates that the body spontaneously produces, which is the source of most oxalates. The ease of including YoChee throughout the day and its natural compatibility with many high-oxalate foods makes it a valuable resource in preventing painful kidney stones.

PROTEIN

½ cup YoChee provides 10 grams protein.

Most protein-rich animal products, including meat, cheese and all but skim milk, come laden with the fats that can erode health. But not nonfat YoChee. YoChee supplies more protein in a half cup than you find in a full cup of milk or an ounce of cheese, meat, fish or poultry. YoChee actually has twice the protein you get from the same volume of yogurt.

Since people who are on low-fat diets avoid many traditional protein foods, YoChee can be especially valuable.

The need for protein varies according to age. The recommended intakes are:

* Ages 2 to 10 – 14 to 28 grams protein daily
* Age 11 and over – 44 to 73 grams protein daily

Note that every living cell requires protein. It is found in muscles, organs, hair, nails and blood. The enzymes, hormones and genetic messengers that comprise the body's regulatory system all depend on protein. Protein is also part of the transport system that carries many essential nutrients to their destination.

WITH OR WITHOUT FAT

½ cup nonfat YoChee provides 0 grams fat.
½ cup low-fat YoChee provides 3 grams fat.

YoChee made from nonfat yogurt is, of course, fat-free. When you compare it with foods that it can easily replace, the results are compelling. For example, an ounce of hard cheese (a 1-inch cube or modest slice) averages about 7 grams of protein and has 7 to 9 grams of fat. One-half cup of sour cream supplies only 3.5 grams of protein, but 24 grams of fat. The 9 grams of protein found in a half cup of cream cheese come with 40 grams of fat. The same volume of mayonnaise doesn't add any protein but contains a whopping 90 grams of fat. Obviously, using nonfat

YoChee instead of these foods is the way to go in order to get protein, yet maintain a sensible fat intake. The same can be said for YoChee made from low-fat yogurt, even with its 3 grams of fat.

Nonfat YoChee 0 grams fat

Nonfat YoChee 10 grams protein

Low-Fat YoChee 3 grams fat

Low-Fat YoChee 9 grams protein

Hard Cheese 7-9 grams fat

Hard Cheese 7 grams protein

Sour Cream 24 grams fat

Sour Cream 3.5 grams protein

Cream Cream 40 grams fat

Cream Cheese 9 grams protein

Mayonnaise 90 grams fat

Mayonnaise 0 grams protein

Fat and Protein Comparisons

The Benefit of Some Fat

When YoChee is made with lowfat or whole milk yogurt, it has a corresponding fat content. (Since very little of the fat is lost in the draining process, the amount of fat will be about what you find in the original quantity of yogurt.) The presence of a particular fat here may actually be a bonus.

Research has shown that an unusual polyunsaturated fatty acid found in the milk of cows, sheep and goats can inhibit certain cancer tumors and may also decrease heart disease by lowering the activity of fats and cholesterol in the bloodstream. It is called conjugated linoleic acid (CLA), and because the effect of CLA may be increased by heat, yogurt (which is made from heated milk) presumably has more CLA than milk. It is also possible that humans, like some animals, can make their own CLA with the aid of intestinal microflora. If so, the fact that YoChee promotes the growth of friendly bacteria in the colon should add to its protective potential.

Potassium

½ cup YoChee provides 290mg. potassium.

The mineral potassium doesn't get much public attention, but it is extremely important nonetheless. In fact, potassium has a wide range of activity. Along with sodium, it helps regulate the balance of fluids in the body. These two minerals also work together to regulate heartbeat.

Potassium is essential for proper muscle contraction, nerve-impulse transmission and the delivery of oxygen to the brain. It assists in the storage and release of energy by the liver, stimulates the kidneys to remove toxins from the body and is involved in keeping the skin healthy and youthful.

It has been observed that dairy foods take part in preventing hypertension. It is likely that the presence of potassium plays a supporting role, along with calcium. Potassium appears to protect against stroke and kidney damage, as well.

The suggested level of potassium intake for adults is about 3,500mg. daily. With about 290mg. in each half cup, YoChee makes a valuable contribution.

B Vitamins

YoChee furnishes the B vitamins riboflavin and B_{12}. Riboflavin helps the body process carbohydrates, fats and proteins. It assists in the manufacture of infection-fighting antibodies and is an essential component in a number of enzymes produced in the body. Riboflavin intake has been linked to a reduced cancer risk, which may be explained by the capacity of some of these enzymes to disarm carcinogens.

In meatless diets, YoChee can be a critical source of vitamin B_{12}. This vitamin, although only needed in small amounts, is mighty. Among other jobs, it is essential for making red blood cells, it helps maintain the central nervous system and it aids in tissue growth and energy production. It also participates in the system that prevents the build-up of a compound in the blood called homocysteine, which in excess damages blood vessels.

Lactose Intolerance and Other Health Issues

The manufacture of yogurt is dependent on the addition of specific strains of bacteria to milk. The presence of this friendly bacteria is something else that makes yogurt and YoChee special.

Consuming YoChee on a regular basis can improve the balance of microflora in the intestines. This can be extremely useful following antibiotic therapy. It also offers protection against diarrhea caused by unsanitary environmental conditions, such as bacteria-contaminated food or water. Long-term daily consumption of yogurt has been shown to enhance the immune system and to reduce the incidence of vaginal yeast infections in susceptible women. In addition, the *Lactobacillus acidophilus* strain of bacteria found in most yogurts can inhibit the activity of certain cancer-causing substances.

People who are sensitive to lactose, the sugar found in dairy-based foods, can often eat yogurt and YoChee. This is because from 30 to 50 percent of the lactose has been "predigested," or changed to harmless lactic acid by the bacterial culture. This amount is further reduced in YoChee, since from one-third to one-half of the remaining lactose is in the liquid (whey) that drains off.

When people are lactose-intolerant, they don't digest lactose, causing the undigested particles to pass into the intestines. There it is broken down by fermentation, resulting in the production of gases that cause cramps, bloating, flatulence and diarrhea. Interestingly, a new approach to treating lactose intolerance is to eat small quantities of lactose-containing foods on a regular basis in an attempt to get the body to adapt. Since YoChee fits the description of a low-lactose food, it may actually have therapeutic value for those who are lactose-intolerant.

The decreased levels of lactose in YoChee may also have a heart-protective influence. Research has shown that the combination of lactose and dietary cholesterol increases the level of artery-clogging fats. Because YoChee is low in lactose, it is less likely to cause this problem than the milk it is made from.

Oᴜʀ Rᴇᴄɪᴘᴇs ᴀɴᴅ Tʜᴇɪʀ Nᴜᴛʀɪᴛɪᴏɴᴀʟ Cᴏɴᴛᴇɴᴛ

In order to provide a reliable nutritional profile of YoChee and our recipes, we had samples of YoChee analyzed for us by an independent laboratory. The results are based on YoChee samples of nonfat and low-fat cow's milk yogurt that were drained for 24 hours. Since yogurts are not all identical in composition, YoChee made with different brands may vary somewhat.

The nutritional analysis provided with our recipes is based on the nonfat YoChee sample. If you use low-fat or full-fat YoChee, the amount of fat will rise proportionately. Since most of the fat is retained in the solids, you can expect the fat in one-half cup of YoChee to be about what you find in one cup of yogurt. Moreover, while YoChee made from cow, goat, sheep or soy milk yogurt can be used in the recipes, nutritional composition, especially when soy is the main ingredient, will not be the same.

Nutritional analysis is popular for recipes today. It is important to understand that this is not an exact science. In all instances, the numbers you see are derived using comprehensive tables of nutritional composition and are based on the recipe, not direct laboratory analysis of the finished dish. To compute our nutritional analysis we used The Food Processor Recipe Analysis Software from ESHA Research to provide our data. Because potential nutritional differences exist among all foods, the nutritional analysis of a recipe is never definitive, despite the fact that it often seems so precise. This doesn't mean it isn't useful, for you do get a reasonable picture of how a dish can influence the overall nutritional value of your diet. The nutritional data also offers a basis on which to compare recipes.

In the nutritional information provided with our recipes, some numbers are rounded off for better comprehension. Where recipes contain an insignificant amount of any nutrient, or less than 1 gram, we use the notation <1.

A Summary of YoChee's Benefits

* No fat or low in fat, depending on the type of yogurt used.
* Low calorie content.
* Takes the place of some or all of the mayonnaise, sour cream, cream cheese, solid shortenings, oil, heavy cream, whipped cream and even eggs in many familiar dishes.
* Tolerates heat well, making it more practical in cooking than yogurt.
* Pleasurable mouthfeel of high-fat foods.
* Mild flavor that is less tart than the yogurt it came from.
* Concentrated, so you get more nutritional value than from an equal volume of yogurt.
* Easy to make—even a child can do it. There is no cooking and it takes just seconds of your time. All you need is a simple draining device and gravity. (While it is easiest to make YoChee with a specially designed drainer, it can also be made by using cheesecloth or coffee filters as the draining mechanism.)
* Even unskilled cooks can easily find new applications.
* An excellent source of protein, calcium, potassium, riboflavin and vitamin B_{12}.
* Provides the body with disease-fighting microorganisms.
* Suitable for many people who are lactose-intolerant.

MAKING YOCHEE

One of the most colorful names for YoChee is "hung cheese," a reference to the traditional way it is made by hanging yogurt in a bag made of cheesecloth or muslin. Today there are several devices on the market that make this process neater, more sanitary and close to effortless.

EQUIPMENT

To make YoChee all you have to do is spoon yogurt into a specially designed draining device or similar homemade apparatus. No complicated equipment is needed. Gravity does all the work. For more information on these draining devices, contact Ceres Press online at YoChee.com or HealthiestDiet.com, tollfree at 1-877-YoChee1 (1-877-962-4331) or see the ordering information at the back of the book.

You can also set up your own draining apparatus. One option is a drip coffee filter set over a container to hold the liquid (whey) that drips out. Disposable paper filters are a little messier than using a ready-made device and need constant replacement. They also may transfer a slight taste and leach some of the papermaking chemicals they contain.

A more traditional approach is to drain the yogurt in a colander or strainer lined with cheesecloth and set over a bowl to catch the drippings. This method is more cumbersome, messier yet and takes up more space, and it is harder to remove all of the finished product. Moreover, although the cheesecloth can be washed and reused a few times, it still needs frequent replacement.

CHOOSING YOGURT FOR YOCHEE

YoChee can be made with cow, goat, sheep or even soy milk yogurt. The yogurt can be nonfat, low-fat or whole-milk. YoChee can also be made using flavored yogurt, although this will obviously limit its use. The recipes in this book were all tested using nonfat cow's milk YoChee.

Do not use a yogurt that contains thickeners such as modified starch, gelatin or gums. Their purpose is to bind the solids and liquids. As a result, these yogurts will not drain as well as those without thickeners. We have been successful making YoChee from many brands of plain yogurt (for a list of satisfactory brands, go online to YoChee.com or HealthiestDiet.com).

To receive the full health potential, choose a yogurt that has live cultures. Individual companies may add one or more types of bacterial cultures, including

L. acidophilus, B. bifidus, L. casei, S. thermophilus, L. bulgaricus and *L. reuteri.* Somewhere on the label it should state that there are "live and active cultures." Brands that make this statement must meet criteria set by the National Yogurt Association.

It is important to check on the label that the yogurt hasn't been pasteurized or heat-treated *after* processing. A few companies treat yogurt this way to extend its shelf life. This exposure to high heat kills the beneficial bacteria along with the other microbes. Therefore, YoChee made with one of these brands won't offer the health-enhancing properties associated with these friendly flora.

You may also have a choice of buying yogurt made with organic milk. This means the cows are raised on farms where no chemical pesticides are used and the herds aren't given growth hormones or antibiotics. Other brands may not meet these strict standards for organic, but may indicate that they are free from the genetically modified growth hormone BST (or rBGH) that some dairies use to boost milk output. This hormone has been a topic of considerable controversy. The subject of organic foods and biotechnology is beyond the scope of this book. We will simply state here that our preference is to support organic farmers and avoid genetically modified products whenever possible.

READING YOGURT LABELS

Read labels for the following ingredients and processes.
Avoid:
> *Thickeners and stabilizers, including modified starch, gelatin, gums
> *Pasteurized or heat-treated after processing

Desirable:
> *Live and active cultures
> *BST- or rBGH-free
> *Organic

Instructions for Making YoChee

Once you have your yogurt and draining device, you are ready to start.

1. If your drainer doesn't come with its own drip container, place it on something large enough to hold the liquid that drains off. For each cup of yogurt there will be approximately one-half cup of liquid.

2. Fill the draining device with yogurt, keeping in mind that the final volume of YoChee will be about half that of the amount of yogurt you start with. Cover with a suitable-size lid, plate or piece of waxed paper for cleanliness.

Deluxe YoChee Maker

YoChee Funnel

Colander with Cheesecloth

3. Place in the refrigerator. Over the course of a day you will witness a magical transformation to a unique food that ranges in texture from smooth and creamy to a dense spread. The thickness of the final product depends on how long you let it drain. As these textural changes take place, the flavor becomes more mellow and less acidic than that of the original yogurt.

> * In 2 to 4 hours you have what we refer to as YoChee cream, a substance not much thicker than yogurt but with a silkier texture that performs much better than plain yogurt in recipes.

> * In 4 to 6 hours it is akin to sour cream.

> * After 8 to 12 hours it reaches a semi-firm form that qualifies as YoChee.

> * By 24 hours you can assume that all the separable moisture is gone.

Storage

Once the YoChee is done draining, pour off the whey and transfer the YoChee to a covered storage container. Rinse the device clean and make another batch.

It is best to use your fresh, refrigerated YoChee within a week. If additional liquid has separated out during storage, simply pour it off or mix it in, according to how thick you want your YoChee to be.

If you have more YoChee than you can use within a week, it can be frozen in a covered freezer-proof container. The texture becomes a bit grainy, but once defrosted it can be stirred smooth again.

COOKING THE YOCHEE WAY

Recipe Key:

A alongside the recipe title indicates something especially quick and simple.

A "<1" in a recipe's nutritional analysis indicates an amount too small to be significant.

Starting Out with YoChee

Replacing Butter, Cream Cheese, Sour Cream & Mayonnaise

An easy way to start using YoChee is as you would butter or cream cheese on bread, rolls, bagels, muffins and crackers. It also easily replaces butter or sour cream for flavoring vegetables, beans, pasta and grains.

Another simple introduction is to substitute YoChee for the mayonnaise, sour cream and cream cheese in many of your standard recipes. If at first you find YoChee alone is not to your liking, begin by using a combination of YoChee with these ingredients. Start out with equal amounts; increase the YoChee over time to taste.

Favorite Quick Applications

Here are some quick ideas to get you started using YoChee. Before long you will get into the habit of using this remarkable food wherever you can.

* Serve on baked potatoes. A few chopped chives make this especially nice.

* Use in dips in place of sour cream or mayonnaise.

* Use in place of butter or mayonnaise to moisten the bread for sandwiches. You might want to add a touch of salt for extra flavor.

* Spread on bread along with some all-fruit preserves for a "creamy YoChee and jelly" sandwich.

* Spread on hot toast, warm muffins, French toast or pancakes and let it melt in like butter. If desired, you can add a touch of maple syrup or honey for flavoring.

* Garnish green salads before or after dressing by topping with several "pearls" of YoChee.

* Spoon a generous dollop on chili, tacos, burritos and bean stews. For extra gusto, season with a dash of hot pepper sauce.
* Stir into pasta sauces to taste just before serving to make them creamy.
* Spread a thin layer on top of casseroles before baking.
* Serve soups and stews with a heaping spoonful of YoChee on top.
* For instant hors d'œuvre, spread on crackers or toasted bread cut in quarters. Top with cucumber slices, diced sun-dried tomatoes, slivers of green and red peppers, thin wedges of artichoke hearts, a few capers, olive paste or something similar.
* For dessert, sweeten YoChee lightly with pure maple syrup and a few drops of vanilla extract. Use on top of berries, baked apples or other fruit desserts as you would whipped cream.

Nutrition Notes

For every 2 tablespoons of YoChee you receive 21 calories, 2.5gm. protein, 2.5gm. carbohydrate, 60mg. calcium

YoChee made from nonfat yogurt is fat-free; YoChee made from low-fat yogurt has <1mg. fat per 2 tablespoons

SIMPLE SPREADS AND TOPPINGS

Here are some ideas for quickly transforming YoChee for use as a spread on bread or for flavoring vegetables. These recipes are especially useful on sandwiches to replace high-fat butter, margarine and mayonnaise, which all contain about 100 calories and 11 grams of fat per tablespoon and no other significant nutrients.

As you become more comfortable with YoChee, you will discover many more applications. Keep in mind that in most cases exact amounts aren't critical. Just add and taste as you go until the flavor and texture are to your liking.

The recipes in this section (and many others) demonstrate the versatility of YoChee in yet another way. That is, spreads also make excellent vegetable toppings, while dips can often double as sauces for pasta and grains.

INSTANT MUSTARD SPREAD

Use on sandwiches, to season vegetables or to slather on an ear of corn instead of butter.

A good general ratio is ¼ cup YoChee to 1 tablespoon mustard, although the exact proportion will vary with the potency of the mustard. Add the mustard in increments, tasting as you go, to determine when to stop.

PER 1 TABLESPOON: 13 CALORIES, <1 GM. FAT, <1 GM. SATURATED FAT, 1.5 GM. PROTEIN, 1.5 GM. CARBOHYDRATE, 30 MG. CALCIUM

TAHINI BUTTER

This is a good all around spread—a much better choice than butter, with about one-third the calories and one-fourth the fat.

Using a fork, beat together 1 part tahini to 2 parts YoChee. Use as is or alter to taste and suitability with the addition of chopped garlic, fresh or dried herbs and/or a pinch of salt.

PER 1 TABLESPOON: 37 CALORIES, 3 GM. FAT, <1 GM. SATURATED FAT, 2 GM. PROTEIN, 1.5 GM. CARBOHYDRATE, 25 MG. CALCIUM

INSTANT HORSERADISH SPREAD

Use on sandwiches in place of mayonnaise or mustard.

Combine ¼ cup YoChee with 1½ teaspoons prepared horseradish. Taste to determine if additional horseradish is desired.

PER 1 TABLESPOON: 11 CALORIES, 1 GM. PROTEIN, <1 GM. FAT, <1 GM. SATURATED FAT, 1.5 GM. CARBOHYDRATE, 30 MG. CALCIUM

Instant Olive Spread

Spread modestly on toast for an hors d'œuvre or spoon a generous spoonful or two on pasta or into soup for additional flavoring.

Combine equal amounts of YoChee and olive paste (tapenade).

Per 1 tablespoon: 30 calories, 2.5gm. fat, <1gm. saturated fat, 1gm. protein, 2.5gm. carbohydrate, 25mg. calcium

Avocado Cream

A quick spread or dip.

Mash a ripe avocado together with YoChee in any proportion that suits you. Season with a little fresh lemon juice, salt and hot sauce to taste.

Ranch Spread

When you make this recipe, add enough hot sauce to give it a nice bite, bearing in mind that when spread out, its potency will be dispersed.

½ cup YoChee
3 tablespoons ketchup
hot sauce

Combine all ingredients, adding hot sauce to taste.

Makes ⅔ cup

Per 1 tablespoon: 13 calories, <1gm. fat, <1gm. saturated fat, 1gm. protein, 2gm. carbohydrate, 25mg. calcium

Instant Creamy Salsa

Here is an easy way to improve the food value of Mexican dishes or a snack of chips and salsa. Since the YoChee tones down the spiciness, choose a medium or spicy salsa rather than something too tame.

½ cup prepared tomato salsa
¼ cup YoChee

Combine the salsa and YoChee. Use at once or store in the refrigerator. Mix to recombine before serving.

Makes ⅔ cup; about 4 servings

Per 2 tablespoons: 14 calories, <1gm. fat, <1gm. saturated fat, 1gm. protein, 2gm. carbohydrate, 35mg. calcium

Quick Creamy Pesto

Combine prepared pesto with YoChee to taste. The exact ratio will depend on the thickness of the pesto and the intended use.

For a sauce, figure on about ¼ cup YoChee per cup of pesto. For dips or spreads, you may need to increase the amount of YoChee until the desired body and preferred flavor intensity are achieved. As a general guide, dips may approach equal amounts of YoChee and pesto, while in spreads YoChee may dominate.

> Per 2 tablespoons with a ratio of 1 part YoChee to 4 parts pesto: 128 calories, 11.5gm. fat, 3gm. saturated fat, 5gm. protein, 2gm. carbohydrate, 180mg. calcium
>
> Per 2 tablespoons with equal amounts YoChee and pesto: 88 calories, 7gm. fat, 2gm. saturated fat, 4gm. protein, 2.5gm. carbohydrate, 135mg. calcium

Hearty Bean Sandwich Filling

Spread on bread and top with sliced tomato, cucumber, onion and lettuce.

Rinse and drain cooked or canned chickpeas, white beans, red beans or similar bean of choice. Mash coarsely with a potato masher or fork, adding as much YoChee as you wish to make a mixture that holds together when gently compressed. Season according to taste with chopped garlic, mustard, fresh dill, basil, parsley, dried oregano, cumin or other desired seasonings.

All-in-One YoChee and Jelly

Use your favorite fruit-flavored yogurt to make a one-step spread for bread.

Stir until the yogurt and fruit are evenly blended. Spoon into the YoChee draining device and refrigerate. Drain for at least 24 hours.

Preparation Pointer

When using YoChee, mashing is often the preferred technique for melding ingredients. A hand potato masher is a handy tool for this job. This inexpensive item is available in most housewares stores.

⏰ Quick Fruit "Tarts"

Assembling a fruit tart using sliced bread, sweetened YoChee and fresh fruit is quick and easy. Since the character of the bread contributes to the final product, you might consider a specialty variety such as multigrain, oat or nutted. Avoid breads with raisins, as they will scorch. The proportions below are designed for sandwich-size bread. For larger slices, you may need to increase the amounts of sweetened YoChee and fruit.

> ⅔ cup YoChee
> 2 tablespoons honey
> ½ teaspoon vanilla extract
> 4 slices bread
> 1 large apple, pear, peach or banana
> cinnamon
> nutmeg

Preheat the oven to 375°F.

In a bowl, combine the YoChee, honey and vanilla. Using all of this sweetened YoChee, spread a generous layer on each slice of bread.

Peel the fruit and cut into thin slices, discarding any core or pits. Arrange on the bread, overlapping slices if necessary. Place on a baking sheet. Sprinkle some cinnamon and nutmeg over each "tart".

Bake for about 25 minutes or until fruit is tender and bread is crisp on the bottom. Serve while still warm.

Makes 4 servings

> *Per tart:* 180 calories, 1.5gm. fat, <1gm. saturated fat, 6gm. protein, 36gm. carbohydrate, 100mg. calcium

SoBe Lettuce Roll-Ups

A quick savory snack that can be assembled in a jiffy. The pattern below is for one roll-up and can be multiplied as needed. Two to three roll-ups per person create a resourceful appetizer.

> **3 to 4 thin raw asparagus spears, snow peas, fresh young green beans or avocado slices**
> **1 romaine lettuce leaf**
> **2 tablespoons YoChee**
> **alfalfa sprouts**
> **salsa**

Arrange the chosen vegetable along the rib of the lettuce leaf. Top with the YoChee and sprouts. Season to taste with salsa. Roll up the sides of the leaf to cover the filling. Eat out of hand.

Makes 1 roll-up

> **Per Roll-up:** 45 calories, <1 gm. fat, <1 gm. saturated fat, 5 gm. protein, 7 gm. carbohydrate, 90 mg. calcium

LABNEH MAKBUS (YoCHEE BALLS)

Labneh Makbus is a traditional Mideastern recipe in which well-drained yogurt is formed into small balls, chilled and then rolled in selected seasonings. These flavorful balls, similar to the Italian delicacy made from fresh mozzarella cheese, are an excellent addition to an appetizer platter. Or they can be one of the elements on a cooked vegetable plate or Salade Composée (see recipe page 239).

> **YoChee**
> **salt**
> **seasonings of choice, including paprika, oregano, cracked pepper, cumin, dried or chopped fresh dill, basil, parsley or favorite mix**
> **olive oil**

Season the YoChee with salt, using ¼ teaspoon per ½ cup of YoChee. Using a tablespoon at a time, roll gently in your hands to form into small balls. Place in a single layer on a plate or tray. Chill for several hours until firm.

Place a generous amount of the chosen seasoning on a plate. Roll each ball in the seasoning to completely coat. Return to the refrigerator until needed.

At serving time, drizzle some olive oil lightly over the balls. This isn't essential, but it's a very nice touch.

Makes 8 balls per ½ cup YoChee

Variation: For sweet service on a fruit platter, roll the balls in cinnamon or nutmeg.

PER 2 BALLS: 21 CALORIES, <1GM. FAT, <1GM. SATURATED FAT, 2.5GM. PROTEIN, 2.5GM. CARBOHYDRATE, 60MG. CALCIUM

Preparation Tip

If you are making YoChee specifically for Labneh Makbus, start by adding the salt to the yogurt before draining. This makes the balls a little easier to form. Either way, be sure to drain the YoChee for at least 24 hours. The finished Labneh Makbus can be kept in the refrigerator for use over the course of a week.

BREAKFAST & BRUNCH

YOCHEE: THE NATURAL EGG EXTENDER

YoChee is particularly helpful for those who want to cut back on eggs, as it can serve as a natural egg extender. You will see this demonstrated here in the "OneLESS" recipes.

BREAKFASTS WITH STAYING POWER

YoChee is the smart spread—the perfect substitute for fatty butter and cream cheese. It can improve the nutritional quality of carbohydrate-intensive breakfast fare such as toast, muffins, bagels, pancakes, waffles and the like by reducing fat and calories and adding protein. At the same time, this produces a more even release of sugar into the bloodstream. As a result, the chance of your being satisfied until lunch is much greater.

When spread on something hot, YoChee melts in like butter. With foods that are at room temperature, you can apply it in a thick layer for a cream cheese-like effect.

CALORIE-SAVING TOPPINGS

Thanks to YoChee, the delicious pancake toppings in this section surpass the usual high-sugar offerings. Not only are they lower in calories, they also add valuable protein and calcium to the meal.

MORE YOCHEE

Of course, there are many other ways to incorporate YoChee into breakfasts. The recipes that follow will inspire you with their ease and tastiness while they enrich the morning meal with protein and calcium. They will probably spark your imagination for creating other YoChee breakfast and brunch dishes.

❧ YoChievements ❧

OneLESS Egg (pg.31) vs. 2 eggs
    36% less calories
    50% less fat
    50% less saturated fat
    28% less protein
    60% more calcium

Silver Dollar Blueberry & Cream Cakes (pg.41) vs. standard
    blueberry pancakes
    30% less calories
    70% less fat
    Similar protein
    13% more calcium

Maple Cream (pg.42) vs. maple syrup
    40% less calories
    2.5 grams protein per ¼ cup vs. no protein
    46% less carbohydrate
    58% more calcium

 **OneLESS Egg**

Eggs go farther when you combine them with YoChee. This recipe demonstrates how to make a single egg seem like two. For a heartier dish, add chopped scallions, chives, mushrooms, leftover cooked vegetables or assorted herbs, according to taste.

> **2 tablespoons YoChee**
> **1 egg**
> **salt**
> **butter or mild-flavored oil, if needed**
> **pepper**

Using a fork, wire whisk or rotary beater, beat the YoChee to loosen it a little. Beat in the egg until the two are fully blended. Season with a pinch of salt.

Heat an 8-inch nonstick or seasoned frying pan. If not well seasoned, add just enough butter or oil to coat the surface. When the pan is hot, add the egg mixture.

As the egg starts to set, stir gently so the uncooked portion settles to the bottom. Continue until firm or cooked to taste. Season with pepper.

Makes 1 serving

Note: For up to 4 eggs, multiply the ingredients proportionally and prepare in a 10- or 12-inch pan. For more than this, cook in separate batches.

PER SERVING: 96 CALORIES, 5GM. FAT, 1.5GM. SATURATED FAT, 9GM. PROTEIN, 3GM. CARBOHYDRATE, 80MG. CALCIUM (SEE YoChievements FOR COMPARISONS)

OneLess Scrambled Egg

Folding YoChee into an egg after it is cooked, rather than beating the two together as in the previous recipe, creates an entirely different effect. Once again, you can vary this simple recipe by adding vegetables or seasonings of choice.

1 egg
mild-flavored oil, if needed
1 tablespoon YoChee
salt
pepper

Break the egg into a bowl and beat until the yolk and white are integrated.

Heat an 8-inch nonstick or seasoned frying pan. If not well seasoned, wipe generously with oil.

Pour the egg into the heated pan and cook over low to moderate heat, stirring with a spoon or lifting the cooked portion with a spatula as it sets. When the egg is cooked to your liking, drop the YoChee in several dollops on top. Fold the cooked portion of the egg over the YoChee, remove from the heat and let sit briefly, until the YoChee melts.

Season to taste with salt and pepper.

Makes 1 serving

Note: For up to 4 eggs, multiply the ingredients proportionally and prepare in a 10- or 12-inch pan. For more than this, cook in separate batches.

Per serving: 85 CALORIES, 5GM. FAT, 1.5GM. SATURATED FAT, 7.5GM. PROTEIN, 2GM. CARBOHYDRATE, 55MG. CALCIUM

OneLESS Peppers, Onions and Eggs

Peppers, onions and eggs are common companions. By whipping YoChee into the eggs, you can produce a tender and flavorful rendition—with one less egg.

1 large green pepper, cut in thin strips
1 small onion, cut in thin crescents
⅓ cup YoChee
3 eggs
salt
1 teaspoon butter or mild-flavored oil
pepper

Combine the green pepper and onion in a 10-inch omelet pan or skillet. Cover, place over medium heat and let the vegetables cook in their own juices for about 10 minutes or until they are quite tender. Stir occasionally to promote even cooking and prevent sticking.

Place the YoChee in a bowl. Using a fork, wire whisk or rotary beater, beat the eggs in one at a time until fully blended. Season with a generous pinch of salt.

When the vegetables are tender, add the butter or oil and heat until the bottom of the pan is coated. Add the eggs.

As the eggs start to set, stir gently so the uncooked portion settles to the bottom. Continue until firm or cooked to taste. Season with pepper.

Makes 2 servings

PER SERVING: 200 CALORIES, 10GM. FAT, 3.5GM. SATURATED FAT, 14GM. PROTEIN, 14.5GM. CARBOHYDRATE, 130MG. CALCIUM

OneLESS Baked Omelets

Flavorful baked omelets—what the Italians call frittatas—are excellent brunch or buffet offerings. The addition of YoChee allows you to use less egg and at the same time boost the health value without detracting from the taste. Baked omelets can be made with almost any freshly cooked or precooked vegetables, rice or pasta, plain or preseasoned, individually or in combination. This makes them a good vehicle for leftovers. In fact, the recipe for this dish allows for a lot of flexibility. The basic technique is to cover the other ingredients with just enough YoChee-egg mix to bind them together. Seasoning with fresh or dried herbs compatible with the filling is up to the cook.

> 4 eggs
> ½ cup YoChee
> 2 cups cooked pasta, grain (brown rice, cracked wheat, couscous, barley, kasha) or vegetables, individually or in combination
> ⅓ cup grated Parmesan cheese, optional
> salt
> pepper
> herbs of choice
> 1 tablespoon olive oil

Preheat the oven to 350°F.

Beat the eggs in a large bowl. Add the YoChee, cooked pasta, grain or vegetables, grated cheese if using, and seasonings of choice. Mix well so that the YoChee is completely incorporated.

Heat the oil in a 12-inch ovenproof omelet pan. Pour in the egg mixture. Cook over low heat for about 5 minutes, until the bottom is set. Transfer the pan to the oven and cook for about 15 minutes, or until the omelet is firm.

Transfer to a plate and cut into wedges. Serve warm or at room temperature.

Makes 4 servings

Notes: You can make individual or 2-person omelets by cutting the recipe in half and cooking in a 6- to 8-inch skillet. Or, you can double the recipe in a large cast-iron skillet. You may need to bake the larger volume for an additional 5 to 10 minutes.

NUTRITION VARIES WITH THE FILLING. VALUES HERE BASED ON USING PLAIN PASTA.

PER SERVING, WITHOUT OPTIONAL CHEESE: 212 CALORIES, 9GM. FAT, 2GM. SATURATED FAT, 13GM. PROTEIN, 22GM. CARBOHYDRATE, 95MG. CALCIUM

PER SERVING, WITH OPTIONAL CHEESE: 250 CALORIES, 11GM. FAT, 4GM. SATURATED FAT, 16GM. PROTEIN, 22GM. CARBOHYDRATE, 208MG. CALCIUM

MEXICAN EGGS

A quick, satisfying dish in which the YoChee adds creaminess to the filling. The total cooking time is just about 5 minutes. To give it a Mexican flair, serve with red tomato or green tomatillo salsa and scoop up with corn tortillas.

> **4 eggs**
> **salt**
> **cayenne pepper**
> **1 tablespoon olive oil**
> **½ cup corn kernels**
> **2 tablespoons chopped cilantro or flat-leaf Italian parsley**
> **¼ cup YoChee**
> **¼ cup shredded cheddar or Monterey Jack cheese, optional**

Beat the eggs in a bowl. Season with a pinch of salt and a pinch of cayenne pepper.

Heat the oil in a 10- to 12-inch omelet pan or skillet. When hot, pour in the eggs. Cook until the bottom just begins to set. Stir gently, lifting the set portion and allowing the uncooked eggs to filter down into the bottom of the pan.

When the eggs are just about done, add the corn kernels and cilantro or parsley. Continue to cook, stirring a few times, until the eggs are firm.

Loosen the eggs from the pan with a spatula. Drop the YoChee in dollops all over the top. Using the spatula, fold the eggs over the YoChee. Remove from the heat, sprinkle the shredded cheese on top if desired, cover and let sit for a minute for the cheeses to melt.

Makes 2 servings

Note: To serve 4, double and cook in a 15-inch skillet.

> PER SERVING, WITHOUT CHEESE: 269 CALORIES, 17.5GM. FAT, 4GM. SATURATED FAT, 15.5GM. PROTEIN, 12GM. CARBOHYDRATE, 110MG. CALCIUM
>
> PER SERVING, WITH OPTIONAL SHREDDED CHEESE: 326 CALORIES, 22GM. FAT, 7GM. SATURATED FAT, 20GM. PROTEIN, 12.5GM. CARBOHYDRATE, 212MG. CALCIUM

Ze Best Brunch Eggs

This recipe was inspired by good friends and has become one of our brunch favorites. We use YoChee here instead of cream cheese.

> **1 large onion, cut in half lengthwise and thinly sliced**
> **1 tablespoon soy sauce**
> **6 cups coarsely chopped Swiss chard or other greens**
> **8 eggs**
> **salt**
> **1 tablespoon butter or olive oil**
> **½ cup YoChee**
> **pepper**

Combine the onion and soy sauce in a 12- to 15-inch skillet or omelet pan. Cover and cook over medium-low heat for about 10 minutes, or until the onion is quite limp. Check a few times to make sure the pan is not too dry; add a spoonful of water, if necessary, to keep the onion from sticking.

Add the Swiss chard. Stir until limp, cover and cook for about 10 minutes, until tender.

Break the eggs into a large bowl. Add a pinch of salt and beat with a fork until the yolks and whites are thoroughly mixed.

Push the greens to the side of the pan and add the butter or oil. When the fat is hot and melted over the bottom of the pan, pour in the eggs. Mix well to distribute the greens evenly.

Cook the eggs until the bottom begins to set. Stir gently, lifting the set portion and allowing the uncooked egg to filter down. Continue, stirring a few times, until the eggs are firm and beginning to color at little on the bottom.

Loosen the eggs with a spatula. Drop the YoChee in dollops all over the top. Season with pepper. Using the spatula, fold the eggs over the YoChee, remove from the heat, cover and let sit a few minutes for the YoChee to melt.

Serve right away, or cover the pan and place in a warm (200°F.) oven until needed.

Makes 4 servings

> *Per serving*: 259 calories, 15gm. fat, 4gm. saturated fat, 19gm. protein, 11gm. carbohydrate, 160mg. calcium

Fall/Winter Brunch Menu

Pink grapefruit and orange wedges

Ze Best Brunch Eggs

Baked winter squash

Crusty bread

Skillet Pear Cobbler (page 281)

Spring/Summer Brunch Menu

Melon wedges and fresh strawberries

Ze Best Brunch Eggs

Seasonal vegetable—corn on the cob/sliced summer tomatoes

Crusty bread

Fresh Fruit Coffeecake with peaches and blueberries (page 285)

Fluffy Mushroom Omelet

This cloudlike omelet is as delicate and appealing as a mushroom soufflé, but with far fewer calories and far less effort. You can make the mushroom topping just before or while the omelet is baking. A good choice for brunch, lunch or even a light supper.

> 4 eggs
> salt
> 1 tablespoon butter or olive oil
> ⅓ cup chopped onion
> 1 teaspoon soy sauce
> cayenne pepper
> 1 cup thinly sliced mushrooms
> ½ cup YoChee

Preheat the oven to 300°F.

Separate the eggs. Using an eggbeater or wire whisk, beat the whites until soft peaks form. Beat in a pinch of salt. Beat in the yolks one at a time until just blended.

Heat the butter or oil in a 10- to 12-inch ovenproof omelet pan. Pour in the eggs and cook until the bottom is just set. Transfer the pan to the oven and bake for about 10 minutes, until the top is set. The bottom should be nicely colored by this time, although the top will still be pale.

While the omelet is in the oven or before, combine the onion and soy sauce in a small skillet. Cook for 3 to 5 minutes, until just softened. Add a pinch of cayenne pepper and the sliced mushrooms. Sauté for about 5 minutes, until the mushrooms are just tender. Remove from the heat and stir in the YoChee until the sauce is creamy (see Note). Season with salt to taste.

When the omelet is done, spread the warm mushroom sauce on top to cover. Cut into quarters and serve.

Makes 2 servings

Note: If serving is delayed, wait until the last minute to add the YoChee to the sauce, reheating the mushrooms just before if necessary. If the sauce needs heating after the YoChee is added, cook over very low heat, while stirring, until just warm.

Variations: You can replace the cayenne pepper with ½ teaspoon dried oregano, thyme or sage, or 2 tablespoons chopped fresh parsley or dill.

Per serving: 263 calories, 16gm. fat, 7gm. saturated fat, 19gm. protein, 10gm. carbohydrate, 175mg. calcium

Egg Crepes with Fresh Cheese and Warm Olives

Delicate rolled egg with a creamy filling. A good brunch or lunch choice. Serve with crusty bread and a mixed green salad.

> **4 eggs**
> **2 tablespoons chopped parsley**
> **2 tablespoons grated Parmesan cheese**
> **pepper**
> **olive oil**
> **½ cup YoChee**
> **salt**
> **2 tablespoons crumbled feta or blue cheese**
> **¼ cup sliced cured black olives (see Notes)**

Preheat the oven to 300°F.

Beat the eggs together with the parsley, grated cheese and a generous amout of pepper.

Pour just enough olive oil into a 10-inch omelet pan to coat the bottom. Set over medium-high heat. When the pan is hot, add half the egg mixture. (To facilitate dividing the eggs evenly, pour them into a liquid measuring cup. You should have about 1 cup. This is especially useful if you decide to increase the recipe and need to judge how much egg to use for each crepe.) Swirl the pan quickly to distribute the egg evenly. Lower the heat and cook until just firm. Remove from the heat.

Season the YoChee with a pinch of salt. Place half the YoChee in a strip down the center of the egg crepe. Sprinkle 1 tablespoon of the crumbled cheese over the YoChee. Fold two sides of the crepe over the filling. Transfer to a baking pan.

Repeat the process with the remaining egg and filling ingredients.

Place the pan with the filled egg crepes in the oven for about 5 minutes to warm through. Meanwhile, warm the olives in a small pan over medium heat. Remove the crepes from the oven and garnish with the hot olives.

Makes 2 servings

Notes: Authentic cured olives add a key flavor note. However, if you want a milder-tasting dish, you can substitute canned olives. The crepes can assembled an hour or so ahead and refrigerated. Reheat before serving as instructed in the recipe, increasing the baking time to 10 minutes, or until the filling warms up.

Per serving: 308 calories, 20gm. fat, 6.5gm. saturated fat, 22gm. protein, 8.5gm. carbohydrate, 310mg. calcium

Labneh with Manakeesh and Zaatar

The morning tradition in many Middle Eastern countries is to pair YoChee with a pizza-like bread called manakeesh. An herb mix known as zaatar, composed of savory, thyme, sumac, and sesame seeds, is usually sprinkled on top. In some homes, olive oil is drizzled over the cheese. Flavorful black olives complete the meal.

The easiest way to duplicate this traditional breakfast is to use commercial pita bread, but if you like you can make homemade manakeesh using the Basic Pizza Crust on page 220. Since zaatar isn't readily available, nor is the herb sumac that it customarily contains, we offer a Westernized version that is tasty nonetheless. Since this isn't authentic, feel free to alter the seasonings according to availability and taste.

> 2 tablespoons sesame seeds
> 1 teaspoon dried savory
> 1 teaspoon crushed dried thyme leaves
> 1 teaspoon crushed dried marjoram leaves
> ½ teaspoon ground cumin
> pinch cayenne pepper
> ¼ cup YoChee per serving
> salt
> extra virgin olive oil, optional
> 1 whole wheat pita bread per serving
> black olives

Combine the sesame seeds and herbs, crushing the savory, thyme and marjoram between your fingers as you add them to release their flavor oils and make them as fine as possible. Place the mixture in an airtight jar and keep on hand for use as needed.

Allowing at least ¼ cup YoChee per serving, season modestly with salt to taste. Place the YoChee on individual plates or in a communal bowl. Sprinkle a generous amount of the sesame-herb mix on top. If desired, drizzle a little olive oil over all.

For each serving, warm up a pita bread either in the oven or by holding it over a gas flame for a minute or so. Serve the bread with the seasoned YoChee and olives.

Makes 1 serving

Per serving: 227 calories, 3gm. fat, <1gm. saturated fat, 12gm. protein, 41gm. carbohydrate, 135mg. calcium

(YoChee is also called labneh, labanah, labne, chaka or suzma, depending on the country of origin.)

Silver Dollar Blueberry & Cream Cakes

Small, delicate pancakes studded with berries.

> 1 egg
> 1 cup YoChee
> 2 tablespoons honey or maple syrup
> ¼ teaspoon salt
> ½ teaspoon vanilla extract
> ½ cup whole wheat flour
> 1 teaspoon baking powder
> ¼ teaspoon baking soda
> ½ cup fresh or frozen unsweetened blueberries

Beat the egg into the YoChee using a fork or wire whisk. Beat in the sweetening, salt and vanilla until blended.

Sprinkle the flour, baking powder and baking soda evenly over the YoChee mixture and stir gently, just until the dry ingredients are completely moistened. Stir in the berries.

Drop the batter by heaping soupspoonfuls onto a hot oiled skillet or griddle. Cook until nicely browned on the bottom. Turn and brown the other side.

Makes 10 pancakes; 2 servings

Per pancake: 60 calories, 1gm. fat, <1gm. saturated fat, 3.5gm. protein, 10gm. carbohydrate, 90mg. calcium (see YoChievements for comparisons)

PANCAKE, FRENCH TOAST & WAFFLE TOPPINGS

In order to improve the nutrition and staying power of pancake, French toast or waffle breakfasts, try one of these easy YoChee toppings. Plan on at least one-fourth cup topping per person, keeping in mind that with the superior nutrition profile of these toppings, you can be even more generous.

Note that if you prepare YoChee toppings ahead and refrigerate them, they may thicken a little. If you want them more pourable, just before serving stir in a spoonful or so of the juice called for in the recipe to reach the desired consistency. If the topping has separated a bit during storage, stir before serving.

MAPLE CREAM

Mix together equal parts YoChee and maple syrup for the perfect sweet topping.

PER ¼ CUP: 126 CALORIES, <1GM. FAT, <1GM. SATURATED FAT, 2.5GM. PROTEIN, 29GM. CARBOHYDRATE, 85MG. CALCIUM (SEE YOCHIEVEMENTS FOR COMPARISONS)

BERRIES AND CREAM

1 cup fresh or frozen unsweetened strawberries or raspberries
2 tablespoons honey
½ cup YoChee

Thaw the berries if frozen. Crush with a fork and stir in the honey. Using a fork, beat in the YoChee. Use immediately or refrigerate.

Makes about 1 cup

PER ¼ CUP: 68 CALORIES, <1GM. FAT, <1GM. SATURATED FAT, 3GM. PROTEIN, 15GM. CARBOHYDRATE, 65MG. CALCIUM

ORANGE-HONEY WHIP

1 cup YoChee
¼ cup orange juice
¼ cup honey
1 teaspoon minced orange rind, preferably organic

Beat the ingredients together with a wire whisk or fork until creamy. Use immediately or refrigerate.

Makes about 1 cup

> *PER ¼ CUP*: 114 CALORIES, <1GM. FAT, <1GM. SATURATED FAT, 5.5GM. PROTEIN, 24GM. CARBOHYDRATE, 120MG. CALCIUM

 ## PEACH TOPPING

½ cup peaches canned in juice, drained
2 tablespoons reserved juice
½ cup YoChee
1 tablespoon honey

Cut the peaches into pieces. Combine with the remaining ingredients in a blender or food processor. Puree until smooth. Use immediately or refrigerate.

Makes about 1 cup

> *PER ¼ CUP*: 51 CALORIES, <1GM. FAT, <1GM. SATURATED FAT, 3GM. PROTEIN, 11GM. CARBOHYDRATE, 60MG. CALCIUM

Aᴘʀɪᴄᴏᴛ Tᴏᴘᴘɪɴɢ

½ cup dried apricots
orange juice or apple juice
1 cup YoChee
¼ cup maple syrup or honey
thin slice lemon without peel

Place the apricots in a bowl and pour on enough juice to cover. Let stand 1 hour or longer. Drain, reserving the liquid. Cut the apricots into small pieces. Combine the apricots in a blender or food processor with ¼ cup of the reserved soaking liquid and the remaining ingredients. Puree until smooth and the apricots are reduced to specks. Use immediately or refrigerate.

Makes 1⅓ cups

Note: The dried apricots in this recipe need to be soaked to soften and plump them up. Do this at least one hour in advance, or overnight in the refrigerator.

Pᴇʀ ¼ ᴄᴜᴘ: 120 ᴄᴀʟᴏʀɪᴇs, <1ɢᴍ. ꜰᴀᴛ, <1ɢᴍ. sᴀᴛᴜʀᴀᴛᴇᴅ ꜰᴀᴛ, 5ɢᴍ. ᴘʀᴏᴛᴇɪɴ, 25ɢᴍ. ᴄᴀʀʙᴏʜʏᴅʀᴀᴛᴇ, 110ᴍɢ. ᴄᴀʟᴄɪᴜᴍ

APPETIZERS,

HORS D'ŒUVRE & LIGHT MEALS

Appetizers and hors d'œuvre usually make their appearance when people are entertaining. This is a great opportunity to introduce YoChee to others. Moreover, since many typical pre-meal delicacies are fat-intensive, YoChee is especially welcome here.

A number of the recipes in this section make ideal finger foods. A few are better as a first course. Many can also double as accompaniments to an entrée. Others—such as the pizzas, nachos and quesadillas—might even be selected as light meals in themselves.

In addition to the recipes in this section, you will find other suitable offering in both "Spreads" and "Dips."

☙ YoChievements ☜

Parmesan Toast (pg.47) vs. typical garlic bread
      23% less calories
      56% less fat
      27% more calcium

Mushroom Pâté (pg.53) vs. pâté de foie gras (goose liver pâté)
      57% less calories
      74% less fat
      87% less saturated fat
      Similar protein

more ...

Angelic Deviled Eggs (pg.55) vs. traditional deviled eggs
        30% less calories
        40% less fat
        Similar protein
        44% more calcium

Quick Mexican Pizza (pg.63) vs. Patio® Frozen Nacho Cheese Burrito
        33% less calories
        36% less fat
        33% more protein
        150% more calcium

Quick White Pita Pizzas (pg.64) vs. Amy's® Frozen Roasted Vegetable Pizza
        40% less calories
        82% less fat
        150% more protein
        8.5 times as much calcium

PARMESAN TOAST

A very simple recipe that provides an instant amuse-bouche—French for "amusement for the mouth." Also a good choice if you are looking for a quick tidbit that can make even basic meals distinctive.

> **8 slices French or Italian bread**
> **about 2 tablespoons YoChee**
> **about ¼ cup grated Parmesan cheese**

Toast the bread lightly. Spread a thin layer of YoChee on each slice of toast. Sprinkle some Parmesan cheese on top. Broil or top brown in a toaster oven until bubbly.

Makes 4 servings

Notes: The exact measure of ingredients will vary with the diameter of the bread. If using a larger bread, use 1 slice per serving and cut in halves or quarters.

Variation: Mash a clove of roasted garlic into the YoChee before spreading on bread, or prepare this with Roasted Garlic YoChee (see recipe page 73).

PER PIECE: 85 CALORIES, 2 GM. FAT, 1 GM. SATURATED FAT, 4 GM. PROTEIN, 13 GM. CARBOHYDRATE, 70 MG. CALCIUM (SEE YOCHIEVEMENTS FOR COMPARISONS)

Choice Cheese

Throughout the book we use Parmesan cheese to encompass a range of hard grating cheeses. Feel free to use Romano, locatelli, sardo or something similar in its place. Fresh grated cheese is preferred for its superior flavor.

Ginger-Soy Mushroom Toast Topping

Serve on toast or grilled bread for what Italians call a bruschetta appetizer. Also makes a tasty topping for salad greens. Can be stored in the refrigerator for a few days.

> **2 ounces mushrooms, finely chopped (½ cup)**
> **½ cup finely chopped tomato**
> **2 tablespoons finely chopped sweet onion, such as Vidalia or Walla Walla**
> **2 tablespoons Creamy Ginger-Soy Dressing (see recipe page 246)**
> **chopped parsley, optional**

Combine all the ingredients except the parsley in a bowl. Let rest for 30 minutes or longer for flavors to meld. Garnish with the chopped parsley, if desired, before serving.

Makes 1 cup topping; 4 servings

> *Per ¼ cup topping*: 37 calories, 3gm. fat, <1gm. saturated fat, 1gm. protein, 2.5gm. carbohydrate, 13mg. calcium

Appetizer Toasts

For more appetizer toast ideas, see "Spreads." For example, Roasted Garlic YoChee, Walnut YoChee Spread or Mediterranean Olive Spread on toasted slices of high-quality bread make excellent pre-meal finger foods.

SUCCULENT STUFFED MUSHROOMS

Plan on serving two to four of these stuffed mushrooms per person, depending on the size of mushrooms, mode of service (first course or hors d'œuvre), the rest of the menu and, of course, people's appetites.

> ½ **cup YoChee**
> 1½ **teaspoons mixed herbs of choice: oregano, parsley, basil, sage, thyme or favorite seasoning mix**
> 8 **medium-large mushrooms**

Preheat the oven to 350°F.

Combine the YoChee with the herbs and mix well.

Remove the stems from the mushrooms and reserve for another use. Clean the caps. Fill each cap with the seasoned YoChee.

Place the mushrooms on a baking sheet and bake for 15 to 20 minutes, until tender. Remove from the oven and let cool briefly before serving.

Makes 2 to 4 servings

> **PER MUSHROOM:** 15 CALORIES, <1 GM. FAT, <1 GM. SATURATED FAT, 2 GM. PROTEIN, 2 GM. CARBOHYDRATE, 30 MG. CALCIUM

PESTO-STUFFED MUSHROOMS

Pass on a platter for an hors d'œuvre or serve at the table as a first course.

> ¾ to 1 cup Creamy Walnut YoChee Pesto or NoWorry Spicy Chickpea YoChee Pesto (see recipes pages 250-251)
>
> 12 to 16 medium to large mushrooms or about 24 small mushrooms

Preheat the oven to 350°F.

Prepare the pesto of choice. Carefully remove the stems from the mushrooms without breaking the caps. Reserve the stems for another use. Clean the mushroom caps.

Fill each of the caps with a spoonful of pesto. Depending on their size, they will hold a little more or less than a tablespoonful; if you choose small mushrooms for platter service, each will hold a generous teaspoonful of filling.

Place the mushrooms, filling up, in a baking dish. Bake for 15 minutes, or until the mushrooms are tender. Very large mushrooms may take 5 minutes longer, or about 20 minutes, to cook.

Makes 4 to 6 servings

> PER LARGE MUSHROOM (BASED ON USING 12) WITH CREAMY WALNUT YOCHEE PESTO: 30 CALORIES, 2GM. FAT, <1GM. SATURATED FAT, 1.5GM. PROTEIN, 3GM. CARBOHYDRATE, 35MG. CALCIUM
>
> PER LARGE MUSHROOM WITH NOWORRY SPICY CHICKPEA YOCHEE PESTO: 25 CALORIES, 1GM. FAT, <1GM. SATURATED FAT, 1.5GM. PROTEIN, 3.5GM. CARBOHYDRATE, 30MG. CALCIUM

Spinach-Stuffed Mushrooms

No matter what the event or who the audience is, Spinach-Stuffed Mushrooms are always appreciated.

> **20 medium mushrooms**
> **¼ cup chopped shallots, scallions or onion**
> **2 cloves garlic, chopped**
> **1 tablespoon balsamic vinegar**
> **½ teaspoon soy sauce**
> **2 cups chopped fresh spinach (see Note)**
> **½ cup YoChee**
> **salt**
> **pepper**

Wash the mushrooms and carefully remove the stems without breaking the caps. Chop the stems until they are quite fine.

Combine the shallots, garlic and vinegar in a small skillet or saucepan and cook for 1 to 2 minutes. Add the chopped mushroom stems and soy sauce and cook, stirring occasionally, for 3 to 5 minutes, until the mushrooms soften and release their juices.

Add the spinach and cook, continuing to stir, until it is wilted and the liquid in the pan is absorbed. Remove from the heat, let cool for a few minutes, then stir in the YoChee. Season with salt and pepper to taste.

Stuff the spinach filling into the mushroom caps. The mushrooms can baked at once or the recipe can be prepared to this point and refrigerated for baking later.

Preheat the oven to 350°F. If the mushrooms were stuffed ahead and refrigerated, bring them back to room temperature while the oven preheats.

Place the mushrooms in a baking pan and bake for 20 minutes, until tender. Remove from the oven and let sit for a few minutes for the filling to set before serving.

Makes 20 mushrooms; 4 to 6 servings

Note: Fresh spinach can be replaced with an equal amount of arugula or half the volume of thawed frozen chopped spinach.

Per mushroom: 11 calories, <1gm. fat, <1gm. saturated fat, 1gm. protein, 2gm. carbohydrate, 15mg. calcium

Stuffed Portobello Mushrooms

A very elegant appetizer for a sit-down dinner. Serve one medium mushroom per person, or cut large mushrooms in half just before serving.

4 medium or 2 large portobello mushrooms, approximately 1 pound total
½ cup cooked brown rice or a combination of brown rice and wild rice
1 tablespoon chopped parsley
½ teaspoon oregano
1 large clove garlic, minced
1 tablespoon balsamic vinegar
2 tablespoons YoChee
3 tablespoons grated Parmesan cheese
salt
pepper
olive oil

Carefully remove the stems from the mushrooms, keeping the caps intact. Clean the stems, discarding tough or uncleanable ends. Chop enough to make ¼ cup. Save any remaining stems for another use.

In a bowl, combine the chopped mushroom stems, rice, parsley, oregano, garlic and vinegar. Add the YoChee and 2 tablespoons of the Parmesan cheese. Mix until thoroughly combined and the rice is coated with Yochee. The mixture should be sticky enough to hold together. If not, add more YoChee.

Season with salt and pepper to taste, according to the saltiness of the Parmesan cheese and whether the rice was preseasoned or not.

Clean the mushroom caps, pat dry and wipe the outer surface with olive oil. Place bottom side up on a baking pan and broil for 6 to 8 minutes, until barely tender and starting to release juices on the under side.

Remove the mushrooms from the broiler, invert and pack the filling into the hollows, creating a mound if need be. Sprinkle the remaining Parmesan cheese on top.

Return the mushrooms to the broiler and broil for 8 to10 minutes, until tender and juicy.

Makes 4 servings

Per serving: 123 calories, 3 gm. fat, 1 gm. saturated fat, 11 gm. protein, 17 gm. carbohydrate, 140 mg. calcium

MUSHROOM PÂTÉ

This savory pâté combines common white cultivated mushrooms with the more intense exotic varieties, such as portobello, cremini, porcini or shiitake. The best flavor balance comes when mild cultivated mushrooms compose about half of the mix. Mushroom Pâté should be prepared at least several hours ahead and keeps well in the refrigerator. Serve on thin slices of toasted bread, or mound on a serving plate with crackers and garnish with parsley sprigs and cherry tomato wedges.

> ¾ pound mixed cultivated white and exotic mushrooms, chopped (4 cups)
> ½ cup chopped shallots
> 2 cloves garlic, chopped
> 3 tablespoons cooking sherry
> 2 teaspoons soy sauce
> ½ cup pumpkin seeds
> ¼ cup sliced hazelnuts or almonds
> ⅓ cup YoChee
> ¼ teaspoon salt
> ¼ teaspoon hot pepper sauce or to taste

Combine the mushrooms, shallots, garlic, sherry and soy sauce in skillet. Cook, stirring frequently, until the mushrooms release their juices and are tender. This will take 8 to 10 minutes. Cook 3 to 5 minutes longer, until most of the liquid evaporates.

While the mushrooms cook, grind the pumpkin seeds and nuts to a fine meal in a blender or food processor. Transfer to a mixing bowl.

Transfer the cooked mushroom mixture to the blender or processor and puree to a coarse texture. Scrape into the bowl with the ground nuts. Incorporate the mushrooms into the nuts along with the YoChee, salt and hot pepper sauce.

Chill for several hours. Adjust the salt and hot pepper sauce to taste before serving.

Makes 2 cups; 8 or more servings

PER ¼ CUP: 103 CALORIES, 6GM. FAT, 1GM. SATURATED FAT, 6GM. PROTEIN, 7.5GM. CARBOHYDRATE, 40MG. CALCIUM (SEE YOCHIEVEMENTS FOR COMPARISONS)

Soy Sauce Selection

Choose a genuine soy sauce, not one doctored with corn syrup and caramel coloring. Real soy sauce is sold in Oriental groceries and natural food stores.

Rolled Eggplant Stuffed with Mushroom Pâté

A bite-size hors d'œuvre suitable for elegant entertaining. Make at least several hours or as long as a day in advance.

> **1 medium eggplant, about 6 inches long (¾ pound)**
> **olive oil**
> **1 cup Mushroom Pâté (preceding recipe)**

Preheat the broiler.

Peel the eggplant and cut lengthwise into slices about ¼ inch thick. Use the 6 largest slices for this recipe. Reserve any remaining eggplant for another use (see Note.)

Generously oil a baking sheet with olive oil. Place the eggplant slices on the baking sheet, then turn them over so both sides are lightly coated with oil. Broil about 6 inches below the heat for about 5 minutes on each side, or until tender and lightly browned.

Arrange 3 scant tablespoons of the Mushroom Pâté in a lengthwise strip down the center of each eggplant slice. Roll jellyroll style along the long edge to cover the filling. Chill.

To serve, use a very sharp knife to cut the eggplant rolls into 1-inch pieces.

Makes about 30 pieces

Note: Any remaining eggplant slices can be broiled at the same time, cut into strips, tossed with a favorite salad dressing and served as a side dish.

Per piece: 20 calories, 1gm. fat, <1gm. saturated fat, 1gm. protein, 2gm. carbohydrate, 8mg. calcium

ANGELIC DEVILED EGGS

A new version of a 1950s classic that is equally tasty, yet has far less fat.

> 6 hard-cooked eggs
> 1 teaspoon balsamic or wine vinegar
> 3 to 4 tablespoons YoChee
> 2 to 2½ teaspoons prepared mustard
> salt
> paprika or minced fresh parsley or dill

Cut the eggs in half lengthwise and carefully scoop out the yolks without damaging the whites.

Using a potato masher or fork, mash the egg yolks with the vinegar and the smaller amounts of YoChee and mustard. When thoroughly mashed, beat gently with a fork to make the mixture light and creamy. If needed, add the remaining YoChee. Adjust mustard and salt to taste.

Mound the mixture into the hollows of the egg whites. Sprinkle generously with the paprika, parsley or dill.

Makes 12 halves

> *PER ½ EGG*: 43 CALORIES, 3 GM. FAT, 1 GM. SATURATED FAT, 3.5 GM. PROTEIN, 1 GM. CARBOHYDRATE, 23 MG. CALCIUM (SEE YOCHIEVEMENTS FOR COMPARISONS)

Rᴇᴅ & Gʀᴇᴇɴ Lᴀʏᴇʀᴇᴅ Sᴘʀᴇᴀᴅ

By flavoring YoChee with green and red pepper purees, then returning the purees to your YoChee draining device in layers, you can create a tasty work of art for festive occasions.

> 1 medium green pepper (6 to 8 ounces)
> 1 medium red pepper (6 to 8 ounces)
> 2 cloves garlic, sliced
> ½ teaspoon salt
> 1 teaspoon lemon juice
> ¼ cup chopped parsley
> 1 teaspoon balsamic vinegar
> 1½ cups YoChee
> cayenne pepper or hot sauce

Place the peppers on a baking sheet and broil 4 to 6 inches beneath the heat for about 15 minutes, turning as needed until the skins are blistered. Alternatively, place them on a baking sheet and bake in a 450°F. oven for about 30 minutes, until the skins begin to brown and start to pull away from the flesh. When the peppers are done, wrap them in a clean cloth for a few minutes to steam. When cool enough to handle, peel off the skins, cut the peppers open and remove the seeds, stems and any thick ribs. Pat dry and cut into pieces, keeping the two peppers separate.

Place the green pepper pieces into a food processor along with 1 clove of sliced garlic, ¼ teaspoon salt, the lemon juice and parsley. Puree until smooth. Transfer to a bowl.

Clean and dry the processor. Add the red pepper pieces, remaining clove of sliced garlic, ¼ teaspoon salt and the balsamic vinegar. Puree until smooth. Transfer to a separate bowl.

Add ¾ cup of YoChee to the green pepper puree. Mix well. Add the remaining ¾ cup YoChee to the red pepper puree. Mix well and season with cayenne or hot sauce to taste.

Spoon one-third to one-half of the green pepper mixture into your YoChee maker, depending on the shape. That is, if it is cone-shaped or narrower at the bottom, use the lesser amount; if straight-sided use half the mixture. Top with one-third to one-half of the red pepper mixture using the same criteria. Smooth gently to completely cover the first layer. Repeat the layers using the remaining YoChee mixtures.

Chill for several hours. Unmold onto a plate to serve.

Makes 2 cups

> Pᴇʀ ¼ ᴄᴜᴘ: 46 ᴄᴀʟᴏʀɪᴇs, <1ɢᴍ. ғᴀᴛ, <1ɢᴍ. sᴀᴛᴜʀᴀᴛᴇᴅ ғᴀᴛ, 4ɢᴍ. ᴘʀᴏᴛᴇɪɴ, 7ɢᴍ. ᴄᴀʀʙᴏʜʏᴅʀᴀᴛᴇ, 95ᴍɢ. ᴄᴀʟᴄɪᴜᴍ

GREEK-STYLE STUFFED ARTICHOKES

Stuffed fresh artichokes are always a treat. Here they appear with a flavorful rice-cheese filling that makes good use of leftover cooked brown rice.

> 4 medium artichokes
> 1 cup cooked brown rice
> 1 tablespoon lemon juice
> 1 teaspoon oregano
> ¼ cup chopped parsley
> 1 tablespoon chopped capers
> ½ cup YoChee
> ¼ cup crumbled feta cheese
> pepper
> ½ cup dry breadcrumbs
> 1 large clove garlic, minced
> ¼ teaspoon salt
> 1 tablespoon olive oil

Remove the stems from the artichokes so they sit steadily. Cut the sharp tips off the leaves using a kitchen scissors. Steam for 35 to 45 minutes or pressure-cook 13 to 15 minutes, until tender. When cool enough to handle, remove the hairy choke from the center. A grapefruit spoon is a handy tool for this job.

Preheat the oven to 375°F.

Combine the rice, lemon juice, oregano, parsley, capers, YoChee, feta and a generous amount of pepper. Mix well. Pack into the center of each artichoke. If there is any filling left, spread the leaves and insert it carefully into the spaces.

Combine the breadcrumbs, garlic and salt. Moisten with the olive oil. Top each artichoke with 2 tablespoons of the crumbs.

Place the artichokes upright in a shallow baking pan. Surround with a little water. Bake for 20 minutes, until the filling is hot and the crumbs are browned.

Makes 4 servings

PER SERVING: 250 CALORIES, 7 GM. FAT, 2 GM. SATURATED FAT, 11 GM. PROTEIN, 38 GM. CARBOHYDRATE, 210 MG. CALCIUM

Better Bread & Cracker Crumbs

For best nutrition and taste, we recommend making your own crumbs in a blender, using dried whole grain bread or crackers.

Creamy Stuffed Italian Artichoke Bottoms

The firm earthiness of the artichoke is perfectly counterbalanced by the tangy flavor and creamy texture of the YoChee crown. As these are quite rich, two bottoms are generally enough for a serving. However, you may wish to provide extra, depending on the rest of the menu and appetites.

½ cup YoChee
½ teaspoon oregano
3 tablespoons minced parsley
1 clove garlic, finely minced
¼ cup shredded and finely chopped zucchini or thawed and squeezed-dry chopped frozen spinach
2 tablespoons grated Parmesan cheese
8 canned artichoke bottoms

Preheat the oven to 350°F.

Combine the YoChee with the remaining ingredients, except the artichoke bottoms. Before adding the zucchini or spinach, press out as much of the moisture as possible.

Drain the artichoke bottoms and pat dry. Mound a spoonful of the seasoned YoChee onto each artichoke bottom. Sprinkle with a little additional Parmesan cheese, if desired.

Place on a baking pan and bake for 12 to 15 minutes, until the stuffing is hot.

Makes 4 servings

Variation: For Creamy Stuffed Greek Artichoke Bottoms, replace the parsley with dill and the Parmesan cheese with feta.

Per artichoke bottom: 31 calories, <1gm. fat, <1gm. saturated fat, 3gm. protein, 4gm. carbohydrate, 70mg. calcium

BAKED ARTICHOKE CHEESE SQUARES

These bite-size squares are ideal for entertaining. Everything can be assembled in advance and then baked just before serving, or the entire operation can be completed ahead since service can be hot, warm or at room temperature. As an added bonus, refrigerated leftovers are delicious as a snack or sandwich filling.

14-ounce can artichoke hearts in water
1¼ cups YoChee
½ cup grated cheese of choice (Parmesan, provolone, cheddar, Monterrey Jack, feta or other natural cheese, alone or mixed)
2 tablespoons sun-dried tomatoes
2 tablespoons coarsely chopped walnuts
⅛ teaspoon hot sauce
¼ cup chopped fresh dill or parsley

Preheat the oven to 350°F.

Drain the artichoke hearts. Chop into small pieces. Combine with the remaining ingredients. Transfer to a 9-inch-square or shallow 1-quart baking dish. If assembled more than one hour ahead, refrigerate.

Bake for 30 minutes, until firm and lightly browned on top. Let sit at room temperature for at least 10 minutes to set before cutting. Cut into 2-inch squares and arrange on a platter to serve.

Makes 16 2-inch pieces

PER 2-INCH PIECE: 43 CALORIES, 1.5 GM. FAT, <1 GM. SATURATED FAT, 3.5 GM. PROTEIN, 4 GM. CARBOHYDRATE, 90 MG. CALCIUM

BROCCOLI PANCAKES

These miniature vegetable-studded pancakes provide a generous appetizer for four or make a nice addition to a vegetable plate dinner. They are sufficiently tasty plain but can be garnished with a YoChee sauce (for example, YoChee Aioli, page 254), or served with a flavorful mustard, chutney or soy dipping sauce.

> **3 cups cut-up broccoli (about 10 ounces)**
> **¼ cup minced onion**
> **1 small clove garlic, minced**
> **dash hot pepper sauce, optional**
> **⅓ cup cornmeal**
> **¼ cup YoChee**
> **2 eggs**
> **½ teaspoon salt**
> **olive or canola oil**

To prepare the broccoli, peel the stalks and cut them into even-size chunks. Separate the tops into individual florets. Steam for 5 minutes.

Chop the steamed broccoli into very tiny pieces. Combine with the onion, garlic and hot pepper sauce. Stir in the cornmeal.

Place the YoChee in a separate bowl. Beat in the eggs and salt. Don't worry if it is a little lumpy.

Add the YoChee-egg mixture to the vegetable mixture. Stir until thoroughly combined and no dry spots remain.

Heat enough oil to just cover the bottom of a large skillet or griddle. When hot, drop in the pancake mixture by heaping tablespoonfuls. Flatten slightly. The pancakes should be just 2 inches in size.

Cook 3 to 5 minutes, until the pancakes are set on the bottom. Turn gently and cook the other side. Transfer to a paper towel to dry the surface.

If need be, keep the cooked pancakes warm in a low (300°F.) oven while the remainder cook. If serving time is delayed, they can be warmed up again.

Makes 16 pancakes; 4 servings

> **PER PANCAKE:** 36 CALORIES, 1.5GM. FAT, <1GM. SATURATED FAT, 2GM. PROTEIN, 3.5GM. CARBOHYDRATE, 20MG. CALCIUM

BEAN NACHOS

Adding YoChee to the bean layer of these nachos provides a creaminess that is a nice contrast to the salsa and chopped pepper. Choose medium or spicy salsa according to taste. Likewise, add some jalapenos or other hot peppers for extra zip.

> 3 ounces tortilla chips (about 3 cups)
> 1½ cups cooked black beans, pinto beans or kidney beans, drained
> ½ cup YoChee
> 1 teaspoon chili powder
> ½ cup shredded Monterey Jack or cheddar cheese
> ¼ cup salsa
> 2 tablespoons chopped sweet green or hot peppers

Preheat the oven to 375°F.

Place the chips so they are nestled together in a 9-inch pie pan or shallow 1-quart baking dish.

Mash the beans lightly using a potato masher or a fork. Mash in the YoChee and chili powder. Gently spread to cover the chips.

Scatter the shredded cheese over the beans. Drop the salsa in dollops evenly over all. Top with the chopped peppers.

Bake for 15 minutes, until the cheese is melted and the beans are hot. Transfer to a serving plate.

Makes 4 servings

> **Per serving:** 283 calories, 11 gm. fat, 4 gm. saturated fat, 14.5 gm. protein, 33 gm. carbohydrate, 220 mg. calcium

Corn Quesadillas

Quesadillas are like grilled cheese sandwiches made with tortillas instead of bread. This corn-and-cheese-stuffed version makes a good appetizer, as well as an excellent accompaniment to bean-vegetable entrees.

> **1 cup YoChee**
> **1 cup fresh or thawed frozen corn kernels**
> **¼ cup minced cilantro, or ¼ cup flat-leaf Italian parsley combined with**
>   **½ teaspoon cumin**
> **salt**
> **8 6-inch corn tortillas**
> **½ cup shredded Monterey Jack or cheddar cheese or a combination**
> **tomato or tomatillo salsa**

Mix the YoChee, corn kernels, cilantro or parsley plus cumin, and a pinch of salt.

Place 4 tortillas on a flat surface. Spread one-fourth of the YoChee mixture on each. Scatter 2 tablespoons of the shredded cheese over this. Cover with a second tortilla.

Heat a heavy skillet or griddle. When hot, cook the quesadillas in the dry pan for 3 minutes on each side, until the filling is hot but the tortillas remain soft rather than crisp. Unless you have a large griddle, you will probably have to cook them in batches (see Note).

With a very sharp knife or kitchen scissors, cut each quesadilla into 4 wedges. Serve along with your favorite salsa.

Makes 4 servings

Note: Quesadillas should be served as soon as possible after they are made. If they are cooked individually and need to be kept warm, put them on a baking pan, cover with a clean kitchen towel and place in a very low (200°F.) oven.

Per quesadilla: 247 calories, 6gm. fat, 3gm. saturated fat, 13gm. protein, 38gm. carbohydrate, 315mg. calcium

⏰ Quick Mexican Pizza

In this recipe, corn tortillas provide the crust for a Mexican-style pizza. As a first course, plan on one pizza per person. For an hors d'œuvre, cut each pizza into four wedges. As an entrée or accompaniment, prepare two pizzas per person. If making just one or two at a time, you may want to use a toaster oven.

> **2 corn tortillas**
> **¼ cup YoChee**
> **¼ cup salsa or Mexican-style tomato sauce**
> **¼ cup shredded Monterey Jack or cheddar cheese or a combination**

Preheat the oven to 400°F.

Place the tortillas on a baking sheet. Spread 2 tablespoons of the YoChee to cover the surface of each tortilla. Top each with 2 tablespoons of the sauce and scatter 2 tablespoons of the cheese over all.

Bake for 10 minutes, until the cheese is melted.

Makes 1 to 2 servings

> Per pizza: 143 calories, 5gm. fat, 3gm. saturated fat, 8gm. protein, 17gm. carbohydrate, 220mg. calcium (see YoChievements for comparisons)

Serving Tip

A kitchen scissors is a good tool for cutting pizza into appetizer wedges.

⏰ Quick White Pita Pizzas

These simple pizzas work with a variety of toppings, as shown below. Cut them into triangles for an hors d'œuvre or as part of an antipasto first course. You can also serve two rounds per person as an entrée, or one as an individual pizza to accompany a meal.

> **2 2-ounce pita breads**
> **¾ cup YoChee**
> **Vegetable Topping (see below)**

Preheat the oven to 400°F.

Using a fork, perforate the circumference of the breads. Separate each into two rounds.

Spread each pita round with 3 tablespoons of the YoChee. Top with the Vegetable Topping of choice.

Place on a baking sheet and bake for 15 minutes, until lightly browned at the edges. Let sit for a few minutes to set filling before serving.

Makes 4 to 6 appetizer servings; 2 to 4 servings as an entrée or accompaniment

> *Per round before adding Vegetable Topping*: 117 calories, 1 gm. fat, <1 gm. saturated fat, 7 gm. protein, 21 gm. carbohydrate, 90 mg. calcium (see YoChievements for comparisons)

Vegetable Toppings

These are some of our favorite variations. Use them as is, or for inspiration.

Greens: Top each round with ½ cup shredded raw greens, such as spinach, romaine, leaf lettuce, arugula, endive, radicchio or a combination. Season with ⅛ teaspoon crushed hot red pepper flakes. Top with 1 tablespoon pine nuts, grated Parmesan cheese or crumbled feta.

Mushroom: Top each round with ⅓ cup thinly sliced raw mushrooms and 1 tablespoon frozen green peas. Scatter a clove of slivered garlic on top. Season with ⅛ teaspoon oregano or mixed Italian seasonings.

Artichoke: Follow the directions for mushroom topping, replacing the mushrooms with ⅓ cup thinly sliced canned or cooked artichoke hearts.

Sweet Red Pepper: Follow the directions for mushroom topping, replacing the mushrooms with ⅓ cup thin strips of sweet red pepper. Instead of green peas, use capers.

Rustic Pizza, French-Style

French, rather than Italian in origin, this country-style pizza is easy to make even if you aren't an experienced pizza or pastry maker.

> Amazing YoChee Piecrust (see recipe page 232)
> 1 cup thinly sliced onion, preferably a sweet variety such as Vidalia, Walla Walla or Sweet Texas
> 1 tablespoon dry red or white wine or water
> 1 clove garlic, chopped
> 1 cup chopped plum tomatoes (from 6 to 8 ounces tomatoes)
> ½ teaspoon dried rosemary or 1 tablespoon chopped fresh basil
> salt
> ¾ cup YoChee
> ¼ cup crumbled fresh goat cheese (2 ounces)
> pepper

Prepare the crust as directed in the recipe, using olive oil. Chill for at least 30 minutes.

Put the onions in a skillet along with the wine or water. Cook, stirring frequently, for 10 to 15 minutes, until the onions are quite limp but not browned. Add the garlic, tomatoes, herb of choice and a generous pinch of salt. Continue to cook for about 10 minutes, until the tomato is softened. Turn the heat up and evaporate as much liquid as possible.

Preheat the oven to 425°F.

Place the Amazing YoChee Piecrust on a pastry cloth or wax-paper-lined surface. Roll into an 11-inch circle. Don't worry if the edges are a little ragged. Transfer to an ungreased baking sheet.

Season the YoChee with a generous pinch of salt. Spread over the pastry, leaving a 1-inch border all around. Distribute the onion-tomato mixture evenly over the YoChee. Top with the goat cheese. Season liberally with pepper.

Fold the pastry border over the edge of the filling, pleating the dough every inch or so to make it fit.

Bake for 15 to 20 minutes, or until the crust is crisp and golden around the edges. Serve warm or at room temperature.

Makes 6 slices

Per slice: 150 calories, 8gm. fat, 2gm. saturated fat, 6gm. protein, 16gm. carbohydrate, 108mg. calcium

Three-Layered Mousse I

The appearance of this colorful three-layered mousse is very impressive. Although the preparation isn't difficult, there are several steps, and you need to leave enough time for baking and cooling. For convenience, frozen cauliflower and spinach are used. If you prefer to use fresh ingredients or alternative seasonings, see the Notes. Fortunately, the mousse can be made ahead and refrigerated. In fact, the flavor actually improves with a day of storage.

1 pound carrots, peeled and diced (about 2½ cups)
½ cup water
½ teaspoon ground ginger
¾ teaspoon salt
1 cup YoChee
3 eggs
1-pound package frozen cauliflower
1½ teaspoons curry powder
10-ounce package frozen chopped spinach, thawed
1 large clove garlic, minced
hot pepper sauce

Place the carrots in a skillet or saucepan with ¼ cup of the water, the ginger and ¼ teaspoon of the salt. Bring to a boil, cover and simmer gently over moderate heat for about 15 minutes, until the carrots are very tender. Drain off any liquid. Puree in a food processor or food mill. Mix in ⅓ cup of the YoChee. Beat in 1 egg. Transfer to a well-oiled 8- or 9-inch loaf pan and tamp down firmly into an even layer with a rubber spatula.

Rinse the pot and add the cauliflower along with the remaining ¼ cup water and ¼ teaspoon salt. Bring to a boil. Cover and simmer gently over moderate heat for about 10 minutes, until the cauliflower is very tender. Remove from the heat. Add the curry powder and mash with a potato masher until the cauliflower is reduced to a rough puree. Mash in ⅓ cup of the YoChee. Beat in 1 egg. Spread carefully in an even layer over the carrot and tamp down firmly with a rubber spatula.

If the spinach is not completely thawed, rinse the pan, add the spinach, cover and cook until no ice crystals remain. Squeeze the spinach to remove as much moisture as possible. Add the minced garlic, a generous dash of hot pepper sauce and the remaining ¼ teaspoon salt. Mash in the remaining ⅓ cup YoChee. Beat in the remaining egg. Spread carefully in an even layer over the cauliflower and tamp down firmly with a rubber spatula.

Preheat the oven to 375°F.

Place the loaf pan in a larger pan and add hot water to reach about halfway up the sides of the loaf pan. Bake for 1 hour or until the loaf is firm.

Remove from the oven and take the loaf pan out of the hot water bath. Let it rest for about 1 hour, until lukewarm, before unmolding onto a platter. At serving time, carefully cut into ½-inch thick slices. Serve lukewarm or at room temperature. If refrigerated, bring back to room temperature before serving.

Makes 16 slices; 8 servings

Notes: The frozen vegetables can be replaced with 5 cups of fresh raw cauliflowerets (3 cups cooked) and 1 cup of cooked chopped fresh spinach. If you want to be creative, you can vary the seasonings; suggestions include using mustard with the cauliflower and nutmeg, tarragon or fresh dill with either the carrots or spinach.

PER SLICE: 50 CALORIES, 1 GM. FAT, <1 GM. SATURATED FAT, 4 GM. PROTEIN, 6.5 GM. CARBOHYDRATE, 70 MG. CALCIUM

THREE-LAYERED MOUSSE II

Much like the preceding recipe, but with a different selection of vegetables. The Notes at the end of the recipe provide instructions for using fresh rather than frozen vegetables, for making adjustments if using canned beans and for alternative seasonings. Remember that if you plan ahead, the flavor actually improves when the mousse is refrigerated for a day.

> **1-pound package frozen broccoli florets or cuts**
> **¼ cup water**
> **¾ teaspoon salt**
> **1½ teaspoons prepared mustard**
> **1 cup YoChee**
> **3 eggs**
> **1½ cups cooked white beans, drained**
> **1 clove garlic, minced**
> **12-ounce package frozen mashed winter squash, thawed**
> **1 teaspoon cumin**

Place the broccoli in a skillet or saucepan with the water and ¼ teaspoon of salt. Bring to a boil, cover and cook over moderate heat for about 20 minutes or until the broccoli is very tender. Remove from the heat. Add the mustard and mash with a potato masher until the broccoli is reduced to a rough puree. Mash in ⅓ cup of the YoChee. Beat in 1 egg. Transfer to an oiled 8- or 9-inch loaf pan and tamp down firmly in an even layer with a rubber spatula.

Combine the beans in a bowl with the garlic and ¼ teaspoon of salt if they are unsalted, or salt to taste. Mash thoroughly with a potato masher. Mash in ⅓ cup of the YoChee. Beat in 1 egg. Spread carefully in an even layer over the broccoli and tamp down firmly with a rubber spatula

If the squash isn't completely thawed, cook until no ice crystals remain. Combine the squash with the remaining ¼ teaspoon salt and the cumin. Mix in the remaining ⅓ cup YoChee. Beat in the remaining egg. Spread carefully in an even layer over the beans and tamp down firmly with a rubber spatula.

Preheat the oven to 375⁰F.

Place the loaf pan in a larger pan and add hot water to reach about halfway up the sides of the loaf pan. Bake for 1 hour, until the loaf is firm. Remove from the oven, take the loaf pan out of the hot water bath and let it rest for about 1 hour, until lukewarm, before unmolding onto a platter. At serving time, carefully cut into ½-inch thick slices. Serve lukewarm or at room temperature. If refrigerated, bring back to room temperature before serving.

Makes 16 slices; 8 servings

Notes: If fresh vegetables are preferred, begin with 5 cups of fresh raw broccoli florets (3 cups cooked) or 2½ cups chopped cooked broccoli. For the squash, use 1½ cups mashed cooked winter squash of any variety. Canned white beans can be used but need to be rinsed and drained. A 15- or 16-ounce can contains 1½ cups of beans. If they are salted, do not add more. If you want to vary the seasonings, try nutmeg, tarragon or fresh dill with either the broccoli or the squash.

Per slice: 69 calories, 1gm. fat, <1gm. saturated fat, 5gm. protein, 10gm. carbohydrate, 73mg. calcium

SPREADS

YoChee is the base for many tasty low-fat spreads that can successfully replace popular high-fat cheese spreads and butters. Use these spreads on sandwiches or as a snack or appetizer on crackers or bread. They also make excellent nutritious stuffings for celery, cherry tomatoes or raw pepper wedges, or decorations for rounds of cucumber or zucchini.

Spreads made with YoChee can be served at once, but they generally benefit by being prepared an hour or more ahead so flavors have a chance to develop fully. Chilling also brings about a slightly firmer consistency. Most spreads will keep for about one week in the refrigerator.

↝ YoChievements ↜

Herb YoChee (pg.71) vs. Philadelphia® Soft Herb and Garlic
    Cream Cheese
        85% less calories
        No fat vs. 5 grams fat per tablespoon
        150% more protein
        50% more calcium

Roasted Garlic YoChee (pg.73) vs. butter
        84% less calories
        No fat vs. 11 grams fat per tablespoon
        1.5 grams protein vs. no protein per tablespoon
        12 times more calcium

more...

Olive and Pimiento YoChee Spread (pg.78) vs. Kraft® Olive and
 Pimiento Cheese Spread
  20% less calories
  50% less fat
  50% less saturated fat
  175% more protein
  7 times as much calcium

Lentil Pâté (pg.81) vs. canned chicken liver pâté
  15% less calories
  70% less fat
  Similar protein
  6 times as much calcium

⏰ HERB YOCHEE

There are many ways to flavor YoChee to make a cream-cheese-like spread. We provide several suggestions below in Enhancing Herb YoChee, but feel free to experiment.

½ cup YoChee
1 tablespoon fresh or freeze-dried chives or 1 tablespoon minced fresh scallion
1 tablespoon fresh or 1 teaspoon dried dill
pinch salt, optional

Combine all the ingredients. Refrigerate several hours to stiffen.

Makes ½ cup

PER 2 TABLESPOONS: 22 CALORIES, <1 GM. FAT, <1 GM. SATURATED FAT, 2.5 GM. PROTEIN, 2.5 GM. CARBOHYDRATE, 60 MG. CALCIUM (SEE YOCHIEVEMENTS FOR COMPARISONS)

Enhancing Herb YoChee

Use the following flavoring ingredients along with those above, or to replace any of them:

✔ Fresh parsley, cilantro or basil (about 1 tablespoon)

✔ Dried herbs such as basil, oregano, rosemary, sage, cumin or curry powder (about 1 teaspoon)

✔ Chopped green or red pepper, radish or water chestnuts (up to 2 tablespoons)

✔ Garlic lovers can add a minced clove of garlic

Sunday Morning Vegetable YoChee

Ideal for smearing on bagels. Serve with the morning newspaper.

> 1 cup YoChee
> ¼ cup finely chopped green pepper
> 2 scallions, finely chopped
> 1 small carrot, shredded
> ½ teaspoon salt

Combine all the ingredients. Use at once or refrigerate.

Makes 1 cup

> PER 2 TABLESPOONS: 26 CALORIES, <1GM. FAT, <1GM. SATURATED FAT, 3GM. PROTEIN, 3.5GM. CARBOHYDRATE, 60MG. CALCIUM

Sunday Morning Muse

This YoChee recipe can be varied by adding sliced radishes, chopped celery, water chestnuts, sun-dried tomatoes, fresh dill or other herbs or flavorings to taste.

Tomato YoChee

A rich tomato flavor.

> **3 tablespoons chopped, rehydrated dried tomatoes (see Note)**
> **½ cup YoChee**
> **1 tablespoon tomato paste**
> **1 teaspoon dried basil**

Combine all the ingredients in a small bowl and stir until uniformly mixed. Chill for several hours before serving.

Makes about ½ cup

Note: To rehydrate dried tomatoes, run them quickly under cold water. Let sit for about 5 minutes to soften before chopping. The tomatoes can still be a bit firm, as they will continue to soften in the YoChee.

> PER 2 TABLESPOONS: 31 CALORIES, <1 GM. FAT, <1 GM. SATURATED FAT, 3 GM. PROTEIN, 5 GM. CARBOHYDRATE, 65 MG. CALCIUM

Roasted Garlic YoChee

For garlic lovers.

> **1 small head garlic with about 10 cloves**
> **½ cup YoChee**
> **1 tablespoon finely minced parsley**
> **⅛ teaspoon salt or to taste**

For roasted garlic, preheat the oven to 400°F. Place the head of garlic in a baking dish and bake for about 40 minutes, until the individual cloves of garlic are soft. Remove from the oven. When cool enough to handle, separate the cloves and holding the pointed end in your hand, squeeze out the garlic. Continue until you have a tablespoon of garlic puree.

Combine the garlic, YoChee and parsley. Season to taste with salt. Store in the refrigerator until needed.

Makes ½ cup

> PER 1 TABLESPOON: 16 CALORIES, <1 GM. FAT, <1 GM. SATURATED FAT, 1.5 GM. PROTEIN, 2.5 GM. CARBOHYDRATE, 35 MG. CALCIUM (SEE YOCHIEVEMENTS FOR COMPARISONS)

Feta Herb Spread

Spread on small rounds of toasted French bread, or serve in a bowl surrounded by wedges of crackers or pita bread and olives.

1 cup YoChee
½ cup crumbled feta cheese (3 ounces)
1 clove garlic, mashed
1½ teaspoons olive oil
1 tablespoon minced fresh parsley
½ teaspoon oregano
pepper

Combine all the ingredients in a bowl, seasoning liberally or to taste with pepper. Mash until smooth.

Cover and refrigerate for several hours, if possible, so that the flavor develops and the cheese sets up.

Makes about 1 cup

Per 2 tablespoons: 54 calories, 3gm. fat, 1.5gm. saturated fat, 4gm. protein, 3gm. carbohydrate, 105mg. calcium

Cashew Rubble Butter

This can be prepared with any odds and ends of cheese you have on hand. Store in the refrigerator and use like butter on bread or crackers.

¼ cup raw cashews
¼ pound cheese (1 cup grated)
4 to 6 tablespoons YoChee

Grind the cashews to a powder in a blender or food processor. Transfer to a mixing bowl. Grate the cheese finely.

Combine the grated cheese with the ground nuts. Incorporate the YoChee as needed by mashing with a fork until the mixture is of stiff spreading consistency.

Use at once or refrigerate.

Makes 1 cup

Per 1 tablespoon: 73 calories, 6gm. fat, 3gm. saturated fat, 4gm. protein, 1gm. carbohydrate, 110mg. calcium

WALNUT YOCHEE SPREAD

Especially good on dark rye bread, cucumber rounds, celery, endive spears or sliced pears.

> ½ cup YoChee
> ¼ cup crumbled blue cheese
> ¼ cup chopped walnuts
> dash hot pepper sauce or pinch cayenne, optional

Combine the YoChee with the blue cheese and mash with a fork until evenly mixed. Add the walnuts and season to taste with hot pepper sauce or cayenne.

Use at once or refrigerate.

Makes ⅔ cup

> **PER 1 TABLESPOON:** 38 CALORIES, 3GM. FAT, 1GM. SATURATED FAT, 2GM. PROTEIN, 1.5GM. CARBOHYDRATE, 40MG. CALCIUM

MEDITERRANEAN OLIVE SPREAD

Use on sandwiches or on toast for an excellent appetizer. A generous teaspoonful is enough for one slice of French or Italian bread or half of a sandwich-size bread slice. You can also use this olive spread as a flavoring for pasta.

> ½ cup pitted black olives (see Note)
> 1 small clove garlic, minced
> 2 tablespoons chopped parsley
> 1 teaspoon balsamic vinegar
> 3 tablespoons YoChee

Combine the olives, garlic, parsley and vinegar in a mini-blender or food processor. Puree quickly until finely chopped but not necessarily smooth. Transfer to a bowl and add the YoChee.

Use at once or refrigerate.

Makes ½ cup

Note: Prepare this with good-quality cured olives, not the bland canned kind.

> **PER 1 TABLESPOON:** 28 CALORIES, 2GM. FAT, <1GM. SATURATED FAT, <1GM. PROTEIN, 1.5GM. CARBOHYDRATE, 15MG. CALCIUM

MELISSA'S OLIVE SPREAD

Unlike the preceding recipe, which calls for flavorful cured olives, Melissa's Olive Spread transforms bland canned olives into something tasty. Spread thinly on bread or crackers, or on sliced raw zucchini. Also great for flavoring pasta.

½ cup grated Parmesan cheese (2 ounces)
6-ounce can pitted black olives, drained (about 1½ cups)
hot pepper sauce
⅓ cup YoChee

If the Parmesan cheese isn't already grated, put it in the blender or food processor first and grate.

Combine the grated cheese, olives and a few dashes of hot pepper sauce in a blender or food processor. Process until everything is minced. You may have to start and stop the machine a few times and stir the ingredients down.

Add the YoChee and process until you have a thick, spreadable mixture. If you want a dip, add additional YoChee.

Use at once or refrigerate.

Makes 1⅛ cup

> *PER 2 TABLESPOONS*: 53 CALORIES, 3.5 GM. FAT, 1 GM. SATURATED FAT, 3 GM. PROTEIN, 2 GM. CARBOHYDRATE, 110 MG. CALCIUM

Choice Cheese

Throughout the book we use Parmesan cheese to encompass a range of hard grating cheeses. Feel free to use Romano, locatelli, sardo or something similar in its place. Fresh grated cheese is preferred for its superior flavor.

MILD YoCHEE AND TOMATO SPREAD

Superior to commercial cheese spreads, which are generally laden with salt and food additives.

> 1 cup shredded cheddar cheese (4 ounces)
> ⅓ cup YoChee
> 1½ tablespoons tomato paste
> ¼ teaspoon hot pepper sauce or to taste

Using a fork, mash the first 3 ingredients together until evenly blended. Add hot pepper sauce to taste. Use at once or refrigerate.

Makes scant 1 cup

> *PER 2 TABLESPOONS*: 66 CALORIES, 5 GM. FAT, 3 GM. SATURATED FAT, 4.5 GM. PROTEIN, 1.5 GM. CARBOHYDRATE, 120 MG. CALCIUM

 ## SHARP YoCHEE AND TOMATO SPREAD

This cheese-and-tomato spread combines cheddar with blue cheese, which gives it more punch.

> ½ cup shredded cheddar cheese (2 ounces)
> ¼ cup crumbled blue cheese
> ¼ cup YoChee
> 1½ tablespoons tomato paste
> ¼ teaspoon hot pepper sauce or to taste

Mash all the ingredients together to make a smooth spread. Use at once or refrigerate.

Makes ¾ cup

Variation: For Cheddar-Blue YoChee, omit the tomato paste and hot pepper sauce.

> *PER 2 TABLESPOONS*: 68 CALORIES, 5 GM. FAT, 3 GM. SATURATED FAT, 4.5 GM. PROTEIN, 2 GM. CARBOHYDRATE, 120 MG. CALCIUM

OLIVE AND PIMIENTO YOCHEE SPREAD

Spread on crackers or use to stuff celery.

> 1 cup shredded cheddar, Monterey Jack or mozzarella cheese (4 ounces)
> 1 tablespoon chopped pimiento or roasted red pepper
> 1 tablespoon chopped green olives
> ¾ teaspoon prepared mustard
> ¼ cup YoChee

Combine all the ingredients, mashing with a fork to a spreadable consistency. Use at once or refrigerate.

Makes ¾ cup

> PER 2 TABLESPOONS: 57 CALORIES, 3GM. FAT, 2GM. SATURATED FAT, 5.5GM. PROTEIN, 1.5GM. CARBOHYDRATE, 140MG. CALCIUM (SEE YOCHIEVEMENTS FOR COMPARISONS)

NY STYLE BAKED VEGETABLE YOCHEE

This flavorful cheese can be served on crackers, toast or a bagel. After you've made it our way, feel free to experiment with other vegetables and seasonings.

> 1 cup YoChee
> 1 stalk celery, finely chopped
> 2 scallions, finely chopped
> 1 small carrot, shredded
> 1 teaspoon dill seed
> ½ teaspoon salt

Preheat the oven to 350°F.

Combine all the ingredients and divide between 2 oven-safe custard cups or place in a single 10-ounce ramekin. Bake for 30 minutes.

Cool to room temperature, pour off any accumulated liquid, unmold and chill completely before serving.

Makes 2 small cheese rounds, or 1 larger round

> PER ¼ SMALL ROUND OR ⅛ LARGER ROUND: 25 CALORIES, <1GM. FAT, <1GM. SATURATED FAT, 3GM. PROTEIN, 3.5GM. CARBOHYDRATE, 65MG. CALCIUM

CURRY CASHEW SPREAD

Spread on pita wedges, crackers, toasted chapatis or fresh apple rings. A good appetizer or accompaniment for an Indian meal.

> ¾ cup YoChee
> ½ to 1 teaspoon curry powder
> ⅓ cup chopped apple
> ¼ cup chopped unsalted dry-roasted cashew nuts

Combine the YoChee with the curry powder, adjusting the amount according to the strength of the curry powder and personal taste. Mix in the apple and nuts.

Use at once or refrigerate.

Makes 1 cup

> **PER 2 TABLESPOONS**: 43 CALORIES, 2 GM. FAT, <1 GM. SATURATED FAT, 2.5 GM. PROTEIN, 4 GM. CARBOHYDRATE, 45 MG. CALCIUM

FRUIT-STUDDED BAKED YOCHEE

A sweet cheese that is excellent on crackers or toast.

> 1 cup YoChee
> ¼ cup chopped raisins, dried apricots and/or pitted dried cherries
> 1 tablespoon honey
> 2 tablespoons orange juice
> ½ teaspoon minced orange rind, preferably organic

Preheat the oven to 350°F.

Combine all the ingredients and divide between 2 oven-safe custard cups or place in a single 10-ounce ramekin. Bake for 30 minutes.

Cool to room temperature, pour off any accumulated liquid, unmold and chill completely before serving.

Makes 2 small cheese rounds, or 1 larger round

> **PER ¼ SMALL ROUND OR ⅛ LARGER ROUND**: 47 CALORIES, <1 GM. FAT, <1 GM. SATURATED FAT, 3 GM. PROTEIN, 9 GM. CARBOHYDRATE, 60 MG. CALCIUM

SWEET YOCHEE

This spread is great on bread but can also be slathered on apple or pear slices or even kiwi rounds. Try it as a topping for pancakes too.

½ cup YoChee
¼ cup mashed banana (½ small)
splash orange juice
flavoring ingredients (see Accessorizing, below), as desired

Mash together the YoChee, banana and juice. Add the flavoring ingredients individually or combined, as desired. Store in the refrigerator.

Makes about ¾ cup spread

> **PER 1** *TABLESPOON WITHOUT ADDED FLAVORING INGREDIENTS*: 11 CALORIES, <1 GM. FAT, <1 GM. SATURATED FAT, 1 GM. PROTEIN, 2 GM. CARBOHYDRATE, 20 MG. CALCIUM

Accessorizing

Choose from the following flavoring ingredients to personalize Sweet YoChee:

- ✔ 2 tablespoons chopped raisins or dates
- ✔ 2 tablespoons chopped dried apricots or figs
- ✔ 2 tablespoons chopped cashews, walnuts or pecans
- ✔ 2 tablespoons well-drained crushed pineapple
- ✔ 2 tablespoons chopped or grated pear or apple

LENTIL PÂTÉ

Lentil Pâté makes a good appetizer stuffed into celery or spread on crackers or French bread. Or use in a sandwich with red onion and romaine lettuce. As with most spreads, it can be eaten right away, but making it ahead gives the flavors a chance to develop.

- ¾ cup dried lentils
- 1 stalk celery without leaves, finely chopped
- 1 bay leaf
- 1½ cups water
- ¼ cup walnuts
- 1 clove garlic
- ½ teaspoon salt
- ½ cup finely chopped spinach, arugula or watercress
- ¼ cup YoChee
- pepper

Combine the lentils, celery, bay leaf, and water in a pot. Bring to a boil over high heat. Reduce heat to low, cover and cook for about 35 minutes, or until the lentils are very tender and the water is absorbed. Drain if necessary to remove any liquid. Discard the bay leaf.

In a blender or food processor, grind the walnuts completely. Add to the lentils. Using a fork or potato masher, mash together until smooth.

Remove the outer peel from the garlic. On a cutting board, cut in half and sprinkle with ¼ teaspoon of the salt. Chop. Using the flat side of a knife, mash the salt into the garlic to extract the juices. Scrape into the lentil-walnut mixture along with the chopped greens, YoChee, remaining ¼ teaspoon salt and a generous amount of pepper. Mix well.

Use at once or cover and refrigerate. Taste before serving and adjust the seasonings if needed.

Makes 2 cups

Note: In a pinch, 2 cups cooked or canned lentils can replace dried. Drain well, and adjust salt if lentils are presalted.

PER 2 TABLESPOONS: 44 CALORIES, 1 GM. FAT, <1 GM. SATURATED FAT, 3 GM. PROTEIN, 6 GM. CARBOHYDRATE, 15 MG. CALCIUM (SEE YOCHIEVEMENTS FOR COMPARISONS)

CHICKPEA SPREAD

Delicious on a sandwhich or as a snack on crackers, toasted rounds of French bread or pita wedges. Try to refrigerate for at least one hour for flavors to develop.

- ⅓ cup boiling water
- ¼ cup sun-dried tomatoes
- 1½ cups cooked or canned chickpeas, drained
- 1 clove garlic
- 1 tablespoon lemon juice
- 1 tablespoon fresh parsley or basil
- ¼ cup YoChee
- ½ teaspoon salt (omit or adjust to taste if beans are salted)
- pepper

In a small bowl, combine the water and sun-dried tomatoes. Let sit for about 15 minutes to soften.

Transfer the tomatoes and the soaking water to a food processor. Add the chickpeas, garlic, lemon juice, and parsley or basil. Process until the chickpeas are smooth and the tomatoes are in very small pieces.

Add the YoChee and process quickly until completely absorbed into the spread.

Season with salt and pepper to taste.

Makes 1½ cups

> **PER 2 TABLESPOONS**: 40 CALORIES, <1GM. FAT, <1GM. SATURATED FAT, 2.5GM. PROTEIN, 7GM. CARBOHYDRATE, 20MG. CALCIUM

DIPS

YoChee is the perfect medium for dips, owing to its rich creamy texture and mild flavor. It can be substituted for sour cream or mayonnaise in almost any dip recipe for a substantial savings in fat and calories. Unlike dips made with yogurt, which tend to separate or become liquidy, those made with YoChee stay thick and cling perfectly to vegetables or chips.

Dips benefit from an hour or more advance preparation to meld the flavors. If made more than an hour ahead, they should be stored in the refrigerator and used within a few days. It is difficult to predict servings where dips are concerned. As a general rule, plan on one-fourth cup per person.

☙ YoChievements ❧

Onion Dip (pg.85) vs. typical onion dip
   50% less calories
   No fat vs. 4 grams fat per 2 tablespoons
   175% more protein
   200% more calcium

more…

Superior Spinach Dip (pg.87) vs. typical spinach dip
    85% less calories
    No fat vs. 14 grams fat per 2 tablespoons
    5 times as much protein
    100% more calcium

Roasted Red Pepper-Chickpea Dip (pg.89) vs. commercial red pepper hummus
    22% less calories
    75% less fat
    25% less protein

Beyond Dips

If you like to experiment, try using a YoChee dip as a filling or topping for an omelet. Or use one of these recipes to liven up plain pasta or rice.

🕰 ONION DIP

Not just for chips—try it with celery sticks, carrot sticks, broccoli florets and strips of red and green pepper.

1 cup YoChee
2 tablespoons dehydrated minced onion
1½ teaspoons soy sauce

Beat all the ingredients together with a fork. Let stand for at least 20 minutes for the flavors to develop.

Makes 1 cup

> PER ¼ CUP: 51 CALORIES, <1GM. FAT, <1GM. SATURATED FAT, 5.5GM. PROTEIN, 6.5GM. CARBOHYDRATE, 120MG. CALCIUM (SEE YOCHIEVEMENTS FOR COMPARISONS)

Soy Sauce Selection

Use a genuine soy sauce, not one doctored with corn syrup and caramel coloring. Real soy sauce is sold in Oriental groceries and natural food stores.

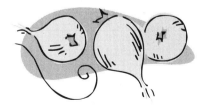

Blue Cheese Dip

The refreshing flavors of cucumber and dill act as a counterbalance to the pungent blue cheese in this dip.

> 1 cup YoChee
> 1 cup diced peeled cucumber
> 2 teaspoons lemon juice
> 1 tablespoon minced dill, plus more to garnish
> ½ cup crumbled blue cheese
> salt
> pepper

In a blender or food processor, puree the YoChee, cucumber and lemon juice until no visible pieces of cucumber remain.

Transfer the puree to a bowl. Using a fork, mash in the dill and blue cheese so that the cheese is well incorporated but tiny pieces remain.

Season with salt and pepper to taste. Serve at once or chill.

At serving time, sprinkle additional minced dill on top for appearance

Makes 1½ cups

> **Per ¼ cup:** 70 calories, 3gm. fat, 2gm. saturated fat, 6gm. protein, 4gm. carbohydrate, 140mg. calcium

Superior Spinach Dip

As luscious as spinach dips made with sour cream and mayonnaise, but with virtually no fat and a fraction of the calories.

>10-ounce package frozen spinach, thawed
>1½ cups YoChee
>¼ cup chopped fresh dill
>¼ cup chopped parsley
>¼ teaspoon hot pepper sauce
>1 tablespoon lemon juice
>½ teaspoon salt
>2 tablespoons minced scallion

Drain the spinach and squeeze out as much liquid as possible. Chop finely.

In a bowl, combine the YoChee, dill, parsley, hot pepper sauce, lemon juice and salt. Mix well. Stir in the spinach and scallion until evenly blended.

Serve at once, or chill until serving time.

Makes 2 cups

>*Per ¼ cup*: 42 calories, <1gm. fat, <1gm. saturated fat, 5gm. protein, 5gm. carbohydrate, 130mg. calcium (see YoChievements for comparisons)

Serving Tip

Dips made in advance and chilled may thicken. If so, just before serving, beat with a fork to loosen and add a spoonful of plain yogurt if needed.

Greek Eggplant Dip

A marriage of three Greek staples: eggplant, garlic and rich thick yogurt.

- 1 medium eggplant (1 to 1¼ pounds)
- 2 cloves garlic, crushed
- 1 tablespoon lemon juice
- ¼ teaspoon salt
- ¼ cup YoChee
- 1 tablespoon minced parsley

Roast the eggplant by placing it directly on a gas burner or a grill and turning it frequently until the outside is charred and the inside is quite soft. Alternatively, place the eggplant on a baking sheet in a 375° oven and bake for about 45 minutes or until very soft. When cool enough to handle, remove the peel.

Puree the eggplant in a food processor or mash by hand with a potato masher until completely smooth. Add the garlic, lemon juice, salt and YoChee, and mix until evenly blended.

Let rest for at least 30 minutes at room temperature or longer in the refrigerator so flavors have time to develop.

Before serving, beat with a fork to loosen the mixture. Taste and adjust salt and lemon juice if necessary. Sprinkle the parsley on top.

Makes 1½ cup

Note: If using a larger eggplant, increase the YoChee gradually by 1-tablespoon increments, and adjust the salt and lemon juice to taste.

Per ¼ cup: 34 calories, <1gm. fat, <1gm. saturated fat, 2gm. protein, 7gm. carbohydrate, 30mg. calcium

ROASTED RED PEPPER-CHICKPEA DIP

We like to serve this dip with small inner leaves of romaine lettuce, strips of sweet red and green pepper, endive and raw or lightly steamed cauliflower and broccoli florets, as well as pita triangles. It can be made with canned or home-cooked dried chickpeas.

> 1 medium sweet red pepper (4 to 6 ounces)
> 2 cups cooked chickpeas
> about ¼ cup bean cooking liquid
> 2 cloves garlic
> ½ teaspoon salt (omit if beans are salted)
> 2 tablespoons wine vinegar
> ¼ cup YoChee

Place the red pepper on a baking sheet and broil 4 to 6 inches beneath the heat for about 15 minutes, until the skin is blistered. Turn several times to cook evenly. Alternatively, hold the pepper over a flame using tongs and brown on all sides. When the skin is completely blistered, wrap the pepper in a clean cloth to steam for a few minutes. When cool, peel off the skin using a small paring knife. Cut open and remove the seeds and any thick ribs.

Puree the chickpeas in a blender or food processor, adding bean liquid as needed to make a smooth, creamy puree. Add the roasted pepper, garlic, salt, wine vinegar and YoChee. Process again until smooth.

Transfer to a shallow serving bowl. If possible, let sit for 30 minutes or longer to blend the flavors. If made more than an hour ahead, refrigerate.

Makes 2 cups

> PER ¼ CUP: 78 CALORIES, 1GM. FAT, <1GM. SATURATED FAT, 4.5GM. PROTEIN, 13.5GM. CARBOHYDRATE, 35MG. CALCIUM (SEE YOCHIEVEMENTS FOR COMPARISONS)

Black Bean Hummus

The union of black beans and hot sauce with more traditional hummus ingredients creates a dip with a South American flair. You can prepare it with canned or freshly cooked dried beans, and it can be served at once or refrigerated. For best flavor, however, serve at room temperature. Set out raw vegetables, baked tortilla chips or pita bread for dipping.

> **2 cups cooked black beans**
> **¼ cup bean liquid, if needed**
> **2 tablespoons lemon juice**
> **2 cloves garlic, finely minced**
> **½ teaspoon hot pepper sauce or to taste**
> **2 tablespoons tahini**
> **2 tablespoons YoChee**
> **salt**

Drain the beans, conserving the cooking liquid. Do not rinse.

Puree the beans in a blender or food processor, adding bean liquid as needed to make a smooth puree. The need for added liquid will depend on how soft the beans are and the amount of liquid that clings to them.

Transfer the bean puree to a shallow bowl. Using a fork, beat in the lemon juice, garlic and hot pepper sauce. Then beat in the tahini and YoChee.

Add salt to taste if the beans were unsalted. Adjust hot sauce according to taste.

If made more than an hour ahead of serving, refrigerate.

Makes 2 cups

Per ¼ cup: 85 calories, 2gm. fat, <1gm. saturated fat, 5gm. protein, 12gm. carbohydrate, 25mg. calcium

Soup

No Fat Creamy Soups

Imagine creamy soups with little or no fat. This sounds impossible, but soups are another area (like sauces) where YoChee really performs. With it you can make velvety soups that mirror the richness of cream with far less fat and fewer calories. Moreover, YoChee works well with both hot and cold soups.

Soup Garnish

In addition to its use as a soup ingredient, with YoChee on hand, a dollop is always available as the perfect soup garnish. It is especially nice on bean soups such as lentil, black bean and minestrone, and hearty vegetable-grain soups like mushroom-barley and tomato-rice. It adds not only a creamy cool contrast but extra fortification as well.

❧ YoChievements ❧

Quick Cream of Tomato Soup (pg.93) vs. tomato soup prepared
    with milk
        50% less calories
        No fat vs. 6 grams fat per cup
        Similar protein
        40% less carbohydrate

more...

Fresh Corn Chowder (pg.96) vs. canned corn chowder
20% less calories
77% less fat
20% more protein

Potato Soup (pg.101) vs. canned vichyssoise
33% less calories
64% less fat
85% less saturated fat
33% less protein

Quick Cream of Tomato Soup

This quickly made soup can be jazzed up by adding any number of seasonings, including chopped parsley, dill, fresh or dried basil, garlic, rosemary or other favorite herbs. You can formulate it to go with an Indian meal by adding curry powder, or make it Mexican with chili powder.

1 cup YoChee
4 cups tomato juice
1 teaspoon honey
pepper

Place the YoChee in a 2-quart saucepan. Using a fork or wire whisk, gradually beat in the tomato juice until smooth and perfectly blended. Add the honey.

Place over low heat and cook, stirring frequently, until the soup is hot. Do not boil. Taste and if the flavor seems a bit sharp, add a little more honey. Season with pepper to taste.

Makes 5 cups; 4 servings

Per serving: 90 calories, <1gm. fat, <1gm. saturated fat, 7gm. protein, 17gm. carbohydrate, 140mg. calcium (see YoChievements for comparisons)

Aztec Soup

A tomato-based soup with strips of toasted corn tortillas is typical Mexican fare.

>1 tablespoon oil
>2 cups chopped onions (2 medium)
>3 cups water or vegetable broth
>2 cups tomato juice
>hot pepper sauce
>4 corn tortillas
>1 teaspoon ground cumin
>salt
>1 cup YoChee
>1 small avocado
>½ lemon

Combine the oil and onion in a soup pot and cook over low heat, stirring occasionally, for about 10 minutes or until the onions begin to color lightly. Add the water or broth, bring to a boil, cover and simmer for 10 minutes. Stir in the tomato juice and return to a boil. Season with hot sauce to taste.

Meanwhile, toast the tortillas by placing them over a gas flame or cooking them in a dry skillet. Cut the toasted tortillas into ¼-inch wide strips. A scissors is a handy tool for this job. Just before serving, add the tortilla strips to the soup and cook for 2 to 3 minutes.

At any time, use a fork to beat the cumin and a pinch of salt into the YoChee. Just before serving, peel the avocado, cut it into bite-size cubes and sprinkle them with some lemon juice to prevent browning.

Place an equal portion of avocado in each person's soup bowl. Ladle the soup into the bowls, allotting an equal portion of tortilla strips to each. Spoon ¼ cup of the seasoned YoChee in dollops into each bowl. Serve at once.

Makes 5 cups; 4 servings

Per serving: 253 calories, 11 gm. fat, 1.5 gm. saturated fat, 9 gm. protein, 32 gm. carbohydrate, 200 mg. calcium

VELVET SQUASH SOUP

A very creamy creamless soup. If desired, garnish each bowl of soup with whole wheat croutons.

1 stalk celery, sliced
1 medium carrot, cut in coins
1 medium onion, diced
1 tablespoon olive oil, extra virgin preferred
1 pound butternut or other winter squash, peeled and cubed (about 3 cups)
1½ cups cooked or canned white beans (great northern, cannellini, navy), drained
3½ cups water or vegetable stock
½-inch piece fresh ginger, peeled and chopped
1 teaspoon salt (reduce if beans or stock are presalted)
pepper
⅔ cup YoChee

In a 3- to 5-quart pot, combine the celery, carrot and onion. Drizzle with the olive oil. Stir to coat the vegetables with the oil and place over low to moderate heat. Cook, stirring occasionally, for 10 minutes, or until the vegetables are starting to wilt but are not browned.

Add the squash, beans, water or stock, ginger and salt. If desired the liquid used to cook the beans can be used to replace some of the water. Remember, if the beans or stock are presalted, you will need to reduce the salt.

Bring to a boil, reduce heat to a simmer and cook for about 20 minutes, or until all the vegetables are tender.

Puree the soup in a blender or food mill or with an immersion mixer until smooth. Reheat if necessary so the soup is hot before finishing.

Put the YoChee in a small bowl and beat with a fork to loosen. Remove the soup from the heat. Adjust salt and pepper to taste. Using fork or spoon, swirl the YoChee into the hot soup forming a decorative pattern.

Makes 1½ quarts; 4 ample to 6 smaller appetizer servings

Note: If the soup is prepared ahead, wait until just before serving to add the YoChee. If reheating is necessary after the YoChee is added, use low heat and avoid boiling.

PER SERVING, BASED ON 4 SERVINGS: 225 CALORIES, 4GM. FAT, <1GM. SATURATED FAT, 12GM. PROTEIN, 38GM. CARBOHYDRATE, 205MG. CALCIUM

FRESH CORN CHOWDER

This soup is especially good when corn is in season and, where possible, locally grown. Note that the cobs are used to make a quick broth that enhances the sweet taste and creaminess. Using a rich, buttery variety of potato like Yukon gold can boost the taste another notch. But even without top-notch produce, Fresh Corn Chowder is still a hit.

    4 ears corn
    4 cups water
    2 medium or 5 to 6 small potatoes (about ¾ pound)
    1 tablespoon butter or oil
    1 medium onion, chopped
    salt
    pepper
    2 tomatoes, peeled, chopped (see Note)
    ½ teaspoon paprika
    1 cup YoChee
    pinch cayenne
    2 tablespoons chopped parsley

Shuck the corn and use a paring knife to strip the kernels into a bowl. Put the cobs in a pot with the 4 cups of water and bring to a boil. Cover and simmer while you proceed.

Scrub the potatoes and peel them if skins are thick or unsightly. Thin-skinned potatoes can be left unpeeled. Dice into bite-size pieces.

Heat the butter or oil in a 3-quart pot. Add the onion and potatoes, along with a generous sprinkling of salt and pepper. Cook for about 5 minutes, stirring occasionally, until the onion softens. Add the tomatoes and cook for another minute or two.

After the corncobs have cooked for at least 10 minutes, strain the liquid into the potato mixture. Cover and simmer for 15 to 20 minutes, or until the potatoes are tender. Timing will depend on the variety and size of the pieces.

Add the corn kernels and paprika to the soup. Cook 5 to 10 minutes longer, until corn is cooked to taste.

Place the YoChee in a bowl. Using a fork, beat in a ladle or two of the hot soup until smooth. Make sure the remainder of the soup in the pot is hot, but remove from the heat. Gently stir the tempered YoChee into the hot soup until completely incorporated.

Season with a pinch of cayenne and salt to taste. Garnish with parsley.

Makes about 2 quarts; 6 generous servings

Note: You can skip peeling the tomatoes if you wish, but there will be small pieces of tomato skins in the soup. To peel, plunge into boiling water for a minute or two until the skins crack. If fresh flavorful tomatoes aren't available, use 1 cup chopped canned tomatoes instead.

PER SERVING: 185 CALORIES, 3GM. FAT, 1GM. SATURATED FAT, 8GM. PROTEIN, 36GM. CARBOHYDRATE, 95MG. CALCIUM (SEE YOCHIEVEMENTS FOR COMPARISONS)

Cooking Tip

If you are preparing a soup containing YoChee in advance, wait to add the YoChee to avoid possible curdling on reheating. Shortly before serving, heat the soup and then add the YoChee. If you must heat a soup once YoChee is added, use a low temperature and avoid boiling.

CREAMY GAZPACHO

This chilled tomato soup is spicy and soothing at the same time. A perfect way to cool down on a hot day.

> 1 cup YoChee
> 4 cups tomato juice
> ¼ cup wine vinegar
> ¼ teaspoon hot pepper sauce or to taste
> 1 large clove garlic, minced
> 1 medium cucumber, diced
> 1 medium green pepper, diced
> 2 tablespoons chopped onion or scallion

Place the YoChee in a large bowl. Using a fork or wire whisk, gradually beat in the tomato juice until smooth and perfectly blended. Beat in the vinegar. Add enough hot sauce to make a spicy soup. Stir in the remaining ingredients.

Cover and refrigerate for 1 hour or longer, until well chilled.

Makes about 7 cups; 6 servings

> *Per serving:* 70 calories, <1gm. fat, <1gm. saturated fat, 5gm. protein, 14gm. carbohydrate, 100mg. calcium

COLD CREAMY BORSCHT

Borscht is a cold beet soup with a Russian heritage. This version is sure to captivate you, as its exquisite pink-purple hue is as alluring as its sweet, earthy taste.

> 1 pound beets
> 3 cups water
> 1 teaspoon honey
> ½ teaspoon salt
> 1 tablespoon lemon juice
> 2 tablespoons chopped fresh dill
> 1 cup YoChee
> ½ cup diced cucumber, optional
> 1 large potato, steamed and cubed, optional

Scrub the beets very well. Put them in a pot with the water without cutting or peeling and bring to a boil. Cover and simmer until tender, from 30 to 45 minutes, depending on the size of the beets.

Remove the beets from the cooking water, reserving 2 cups.

When the beets are cool enough to handle, remove the peels, cut the beets into chunks and combine in the blender or food processor with 1 cup of the reserved liquid. Process until shredded.

Add the remaining 1 cup of reserved cooking liquid, along with the honey, salt, lemon juice, dill and YoChee. Process quickly, just until combined. Chill.

To serve, pour the soup into individual bowls and garnish each with some of the cucumber and potato if desired.

Makes 5 cups; 4 servings

> *PER SERVING:* 98 CALORIES, <1GM. FAT, <1GM. SATURATED FAT, 7GM. PROTEIN, 18GM. CARBOHYDRATE, 135MG. CALCIUM

Chilled Avocado Soup

This is a very rich soup despite the modest ingredients, so small portions are recommended. Use a California avocado in this recipe, since they are the most flavorful and creamy.

> 1 medium-size ripe California avocado
> 1 tablespoon lemon juice, plus additional
> 2 cups peeled, diced cucumber (2 small to medium)
> 1 large clove garlic, sliced
> ¼ teaspoon salt
> ¼ teaspoon hot pepper sauce or to taste
> 1¼ cups YoChee (see Note)
> ½ cup chopped tomato
> ¼ cup minced cilantro or flat-leaf Italian parsley

Halve the avocado, remove the pit, scoop out the flesh and measure 1 cup. Set aside any remaining avocado to use as a garnish and sprinkle with a little lemon juice to keep it from browning.

Combine the measured cup of avocado, 1½ cups of the cucumber, 1 tablespoon lemon juice, garlic, salt and hot sauce in a blender or food processor. Puree until smooth and creamy.

Add 1 cup of the YoChee and puree until it is completely incorporated.

Transfer the soup to a container and stir in the reserved ½ cup of diced cucumber. Refrigerate until very cold. Adjust salt and hot pepper sauce to taste.

If you have any avocado left, just before serving the soup make a guacamole garnish by mashing it with lemon juice and seasoning to taste with salt and hot sauce.

Whip the soup with a fork and ladle it into 4 individual bowls. Garnish each serving with 2 tablespoons of diced tomato, 1 tablespoon of minced cilantro or parsley, a dollop of the remaining YoChee and a dollop of guacamole, if available.

Makes 3 cups; 4 servings

Note: Soft YoChee or even YoChee cream can be used with success in this recipe.

PER SERVING: 153 CALORIES, 8GM. FAT, 1GM. SATURATED FAT, 9GM. PROTEIN, 14GM. CARBOHYDRATE, 180MG. CALCIUM

Hot or Cold Potato Soup (Vichyssoise)

The conventional way to serve vichyssoise is very cold. However, this recipe can be served hot or cold. Try it as a tasty hot potato soup before chilling.

> 1 tablespoon olive oil
> ½ cup chopped onion
> 1 cup sliced leeks
> 1 pound potatoes, diced (3 cups), peeled or not according to personal preference and condition of skins
> 4 cups water or vegetable broth
> 1½ teaspoons salt (reduce if broth is salted)
> ¾ cup YoChee
> pepper
> chopped parsley, dill or watercress

Heat the oil in a 3- to 5-quart pot. Add the onion and leeks and cook for a few minutes, until limp. Add the potatoes, water or broth and salt. Bring to a boil. Cover and cook over low heat so liquid is just simmering for about 20 minutes, or until the potatoes are soft enough to puree.

Transfer the soup to a food processor or blender. Puree until smooth. You may have to do this in two batches. Add the YoChee, and puree to combine.

Serve at once, or chill for cold service.

Before serving, adjust salt if necessary and season with pepper to taste. Pour into individual bowls and garnish each with some parsley, dill or watercress.

Makes about 7 cups; 4 to 6 servings

> *Per serving, based on 4 servings:* 174 calories, 4gm. fat, <1gm. saturated fat, 7gm. protein, 29gm. carbohydrate, 115mg. calcium (see YoChievements for comparisons)

WATERCRESS SOUP

Another variation of vichyssoise that is tasty either hot or cold.

> 1 tablespoon olive oil
> ½ cup chopped onion
> 1 cup sliced leeks
> 1 pound potatoes, diced (3 cups), peeled or not according to personal preference and condition of skins
> 3 cups watercress, divided
> 4 cups water or vegetable broth
> 1½ teaspoons salt (reduce if broth is salted)
> ¾ cup YoChee, plus 4 to 6 tablespoons for garnish
> pepper

Heat the oil in a 3- to 5-quart pot. Add the onion and leeks and cook for a few minutes, until limp. Add the potatoes, 2 cups of watercress, water or broth and salt. Bring to a boil. Cover and cook over low heat just so the liquid is simmering for about 20 minutes or until the potatoes are soft enough to puree.

Transfer the soup to a food processor or blender. Puree until smooth. You may have to do this in two batches. Add the ¾ cup of YoChee, and puree to combine.

Serve at once, or chill for cold service.

Before serving, adjust salt if necessary and season with pepper to taste. Pour into individual bowls and garnish each with some of the remaining watercress leaves and a dollop of YoChee.

Makes about 7 cups; 4 to 6 servings

PER SERVING, BASED ON 4 SERVINGS: 188 CALORIES, 4GM. FAT, <1GM. SATURATED FAT, 9GM. PROTEIN, 30GM. CARBOHYDRATE, 175MG. CALCIUM

Vegetable Entrées

What distinguishes these vegetable-based entrées from the vegetables designated as side dishes is that they are a good source of protein, an important feature in meatless menus. Of course, there is no reason that they can't be served along with meat, fish or poultry entrées as the vegetable portion of the meal. If so, you can expect to get six to eight side-dish servings from an entrée designed for four.

❧ YoChievements ❧

Surprising Spinach Quiche (pg.108) vs. typical spinach quiche
       33% less calories
       50% fat
       75% less saturated fat
       22% more protein
       34% more calcium

Cauliflower Gratin (pg.118) vs. frozen cauliflower with cheese sauce
       16% less calories
       80% less fat
       100% more protein
       54% more calcium

more…

YoCheesy Stuffed Baked Potatoes (pg.120) vs. typical cheese-stuffed baked potatoes
- 12% less calories
- 25% less fat
- 38% more protein
- 64% more calcium

Eggplant Lasagna (pg.130) vs. frozen eggplant Parmesan
- 50% less calories
- 82% less fat
- 55% less saturated fat
- Similar protein
- 100% more calcium

Vegetable Potpie (pg.134) vs. frozen vegetable potpie
- Similar calories
- 60% less fat
- 99% less saturated fat
- 150% more protein
- 10 times as much calcium

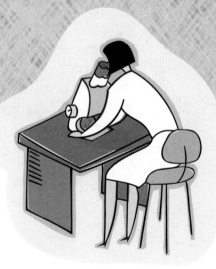

⏰ PORTOBELLO PIZZA

A meaty portobello mushroom makes a terrific foundation for a pizza-like topping. The recipe here is proportioned per serving, although exact measurements aren't critical.

> 1 large portobello mushroom, about 5 inches across
> 1 clove garlic, finely chopped
> ¼ cup YoChee
> salt
> crushed red pepper flakes or hot pepper sauce
> about 1 ounce thinly sliced mozzarella or provolone cheese
> 2 slices fresh tomato
> a few fresh basil leaves, chopped
> ½ teaspoon oregano
> 1 tablespoon grated Parmesan cheese

Preheat the oven to 375°F.

Clean the mushroom, remove the stem and place the cap gills up in a shallow baking pan. Sprinkle with the garlic.

Season the YoChee with a pinch of salt and hot pepper to taste. Spread the YoChee over the surface of the mushroom cap. Cover with the thinly sliced cheese. Top with the tomatoes. Scatter the basil and crush the dried oregano over the tomatoes. Sprinkle the grated Parmesan cheese over all.

Bake for 20 minutes or until the mushroom is fork-tender.

Makes 1 serving

Notes: If the mushroom is larger than 5 inches, increase the YoChee to ⅓ cup. If flavorful fresh tomatoes aren't available, replace them with 2 tablespoons of prepared tomato sauce.

PER SERVING: 178 CALORIES, 6.5GM. FAT, 4GM. SATURATED FAT, 19GM. PROTEIN, 13GM. CARBOHYDRATE, 440MG. CALCIUM

Baked Broccoli & Cheese

This vegetable-cheese casserole is nicely complemented by an orange vegetable such as carrots or baked winter squash, plus a salad and crusty bread.

>   **1 pound broccoli**
>   **2 eggs, separated**
>   **1 cup YoChee**
>   **½ cup shredded provolone cheese**
>   **¼ cup grated Parmesan cheese**
>   **¼ cup chopped scallions**
>   **¼ teaspoon nutmeg**
>   **¼ teaspoon salt**

Chop the broccoli, including the stems, into small pieces. You should have about 5 cups. Steam for 8 minutes.

Preheat the oven to 350⁰F.

Combine the egg yolks, YoChee, provolone, 2 tablespoons of the Parmesan cheese, scallions and nutmeg.

In a separate bowl, beat the egg whites until soft peaks form. Add the salt and continue to beat until stiff.

Fold the egg whites into the YoChee mixture. Fold in half of the broccoli.

Oil a shallow 1½-quart or 9-inch baking dish. Place the remaining broccoli in the dish. Spread the YoChee mixture on top to completely cover. Sprinkle the remaining 2 tablespoons of Parmesan cheese over the top.

Bake for about 25 minutes, until set and lightly colored on top. Let sit at room temperature for 10 minutes before serving.

Makes 4 servings

Note: For 8 servings, or perhaps 6 hearty appetites, double the recipe and bake in a 9x13-inch baking dish or 3- to 4-quart casserole.

Per serving: 203 calories, 9gm. fat, 5gm. saturated fat, 19gm. protein, 12.5gm. carbohydrate, 390mg. calcium

BAKED SPINACH AND FETA

This crustless spinach pie can be divided into four to six large pieces as a main course, or cut into 2-inch squares for an hors d'œuvre. It tastes best when eaten at room temperature.

¾ **pound spinach**
½ **teaspoon salt**
2 **eggs**
¼ **cup chopped scallions**
¼ **cup minced dill**
2 **tablespoons minced parsley**
½ **cup crumbled feta cheese**
1 **cup YoChee**
pepper
1 **tablespoon olive oil**

Chop the spinach so that it is quite fine. You should have about 6 cups lightly packed. Sprinkle with the salt and let it stand for at least 20 minutes to extract the moisture. Squeeze the spinach with your hands to drain off the liquid and press dry before using. You should have about 1 cup of spinach.

Preheat the oven to 350°F.

Beat the eggs and add the pressed spinach, scallions, dill, parsley, feta and YoChee. Mix until evenly blended. Season liberally with pepper.

Spread the mixture in an oiled shallow 1½-quart casserole or a 9-inch baking dish. Drizzle with the olive oil.

Bake for 30 minutes or until firm and just starting to color on top. Let stand at room temperature for at least 20 minutes before serving.

Makes 4 to 6 entrée servings; 16 hors d'œuvre pieces

PER ENTRÉE SERVING, BASED ON 4 SERVINGS: 182 CALORIES, 10.5GM. FAT, 4GM. SATURATED FAT, 13.5GM. PROTEIN, 9.5GM. CARBOHYDRATE, 315MG. CALCIUM

PER 2-INCH HORS D'ŒUVRE PIECE: 45 CALORIES, 2.5GM. FAT, 1GM. SATURATED FAT, 3.5GM. PROTEIN, 2.5GM. CARBOHYDRATE, 80MG. CALCIUM

Surprising Spinach Quiche

Unlike traditional high-fat quiche (with 40 to 60 grams of fat per serving), this version is relatively lean (just 19 grams per slice) without sacrificing any flavor or texture. Serve with a salad for a simple meal. Smaller servings are suitable as appetizers.

> Amazing YoChee Piecrust, page 232 (see Note)
> 1 tablespoon olive oil
> ¼ cup thinly sliced scallions or chopped onion
> 4 cups chopped spinach, Swiss chard or a mixture with arugula (6 to 8 ounces)
> ¼ cup minced fresh dill or parsley
> 2 eggs
> 1½ cups YoChee
> ½ teaspoon salt
> ¾ cup shredded cheese of choice, such as Swiss, Gouda, mozzarella, provolone, cheddar or any mixture

Preheat the oven to 400°F.

Place the crust in a 9-inch pie pan or tart pan with a removable bottom. Press so the bottom is quite thin and there is more support around the sides. Crimp or flute the edges of the crust as desired. Prick the surface of the crust liberally with a fork. Bake for 10 minutes, remove from the oven and reduce the heat to 350°F.

Let the crust cool for a few minutes before filling.

Heat the oil in a large skillet and sauté the scallions or onion, greens and herb of choice for 8 to 10 minutes, until tender and fairly dry.

In a large bowl, beat the eggs into the YoChee. Fold in the salt, shredded cheese and cooked greens. Spread this mixture in the partially baked crust.

Bake for 25 to 30 minutes, until just set and lightly colored on top. Let cool for at least 15 minutes before cutting to allow the filling to set. Serve warm or at room temperature.

Makes 4 entrée servings; 6 appetizer servings

Note: You can use a different piecrust but this will alter the nutritional make-up.

Per entrée serving: 366 calories, 19gm. fat, 5gm. saturated fat, 22gm. protein, 28gm. carbohydrate, 525mg. calcium (see YoChievements for comparisons)

Per appetizer serving: 244 calories, 13gm. fat, 3.5gm. saturated fat, 15gm. protein, 19gm. carbohydrate, 350mg. calcium

Vegetable Quiche Variations

This pattern can be used to create other vegetable quiches.

For Broccoli Quiche, substitute 2 cups chopped broccoli florets for the greens. Add ½ teaspoon prepared mustard for seasoning.

For Mushroom Quiche, use 3 cups sliced mushrooms instead of the greens. Season with ¼ teaspoon nutmeg and omit the fresh herbs.

YOCHEE BAKE

This vegetable-studded custard is one of our YoChee classics. For an entrée we suggest two wedges; one wedge or small squares make good appetizers or hors d'œuvre. The basic version below is open to variation for those who want to be creative (see Deluxe YoChee Bake).

> 1 cup YoChee
> 2 eggs
> ½ cup shredded cheese of choice
> 2 to 4 tablespoons cut-up sun-dried tomatoes
> 1 teaspoon oregano

Preheat the oven to 350°F.

Beat the YoChee with the eggs until smooth. Add the remaining ingredients. Transfer to an oiled 9-inch round baking dish or glass pie plate.

Bake for 30 minutes, until firm and slightly browned on top. Cool at least 10 minutes before serving. Best at room temperature; also good chilled.

Makes 4 entrée servings; 8 wedges

Notes: For a crowd, triple the recipe, bake in a 9x13-inch pan and cut into 2-inch squares.

> PER ENTRÉE SERVING: 145 CALORIES, 7.5GM. FAT, 4GM. SATURATED FAT,12GM. PROTEIN, 7GM. CARBOHYDRATE, 230MG. CALCIUM

> PER APPETIZER WEDGE OR 2-INCH SQUARE: 72 CALORIES, 3.5GM. FAT, 2GM. SATURATED FAT, 6GM. PROTEIN, 3.5GM. CARBOHYDRATE, 115MG. CALCIUM

Deluxe YoChee Bake

Mix and match ingredients as desired:

✓ Add 2 cut-up canned artichoke hearts, or 2 sliced scallions or up to ½ cup cooked diced vegetables of choice.

✓ Replace the shredded cheese with ½ to ¾ cup crumbled feta cheese.

✓ Replace the oregano with 1 tablespoon chopped fresh parsley or dill.

SKILLET STEW

This stew is fast and easy and always gets excellent reviews. Serve it over cooked grains, such as brown rice, kasha, barley or millet, or even as a topping for baked potatoes.

2 tablespoons soy sauce
½ cup chopped green pepper (½ medium pepper)
¼ cup sliced scallions
2 carrots, shredded
10 ounces zucchini or yellow crookneck squash, cut into small sticks (2 cups)
8 medium mushrooms (10 ounces), sliced or cut into bite-size pieces
½ pound broccoli, cut into small pieces
¼ cup chopped parsley
2 tablespoons chopped fresh dill
¼ teaspoon salt
⅔ cup YoChee
⅔ cup shredded cheddar cheese

Combine the soy sauce, vegetables and herbs in a large heavy skillet. Cover and cook over moderate heat for 15 to 20 minutes, stirring occasionally, until the vegetables are tender.

Turn the heat as low as possible. Stir in the salt, YoChee and shredded cheddar. Cook, stirring continuously, until the cheese melts.

Makes 4 servings

Variation: Instead of broccoli, use cauliflowerets or green beans cut in 1-inch pieces.

PER SERVING: 176 CALORIES, 7GM. FAT, 4GM. SATURATED FAT, 13GM. PROTEIN, 18GM. CARBOHYDRATE, 275MG. CALCIUM

Soy Sauce Selection

Use a genuine soy sauce, not one doctored with corn syrup and caramel coloring. Real soy sauce is sold in Oriental groceries and natural food stores.

CREAMY GARDEN VEGETABLES, ITALIAN STYLE

This creamy vegetable dish can be made Italian style or with a Greek flair (as in the next recipe). Serve over a bed of pasta or a favored grain. To complete the meal, add some form of legumes as an appetizer or side dish, plus a green salad and crusty bread.

1 small onion, cut in thin crescents
2 cups coarsely chopped mushrooms
4 cups vegetables of choice, cut in thin 1- to 2-inch-long strips or comfortable bite-size pieces: choose from asparagus, broccoli, carrots, cauliflowerets, celery, corn kernels, fennel, green beans, leeks, sweet red or green pepper, snow peas, zucchini, yellow crookneck squash and/or shredded greens
¼ cup chopped flat-leaf Italian parsley
2 tablespoons chopped fresh basil or ½ teaspoon dried basil
1 teaspoon oregano
2 tablespoons cooking sherry
1 cup YoChee
⅓ cup grated Parmesan cheese
pepper

Combine the onion, mushrooms, vegetables, herbs and cooking sherry in a heavy skillet. Cover and cook over moderate heat for 10 minutes or until the vegetables are just tender and the mushroom liquid runs freely.

Remove from the heat and add the YoChee and Parmesan, stirring continuously until the sauce is creamy. If necessary, return to very low heat to melt the cheese. Season generously with pepper.

Makes 4 servings

Per serving: 135 calories, 3gm. fat, 2gm. saturated fat, 11gm. protein, 16gm. carbohydrate, 270mg. calcium

Choice Cheese

To achieve full flavor, use a high quality, freshly grated cheese. Feel free to use Romano, locatelli, sardo or something similar in place of Parmesan.

CREAMY GARDEN VEGETABLES, GREEK STYLE

Serve over cracked wheat or rice pilaf. Compete the meal with beans in the form of soup, appetizer or side dish, a cucumber-tomato salad and pita or crusty bread.

- 1 small onion, cut in thin crescents
- 2 cups coarsely chopped mushrooms
- 4 cups vegetables of choice, cut in thin 1- to 2-inch-long strips or comfortable bite-size pieces: choose from asparagus, broccoli, carrots, cauliflowerets, celery, corn kernels, fennel, green beans, leeks, sweet red or green pepper, snow peas, zucchini, yellow crookneck squash and/or shredded greens
- ¼ cup minced fresh dill
- 2 tablespoons cooking sherry
- 1 cup YoChee
- ⅓ cup crumbled feta cheese
- pepper

Combine the onion, mushrooms, vegetables, dill and cooking sherry in a heavy skillet. Cover and cook over moderate heat for 10 minutes or until the vegetables are just tender and the mushroom liquid runs freely.

Remove from the heat and add the YoChee and feta, stirring continuously until the YoChee is completely incorporated and the feta is warm and slightly softened. If necessary, return to very low heat to complete the process. Season generously with pepper.

Makes 4 servings

PER SERVING: 132 CALORIES, 3GM. FAT, 2GM. SATURATED FAT, 9.5GM. PROTEIN, 17GM. CARBOHYDRATE, 220MG. CALCIUM

⏰ SUMMER STEW

This stew features seasonal produce in a refreshing sauce.

1 large red onion, chopped
4 cloves garlic, chopped
1 cup diced tomato (1 medium)
1 small eggplant (about 1 pound), cut in ¾-inch cubes
1 pound new potatoes, cut in ¾-inch cubes
2 medium red peppers (4 to 5 ounces each), cut in thin strips
½ pound flat Italian Romano beans or green beans, trimmed
¼ cup chopped parsley
½ teaspoon salt
2 tablespoons chopped fresh basil
1 cup YoChee
pepper

Combine the onion, garlic and tomato in a 5-quart or larger pot with a tight-fitting lid. Cover and place over low heat for 10 minutes.

Prepare the remaining vegetables. You can peel the eggplant and potatoes or not depending on personal preference and the condition of the skins.

Add the vegetables, parsley and salt to the pot. Cover and continue to cook over low heat, stirring occasionally, for about 45 minutes or until the vegetables are very tender and practically melted into a sauce. The vegetables should expel enough of their own juices to cook; however, if the mixture seems dry, a little water or dry wine should be added.

Remove the pot from the heat, take off the cover and let cool for about 10 minutes.

Stir in the basil, YoChee and a generous amount of pepper. Adjust salt to taste.

Serve lukewarm or at room temperature.

Makes 6 servings

PER SERVING: 153 CALORIES, <1GM. FAT, <1GM. SATURATED FAT, 8GM. PROTEIN, 32GM. CARBOHYDRATE, 120MG. CALCIUM

SUMMER TOMATO GRATIN

This flavorful YoChee-tomato casserole is best when made with ripe, summer tomatoes. It is designed to be eaten warm but not piping hot.

1½ cups YoChee
⅓ cup chopped green or black olives
⅓ cup chopped capers
6 large or 8 medium tomatoes (3 pounds)
pepper
4 cloves garlic, finely chopped
2 tablespoons chopped fresh basil
¼ cup chopped parsley
¼ cup pumpkin seeds
2 tablespoons wheat germ
1 tablespoon olive oil

Preheat the oven to 350°F.

Combine the YoChee, olives and capers. Slice the tomatoes into ¼-inch thick rounds.

Place half of the tomato slices in overlapping layers in a shallow 2-quart or 9x13-inch baking dish. Season generously with pepper and sprinkle with half of the garlic, basil and parsley. Top with half of the YoChee mixture, dropping it from a spoon in dollops evenly over the tomato slices. Repeat the layers.

Grind the pumpkin seeds in a blender or food processor. Combine with the wheat germ and sprinkle evenly over the top of the assembled casserole. Drizzle the olive oil evenly over the surface.

Bake for 30 minutes. Serve warm, but not piping hot.

Makes 4 to 6 servings

PER SERVING: BASED ON 4 SERVINGS: 274 CALORIES, 12GM. FAT, 2GM. SATURATED FAT, 17GM. PROTEIN, 29GM. CARBOHYDRATE, 230MG. CALCIUM

Cold Vegetable Terrine

This cold layered vegetable assemblage is a good choice on a warm day. It must be made several hours in advance but can be held for several days. If you don't have a tart pan with a removable bottom, use a straight-sided baking dish or a deep pie plate.

> 1 medium eggplant (1¼ to 1½ pounds)
> 2 medium zucchini (10 to 12 ounces each)
> 2 medium-large sweet red peppers
> olive oil
> 2 cups YoChee
> ½ teaspoon salt
> hot pepper sauce
> ¼ cup minced parsley
> ¼ cup minced fresh dill or basil
> parsley sprigs or fresh basil leaves

Slice the eggplant crosswise into ¼ -inch or thinner rounds. Discard the ends. Cut the zucchinis lengthwise into ¼-inch thick slices.

Preheat the broiler.

Place the vegetables, including the peppers, in a single layer on a shallow, well-oiled baking pan. You may have to use more than one pan. Turn once so that both sides of the vegetables are lightly coated with oil.

Place the pan about 6 inches below the heat of the broiler and broil the vegetables for about 8 to 10 minutes on each side or until nicely browned. The peppers should be turned several times so that all sides are exposed to the heat; cook until the skin is charred and blistered all over. If you have used more than one pan, you may have to do this step in batches. Alternatively, the vegetables can be cooked on a grill.

Remove the vegetables from the heat as they are done. When the peppers are charred, wrap them in a clean cloth for a few minutes to steam. When cool enough to handle, remove the skins using a small paring knife, cut open, remove the seeds and ribs and pat dry. Slice the peppers into 1-inch-wide strips. Cool all the vegetables to room temperature.

While the vegetables are cooking or sometime before, season the YoChee with the salt and a dash of hot pepper sauce to taste. Combine half with the minced parsley and the remainder with the minced dill or basil. If done in advance, refrigerate.

Using a 10-inch tart pan with a removable bottom, place the eggplant slices so they overlap one another and completely cover the bottom. With a rubber spatula, gently spread one batch of the seasoned YoChee to cover the eggplant. Place the strips of roasted red pepper on top. Spread the remaining seasoned YoChee over this layer. Top with a covering layer of broiled zucchini.

Place the pan on a plate to catch any liquid drippings. Cover with a plate, foil or plastic wrap. Refrigerate.

Serve well chilled, cut in wedges. Garnish each serving with the parsley sprigs or basil leaves.

Makes 6 entrée servings; 8 appetizer servings

> **Per entrée serving**: 130 calories, 3gm. fat, <1gm. saturated fat, 9.5gm. protein, 19gm. carbohydrate, 185mg. calcium
>
> **Per appetizer serving**: 98 calories, 2gm. fat, <1gm. saturated fat, 7gm. protein, 14gm. carbohydrate, 140mg. calcium

Cauliflower Gratin

This easily prepared casserole can be cooked at once or, for added convenience, assembled in advance and refrigerated until baking time. For a complete meal, add a grain, a cooked green bean or carrot accompaniment and a tossed salad.

> 1 medium-large cauliflower (about 2 pounds)
> 1½ cups YoChee
> 1½ tablespoons prepared mustard
> ⅓ cup dry bread or cracker crumbs
> 2 tablespoons wheat germ
> ¼ teaspoon salt
> ¼ teaspoon nutmeg

Preheat the oven to 375°F.

Break the cauliflower into florets and steam for 5 to 8 minutes, until just tender. When done, arrange the florets in a shallow 2-quart baking dish to that they are snuggled together.

Combine the YoChee and mustard. Smear over the cauliflower using a rubber spatula or the flat side of a knife blade.

Combine the crumbs, wheat germ and seasonings. Sprinkle evenly over the coated cauliflower. Bake for 20 minutes.

Makes 6 servings

> *Per serving*: 115 calories, 1gm. fat, <1gm. saturated fat, 10gm. protein, 18gm. carbohydrate, 180mg. calcium (see YoChievements for comparisons)

Nuttier Nutmeg

Nutmeg is most commonly bought preground. However, for a superior fresh, aromatic flavor, it is better to purchase the whole nutmeg and grind it yourself as needed. Tiny metal nutmeg graters with a compartment to store the nugget are available in housewares stores. Whole nutmeg keeps for years.

No-Fry Chili Rellenos

Rather than batter-frying the peppers, in this version we stuff them with a succulent corn filling and simmer them in a flavorful tomato sauce. To serve, set the peppers on a bed of brown rice, quinoa, polenta or black beans. Cover with the sauce.

8 4- to 6-inch poblano or Anaheim chilies or Italian frying peppers
1½ cups YoChee
1½ cups fresh or frozen corn kernels
⅓ cup thinly sliced scallions
4 cups Mexican-style tomato sauce

Arrange the peppers on a baking sheet. Broil until the skins are lightly charred, turning to cook all sides. This will take about 15 minutes. When done, wrap the peppers in a clean dishtowel to steam for 5 to 10 minutes. Remove the skins.

Cut a slit in the side of each pepper. Carefully remove any seeds. Pat the inside of the peppers with a paper towel to absorb any moisture.

In a bowl, combine the YoChee, corn and scallions. Spoon the mixture into the peppers. If the surface of the peppers gets messy during filling, wipe with a damp cloth when finished.

Pour the tomato sauce into a skillet large enough to hold the peppers in a single layer. Arrange the peppers slit side up in the sauce; the sauce should generously surround the peppers but not reach as high as the slit.

Bring the sauce to boil over medium heat. Lower the heat so that the sauce simmers gently. Cover, leaving the lid slightly ajar to allow steam to escape. Cook for 20 minutes.

Makes 4 servings

Per serving: 238 calories, 1gm. fat, <1gm. saturated fat, 15gm. protein, 45gm. carbohydrate, 225mg. calcium

YOCHEESY STUFFED BAKED POTATOES

An especially convenient meal when you have prebaked the potatoes. The recipe is based on generously sized potatoes of about 8 ounces each. You may need to make some adjustments according to the size of the potatoes, but exact amounts aren't really critical. A whole potato makes a substantial main dish, while half a potato can serve as an accompaniment.

> 2 baked potatoes (about 8 ounces each)
> ½ cup YoChee
> ¼ cup sliced scallions
> ¼ cup minced sweet red, yellow or green pepper
> ½ to ¾ cup diced gooey melting cheese, such as mozzarella, provolone, Monterey Jack, cheddar or Swiss
> salt
> pepper
> paprika

If the potatoes aren't already baked, bake them.

Preheat the oven to 350^0 to 375^0F.

Cut the potatoes in half lengthwise. If the potatoes are still hot, hold them in a clean kitchen towel while you work with them. Carefully scoop out the insides, leaving the shells intact.

Mash the potatoes with a potato masher, a rotary or electric beater or by pressing through a food mill until no lumps remain. Beat in the YoChee until the potatoes are smooth and creamy. Fold in the scallions, minced pepper and cheese. Season with salt and pepper to taste.

Mound the potato filling back into the skins. Sprinkle paprika liberally on top.

Place the potato halves on a baking pan and put them in the oven for 20 minutes, until very hot and lightly crusted on top.

Makes 2 entrée servings; 4 side-dish servings

Note: The potatoes can be stuffed and refrigerated up to a day ahead; if so, baking time may need to be extended by 5 to 10 minutes.

Variation: For a more exotic flavor, replace the melting cheese with blue cheese, but reduce the amount by about half, as its flavor is strong.

PER WHOLE POTATO WITH THE LESSER AMOUNT OF CHEESE: 385 CALORIES, 10.5GM. FAT, 6GM. SATURATED FAT, 18GM. PROTEIN, 56GM. CARBOHYDRATE, 385MG. CALCIUM (SEE YOCHIEVEMENTS FOR COMPARISONS)

PER WHOLE POTATO WITH THE FULL AMOUNT OF CHEESE: 445 CALORIES, 15.5GM. FAT, 9GM. SATURATED FAT, 22GM. PROTEIN, 56GM. CARBOHYDRATE, 510MG. CALCIUM

Preparation Tip

A serrated grapefruit spoon or curved grapefruit knife is a handy tool for scooping out the potatoes.

Potato Tortilla

A dense omelet in which potatoes are held together by a mixture of egg, YoChee and cheese. Serve warm or at room temperature.

> 1 pound potatoes
> 1 medium onion
> 1 tablespoon olive oil
> salt
> pepper
> 3 eggs
> ½ cup YoChee
> ½ cup shredded cheddar cheese

Scrub the potatoes, peel or not according to personal taste, and slice paper-thin. Slice the onion very thin.

Heat the oil in a 10- or 12-inch ovenproof skillet, then alternate layers of overlapping potato slices and onion, beginning and ending with potato. You should have three layers of potato. Season each layer with salt and pepper to taste.

Cover the pan tightly and cook over moderate heat until the potatoes are tender, about 40 minutes.

In a large bowl, beat the eggs, YoChee and cheddar cheese together until completely blended.

Loosen the potatoes with a spatula to make sure they aren't sticking to the pan. If necessary, add a little more oil. Pour the egg mixture over the cooked potatoes, spread to cover, and move gently with a fork so the egg penetrates through the potato layers.

Cover the pan and cook for about 10 to 12 minutes, until the top is almost set. Remove the cover and place the pan under the broiler for 2 to 3 minutes, just long enough to cook the top.

Cut in wedges to serve.

Makes 4 servings

> *Per serving*: 252 calories, 12gm. fat, 4.5gm. saturated fat, 14gm. protein, 25gm. carbohydrate, 200mg. calcium

POTATO-STUFFED PEPPERS

These peppers have a creamy cheese filling inside. Serve half a pepper per person, plain or with a topping of tomato sauce or salsa.

> 2 very large red, yellow or green peppers
> 2 cups cooked potatoes (see Note)
> ½ cup YoChee
> 1 cup shredded or diced cheese of choice, including cheddar, Monterey Jack, queso blanco, mozzarella, Swiss, blue or other good melting cheese
> salt
> pepper

Preheat the oven to 350ºF.

Cut the peppers in half lengthwise. Remove the seeds and any tough ribs. Steam for 5 minutes to soften slightly.

Use a potato masher or fork to mash the potatoes completely. Mash in the YoChee. Fold in the cheese. Season to taste with salt and pepper.

Stuff the pepper halves with the potato mixture. Place on a wire rack in a baking pan and bake for about 20 minutes, until the filling is hot and firm and the peppers are very tender.

Makes 4 servings

Note: You can cook the potatoes expressly for this dish, plan ahead by making extra potatoes at a previous meal or take advantage of unplanned extra baked or boiled potatoes. You will need 1 very large or 2 smaller potatoes.

PER SERVING: 212 CALORIES, 7.5GM. FAT, 5GM. SATURATED FAT, 12GM. PROTEIN, 24GM. CARBOHYDRATE, 330MG. CALCIUM

Preparation Pointer

When using YoChee, mashing is often the preferred technique for melding ingredients. A hand potato masher is a handy tool for this job. This inexpensive item is available in most housewares stores.

POTATO ENCHILADAS

Creamy mashed potatoes encased in corn tortillas provide the focal point of a Mexican meal. Our recipe was inspired by the fabulous version served in El Repollo Roja in Puerta Vallarta, Mexico.

2 cups cooked cubed potatoes
½ cup YoChee
1 cup shredded or diced cheese of choice, including cheddar, Monterey Jack, queso blanco, mozzarella, Swiss, blue or other good melting cheese
salt
pepper
12 6-inch cornmeal tortillas
1½ cups Mexican-flavored tomato sauce or salsa verde (tomatillo sauce)
1½ cups NoWorry Creamy Tomato Salsa (see recipe page 252)

Preheat the oven to 350⁰F.

Use a potato masher or fork to mash the potatoes completely. Mash in the YoChee. Fold in the cheese. Season to taste with salt and pepper.

If the tortillas are frozen, wrap them in foil and put them in the oven for a few minutes until pliable.

Place each tortilla on a flat surface and put a scant ¼ cupful of the potato filling in a strip down the middle. Roll the tortilla to completely cover.

Place the filled tortillas seam-side down in a shallow baking dish. Continue until all the tortillas are filled, placing them close together in the pan in a single layer.

Spoon the sauce over the enchiladas. Bake for 15 minutes or until hot inside.

Transfer to individual plates and top each serving with some of the Creamy Tomato Salsa. Serve the rest of the salsa on the side.

Makes 4 servings

Note: The potatoes can be cooked expressly for this dish, or use leftover baked or steamed potatoes.

PER SERVING, BEFORE ADDING NoWORRY CREAMY TOMATO SALSA: 384 CALORIES, 11GM. FAT, 5.5GM. SATURATED FAT, 16GM. PROTEIN, 58.5GM. CARBOHYDRATE, 420MG. CALCIUM

Eggplant and Potato Curry

Serve as one element in an Indian meal, along with dal (lentils, split peas or chickpeas) for added protein, chapatis, chutney and a cold Indian-style chopped cucumber, tomato and onion salad. (Recipes for these other dishes can be found in both "American Wholefoods Cuisine" and "The Healthiest Diet in the World.")

> 3 tablespoons oil
> 1 large onion, thinly sliced
> 2 cloves garlic, chopped
> 1 tablespoon finely chopped fresh ginger
> 1 teaspoon cumin
> ¼ teaspoon turmeric
> ¼ teaspoon cayenne
> 1 large eggplant (about 1½ pounds), peeled and cut in 1- to 2-inch cubes
> ¾ cup water
> ¾ teaspoon salt
> 1 pound potatoes
> ¾ cup YoChee

Heat 1 tablespoon of the oil in a 3- to 5-quart pot and sauté the onion, garlic and ginger for 3 to 5 minutes, until softened. Add the cumin, turmeric and cayenne and cook 1 minute longer.

Add the remaining 2 tablespoons of oil and the eggplant cubes. Cook, stirring frequently, until the oil is absorbed and the eggplant starts to cook.

Add the water and salt. Cover and cook over medium heat, stirring occasionally, for about 20 minutes, or until the eggplant is very tender.

Meanwhile, scrub the potatoes, cut into them into chunks and steam for 15 to 20 minutes, or until tender. Remove the peels after cooking and cut the potatoes into bite-size pieces.

Add the cooked potatoes to the eggplant. Remove the pot from the heat. While the curry is still hot, gently stir in the YoChee until it melts.

Serve warm or at room temperature.

Makes 6 servings

> **Per serving:** 175 calories, 7 gm. fat, <1 gm. saturated fat, 6 gm. protein, 25 gm. carbohydrate, 85 mg. calcium

Baked Stuffed Eggplant

This is a recipe where you can be creative about adding other ingredients and seasonings. For example, just varying the cheese, introducing some chopped walnuts, lentils or raisins to the filling or using curry or chili powder according to taste can alter its character dramatically. Serve with cracked wheat or another grain, salad and bread with a YoChee spread.

1 medium eggplant (about 1 pound)
1 tablespoon olive oil
1 small onion, chopped
1 large clove garlic, chopped
½ cup chopped celery and/or red or green pepper
¾ cup diced tomato
1 teaspoon oregano
¼ teaspoon salt
pepper
½ cup YoChee
½ cup Italian-style or spicy tomato sauce
2 tablespoons crumbled feta, shredded mozzarella or grated Parmesan cheese, optional but preferred

Cut the eggplant in half lengthwise. Using a curved grapefruit knife, scoop out the inside, leaving a shell about ¼ inch thick. Salt the shell lightly. Dice the eggplant flesh into small pieces.

Heat the oil in a large skillet. Add the onion and garlic and sauté until just tender, about 5 minutes. Add the diced eggplant, remaining vegetables and oregano. Cook for 10 to 15 minutes, stirring occasionally, until the eggplant is softened. Remove from the heat.

Season with ¼ teaspoon salt or to taste and a generous amount of pepper. Add the YoChee and stir until evenly mixed.

Meanwhile, preheat the oven to 350°F.

Place the eggplant shells in a baking dish. Spoon the YoChee filling into the shells. Pour the tomato sauce on top.

Cover and bake for 30 to 40 minutes, or until the shells are tender.

Uncover the baking dish and top each eggplant half with 1 tablespoon of the cheese, if using. Bake uncovered for 10 minutes longer, whether cheese is used or not.

Makes 2 servings

> **PER SERVING, WITHOUT CHEESE**: 240 CALORIES, 10GM. FAT, 1GM. SATURATED FAT, 10GM. PROTEIN, 32GM. CARBOHYDRATE, 170MG. CALCIUM
>
> **PER SERVING, WITH FETA**: 264 CALORIES, 12GM. FAT, 3GM. SATURATED FAT, 11GM. PROTEIN, 33GM. CARBOHYDRATE, 215MG. CALCIUM
>
> **PER SERVING, WITH MOZZARELLA**: 258 CALORIES, 11GM. FAT, 2GM. SATURATED FAT, 11.5GM. PROTEIN, 33GM. CARBOHYDRATE, 215MG. CALCIUM
>
> **PER SERVING, WITH PARMESAN**: 268 CALORIES, 12GM. FAT, 2.5GM. SATURATED FAT, 12GM. PROTEIN, 33GM. CARBOHYDRATE, 255MG. CALCIUM

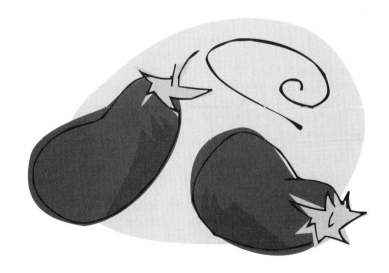

Eggplant Rollatini

As in the following recipe for Eggplant Lasagna, you can peel the eggplant or not, according to personal preference. Bake until the eggplant is quite tender, and don't be surprised if baking takes longer than specified in the recipe.

> 2 medium eggplants (1 to 1½ pounds each)
> ½ pound fresh greens, such as spinach, kale, Swiss chard or arugula, or 10-ounce package frozen chopped spinach
> ¼ cup chopped fresh parsley and/or basil
> 1½ cups YoChee
> ¾ cup shredded mozzarella and/or provolone cheeses, in any proportion
> ¼ cup grated Parmesan cheese
> ¼ teaspoon nutmeg
> salt
> pepper
> 2 cups well-seasoned Italian-style tomato sauce

Cut each eggplant lengthwise into 8 slices, each slice about ¼ inch thick. Place the eggplant slices on an oiled baking sheet, turn once so both sides are lightly coated with oil, and broil 6 inches from the heat for about 5 minutes on each side, until lightly browned. Alternatively, pile the eggplant slices on a vegetable steamer and steam for 10 minutes, until pliable and partially cooked.

If using fresh greens, chop them by hand or in a food processor until very fine; you should have about 3 cups. Place the greens in a strainer and press to remove as much liquid as possible. If using frozen spinach, let it thaw and then press in a similar manner. At the end you should have about 1 cup finely chopped dry greens.

Combine the greens with the fresh herbs, YoChee, shredded cheese, Parmesan, nutmeg and salt and pepper to taste. The amount of salt will vary with the saltiness of the cheeses and may even be unnecessary.

Preheat the oven to 350°F.

Place about 2 tablespoons of the YoChee filling in a strip across the center of each slice of eggplant. Roll to enclose the filling, as illustrated on the next page.

Spoon a layer of the sauce to cover the bottom of a 9x13-inch baking pan. Place the eggplant rolls side by side in the pan. Top with the remaining sauce. Cover the baking dish and bake for 30 minutes.

Remove the cover and bake for 10 more minutes, or until the eggplant is easily pierced with a fork.

Makes 4 ample servings

Note: The casserole can be assembled in advance and refrigerated until baking time. Bring to room temperature while the oven preheats.

> **PER SERVING**: 293 CALORIES, 6.5 GM FAT, 3.5 GM. SATURATED FAT, 23 GM. PROTEIN, 42 GM. CARBOHYDRATE, 535 MG. CALCIUM

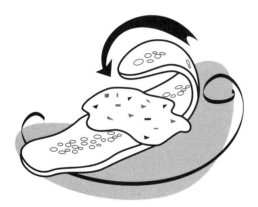

Rolling eggplant slice over the filling

Eggplant Lasagna

Eggplant makes an excellent substitute for pasta in lasagna. Peel the eggplant or not, according to personal preference. Be sure to cook this dish until the eggplant is soft. It may take longer than specified in the recipe, as every eggplant seems to have its own personality when it comes to baking time.

> 2 medium eggplants (2½ to 3 pounds total)
> 2 cups YoChee
> ¼ cup minced parsley
> salt
> 2 cups well-seasoned Italian-style tomato sauce
> 4 ounces thinly sliced or shredded mozzarella cheese (1 cup)
> ¼ cup grated Parmesan cheese

Trim the ends of the eggplants and slice the remaining eggplant crosswise into rounds no more than ¼ inch thick. Place the eggplant slices on a well-oiled baking sheet. Turn once so that both sides are lightly coated with oil. Broil 6 inches from the heat for about 5 minutes on each side or until lightly browned.

Preheat the oven to 350⁰F.

Combine the YoChee with the parsley and a pinch of salt.

Set aside 1 cup of the tomato sauce for the top. Layer the ingredients in a 9x13-inch baking dish or shallow 2-quart casserole, beginning with a little of the remaining sauce (about ¼ cup), one third of the eggplant to cover the bottom of the dish, half of the seasoned YoChee, half of the mozzarella and half of the remaining tomato sauce. Use the back of a spoon or a spatula to spread the YoChee and the sauce to cover the eggplant. Repeat this pattern with another layer of eggplant, YoChee, mozzarella and sauce. Top with a final layer of eggplant, the reserved 1 cup of tomato sauce and the grated Parmesan cheese.

Cover the pan and bake for 30 minutes. Remove the cover and bake 10 minutes longer or until the eggplant is fork tender.

Let the casserole sit at room temperature for at least 15 minutes to set before serving.

Makes 6 servings

Note: The casserole can be assembled in advance and refrigerated until baking time. Bring to room temperature while the oven preheats.

Per serving: 210 calories, 5gm. fat, 3gm. saturated fat, 17gm. protein, 28gm. carbohydrate, 275mg. calcium (see YoChievements for comparisons)

Mushroom Ragout

Earthy mushrooms in a creamy sauce make a satisfying meal served over potatoes, toast or a favorite grain. For additional serving ideas, see Ragout Repertoire (page 133).

½ pound cultivated white mushrooms
½ pound mixed exotic mushrooms of choice, including portobellos, creminis, shiitakes, chanterelles or the like
½ cup thinly sliced shallots
¼ cup cooking sherry or dry wine
2 teaspoons soy sauce
½ cup YoChee
½ teaspoon salt
pepper

Clean the mushrooms and slice the caps and stems into bite-size pieces. You should have about 3 cups.

Combine the mushrooms, shallots, sherry and soy sauce in a skillet. Cook, stirring frequently, for 8 to 10 minutes or until the mushrooms release their juices and are tender.

Remove from the heat and stir in the YoChee and salt. Return to low heat and cook, stirring continuously, for 1 to 2 minutes until creamy and warm. Do not boil. Season with pepper to taste.

Makes 4 to 6 servings

Per serving, based on 4 servings: 85 calories, <1gm. fat, <1gm. saturated fat, 6.5gm. protein, 11gm. carbohydrate, 70mg. calcium

WILD RED MUSHROOM RAGOUT

Meaty mushrooms in a flavorful red sauce. For serving ideas, see Ragout Repertoire.

1 tablespoon olive oil
1 large clove garlic, chopped
1 medium onion, chopped
½ pound portobello mushrooms
¼ pound cremini mushrooms
¼ pound shiitake mushrooms
1½ cups canned crushed tomatoes
½ teaspoon salt
¼ cup chopped fresh basil
¾ cup YoChee
pepper

Heat the oil in a large saucepan. Add the garlic and onion. Cook, stirring frequently, for 5 to 8 minutes, until the onion begins to color.

Cut the mushrooms into small pieces. Add them to the pot and cook for about 5 minutes, until they begin to soften and release their juices.

Add the crushed tomatoes, salt and basil. Bring to a boil. Reduce the heat so it is very low. Cover the pot and cook, stirring occasionally, for about 20 minutes, until the mushrooms are tender.

Remove from the heat. Stir in the YoChee until the ragout is creamy. Season generously with pepper. Taste for salt.

Makes 4 to 6 servings

Pᴇʀ sᴇʀᴠɪɴɢ, ʙᴀꜱᴇᴅ ᴏɴ 4 sᴇʀᴠɪɴɢꜱ: 121 ᴄᴀʟᴏʀɪᴇꜱ, 3.5ɢᴍ. ꜰᴀᴛ, <1ɢᴍ. ꜱᴀᴛᴜʀᴀᴛᴇᴅ ꜰᴀᴛ, 8.5ɢᴍ. ᴘʀᴏᴛᴇɪɴ, 14ɢᴍ. ᴄᴀʀʙᴏʜʏᴅʀᴀᴛᴇ, 135ᴍɢ. ᴄᴀʟᴄɪᴜᴍ

Ragout Repetoire

Here are some creative ways to use the two preceding mushroom ragout recipes. You can also apply these ideas to many other creamy YoChee-vegetable combinations.

✔ Spoon over toast, biscuits or English muffins.

✔ Spoon over rice, polenta, cracked wheat, couscous, barley, kasha, millet or quinoa.

✔ Toss with cooked pasta. Top with grated Parmesan cheese or crumbled feta or blue cheese if desired.

✔ Use as a topping for steamed vegetables such as cauliflower, broccoli, asparagus or green beans.

✔ Serve on baked white or sweet potatoes or winter squash.

✔ Use as a filling or topping for an omelet.

✔ Use to fill or top crepes.

✔ Use as a burger garnish.

VEGETABLE POTPIE

The YoChee in both the crisp crust and the creamy filling makes this homey, old-fashioned potpie a protein-packed meal.

> **Biscuit Crust (see facing page)**
> **6 cups diced cooked vegetables (see Vegetable Vitals)**
> **1 small onion, chopped**
> **1 tablespoon minced fresh parsley, sage or dill or 1 teaspoon mixed dried poultry seasonings**
> **2 cups YoChee**
> **pepper**
> **salt**

Preheat the oven to 425°F.

Prepare the Biscuit Crust. Roll to a thickness of ⅛ to ¼ inch.

Combine the vegetables, herb of choice and YoChee. Season liberally with pepper and salt to taste. Place in an oiled 1½-quart casserole, deep 9- or 10-inch pie pan or 4 individual baking dishes.

Lay the crust on top of the vegetables to cover. Cut a few slits to allow steam to escape. Bake for 15 to 20 minutes, until the top is brown.

Makes 4 servings

> *PER SERVING:* 461 CALORIES, 8.5 GM. FAT, <1 GM. SATURATED FAT, 25.5 GM. PROTEIN, 76.5 GM. CARBOHYDRATE, 460 MG. CALCIUM (SEE YOCHIEVEMENTS FOR COMPARISONS)

Vegetable Vitals

The vegetables for potpie can be cooked leftovers or made expressly for this dish.

Choose a colorful mixture, including fresh or frozen corn, peas, broccoli, cauliflower, white or sweet potatoes, carrots, turnips, green beans, celery or cooked or canned beans.

To prepare fresh vegetables, dice and combine in a skillet with a little water. Cover and cook for 15 to 20 minutes, stirring occasionally, until just tender. Remove from the heat. Add beans or frozen vegetables if using. Let cool slightly before continuing.

BISCUIT CRUST

⅔ cup whole wheat flour
⅓ cup cornmeal or oats
2 tablespoons wheat germ
1 teaspoon baking powder
¼ teaspoon baking soda
¼ teaspoon salt
2 tablespoons olive or canola oil
1½ teaspoons honey
½ cup YoChee

Combine the dry ingredients in a mixing bowl. Stir in the oil and mix with a pastry blender, wire whisk or fork until completely incorporated and crumbly. Stir in the honey and YoChee. Mix until the ingredients are well blended, kneading gently in the bowl with your hands at the end to form a ball of dough.

Pat or roll the dough gently until it is ¼ to ⅛ inch thick. Use as directed in the Vegetable Potpie recipe.

Makes 1 large or 4 individual crusts

> **PER SERVING**: 200 CALORIES, 7 GM. FAT, <1 GM. SATURATED FAT, 7 GM. PROTEIN, 29 GM. CARBOHYDRATE, 150 MG. CALCIUM

Russian Vegetable Pie

The creamy filling of this savory pie is packed with vegetables and infused with dill. The rich taste disguises the fact that it is fat-free. The crust, unlike traditional piecrusts, has no hydrogenated or saturated fat and is practically foolproof. For convenience, the filling can be prepared at the last minute, or well in advance and chilled. Another asset is that the finished pie can be eaten while still warm or at room temperature.

Filling:
1 small onion, thinly sliced (about ½ cup)
1 medium carrot, shredded (about ¼ cup)
1 cup thinly sliced mushrooms
¼ cup slivered green pepper
2 cups coarsely shredded cabbage
¼ cup minced fresh dill
¼ teaspoon salt
1 cup YoChee

Crust:
⅔ cup whole wheat flour
⅓ cup cornmeal
2 tablespoons wheat germ
1 teaspoon baking powder
¼ teaspoon baking soda
2 tablespoons olive oil
½ cup YoChee
1½ teaspoons prepared mustard

To make the filling, combine the vegetables and the dill in a heavy skillet. Cover and steep over medium heat, stirring occasionally, for 15 minutes or until tender. Season with the salt. Cool to lukewarm.

Preheat the oven to 425⁰F.

To prepare the crust, combine the dry ingredients in a mixing bowl. Stir in the olive oil and mix with a pastry blender, wire whisk or fork until completely incorporated and crumbly. Stir in the ½ cup YoChee and mix until the ingredients are well blended, kneading gently in the bowl with your hands at the end to form a ball of dough.

Oil a 9-inch pie pan. Press the dough over the bottom and up the sides of the pan to make a shell. Prick the surface liberally with a fork. Bake for 10 minutes.

Remove the crust from the oven and lower the heat to 375°F.

Complete the filling by combining the cooled vegetables with the 1 cup YoChee. Stir until evenly mixed.

Spread the mustard lightly over the bottom of the partially baked crust. Add the vegetable filling.

Bake for 20 minutes, until the filling is firm and the edges of the crust are golden brown. Remove from the oven and let sit for at least 10 minutes before cutting.

Makes 4 entrée servings; 8 appetizer servings

PER ENTRÉE SERVING: 269 CALORIES, 8.5 GM. FAT, 1 GM. SATURATED FAT, 13 GM. PROTEIN, 37 GM. CARBOHYDRATE, 295 MG. CALCIUM

Zucchini Flatcakes

Zucchini Flatcakes can be eaten sweet or savory. Favorite toppings include apricot preserves, chutney or a sprinkling of soy sauce. In addition, we serve a dollop of YoChee on top of each flatcake. This recipe feeds two generously and can be multiplied as needed.

1½ pounds zucchini
½ teaspoon salt
1 egg
⅓ cup YoChee, plus additional for garnish
½ cup whole wheat flour
1 teaspoon baking powder
1 teaspoon olive or canola oil, plus additional oil for cooking
¼ cup minced parsley

Shred the zucchini, using a box grater or food processor. You should have about 4 cups. Mix with the salt and place in a colander or strainer to drain for 20 minutes or longer. Press to remove as much liquid as possible. (You can save this for soup if you like.) You should have about 2 cups of zucchini.

Transfer the zucchini to a large mixing bowl. Beat in the egg, then the ⅓ cup of YoChee. Stir in the flour, baking powder, teaspoon of oil and parsley, and mix until evenly blended.

Heat enough oil to just cover the surface of a griddle or large skillet. When hot, drop the zucchini batter by ⅓ cupfuls into the pan. Cook until the flatcakes are set on the bottom and nicely browned.

Turn, flatten lightly with a spatula, and cook the other side. Flatcakes can be turned several times if necessary until the outside is well-colored.

Makes 2 generous servings; 8 flatcakes

Per serving: 276 calories, 10gm. fat, 2gm. saturated fat, 14.5gm. protein, 36gm. carbohydrate, 320mg. calcium

Per flatcake: 69 calories, 2.5gm. fat, <1gm. saturated fat, 3.5gm. protein, 9gm. carbohydrate, 80mg. calcium

MAINLY BEANS

These YoChee-bean recipes include both entrées and accompaniments. Note that when cooked beans are called for, either home-cooked or canned beans will do.

BEAN BOOSTER

In addition to its use in the recipes here, plain YoChee is a perfect accessory to many other bean dishes, where it complements the taste, texture and protein. For example, we always top bean chili or black bean soup with a generous garnish of YoChee instead of the traditional sour cream.

᾿ YoChievements ᾿

Stuffed Peppers (pg.144) vs. frozen stuffed peppers with beef
    Similar calories
    70% less fat
    60% more protein
    40% more (high fiber) carbohydrate
    200% more calcium

more…

Mushroom-Tofu Paprikash (pg.146) vs. veal paprikash
   25% less calories
   53% less fat
   86% less saturated fat
   33% less protein
   6.5 times as much calcium

Barbecue-Style Beans (pg.150) vs. canned barbecue baked beans
   10% less calories
   75% less fat
   14% more protein

Bean Tostadas

Tostadas are similar to nachos, only easier to prepare. This recipe is easily multiplied for as many servings as required.

1½ cups cooked red, pink or black beans, drained
4 tostadas (see Tostadas Tips)
½ cup YoChee
½ cup shredded Monterey Jack or cheddar cheese
½ teaspoon cumin
sliced jalapeno peppers, optional
⅓ cup Instant Creamy Salsa or NoWorry Creamy Tomato Salsa
(see recipes pages 24 and 252)

Preheat the oven to 375°F.

Mash the beans lightly using a potato masher or fork. Carefully cover the surface of each tostada with about ⅓ cup of the mashed beans. Drop 2 tablespoons of the YoChee in dollops over the beans on each tostada. Top each tostada with 2 tablespoons of the shredded cheese and a sprinkling of cumin.

Bake for 10 to 15 minutes, until the cheese is melted and the beans are hot.

Garnish with some sliced jalapeno peppers if desired. Serve with the salsa of choice on the side for topping the tostadas to taste.

Makes 2 servings

Per tostada before adding salsa: 225 calories, 8gm. fat, 3.5gm. saturated fat, 13gm. protein, 26gm. carbohydrate, 200mg. calcium

Tostadas Tips

Corn tostadas are flat taco shells. If they're unavailable, or for a lower-fat option, substitute corn tortillas prepared as follows:

Preheat the oven to 500°F. Run cold water quickly over each tortilla and drain. Place the tortillas directly on the oven rack. Bake for 5 minutes. Turn and bake for 2 to 3 minutes longer, until crisp. Remove from the oven and proceed with the recipe.

For nachos, replace the tostadas with a bed of tortilla chips.

Quick Creamy Bean Stew

This is a really simple and quick dish that is adaptable to whatever ingredients you have on hand (see Sumptuous Stews). If desired, serve with a salsa garnish.

> 2 cups cooked beans of choice (kidney beans, pinto beans, chickpeas, pigeon peas, white beans, black beans, etc.), lightly drained
> 3 carrots, cut into coins
> 1 small onion, diced
> 3 cloves garlic, sliced
> ½ cup tomato juice
> ⅓ cup YoChee
> salt

Combine everything but the YoChee in a pot. Bring to a boil, reduce the heat to a gentle simmer and cook for 15 to 20 minutes, or until the carrots are cooked to taste. Stir occasionally during cooking.

Remove from the heat, cool for a few minutes, then stir in the YoChee until creamy.

Season to taste with salt.

Makes 2 entrée servings; 4 side-dish servings

> Per entrée serving: 354 calories, 1gm. fat, <1gm. saturated fat, 23gm. protein, 66gm. carbohydrate, 290mg. calcium

Sumptuous Stews

For a jazzier dish, add any of these herbs and/or vegetables:

> ✔ 2 tablespoons chopped fresh parsley, cilantro or basil
>
> ✔ ½ teaspoon dried oregano, cumin or thyme
>
> ✔ As desired: diced peppers, celery, 1-inch lengths of green beans or corn kernels

If the volume of vegetables is increased, add a little more tomato juice, if necessary, to make a gravy.

BEAN-CHEESE BAKE

This accommodating recipe can also be adapted to the ingredients on hand, as well as the inspiration of the cook. The vegetables can be either leftovers or freshly prepared.

> 3 to 4 cups cooked lentils, black beans, kidney beans or other beans of choice, lightly drained (see Notes)
> 2 to 3 cups diced vegetables of choice, individually or a mixture including precooked white or sweet potatoes, carrots, winter squash, zucchini or green beans; frozen corn or peas; uncooked onion, scallions, celery or green or red pepper
> 2 teaspoons seasoning of choice, such as oregano, cumin, chili powder, or curry powder (see Notes)
> salt
> 1½ cups YoChee
> ½ cup shredded cheddar or other cheese of choice

Preheat the oven to 350°F.

Combine the beans, vegetables and seasoning of choice. Season with salt to taste if the beans are not presalted. Place in a shallow 1½- to 2-quart baking dish.

Cover the surface evenly with dollops of the YoChee dropped from a spoon. Scatter the shredded cheese over all.

Bake for 20 minutes.

Makes 4 servings

Notes: While it is better to use the full 4 cups of beans, if you are using canned beans, two 1-pound cans provide about 3 cups of beans. If using chili powder or curry powder as the seasoning, you can either mix it with the beans or with the YoChee or with both for extra flavor.

Per serving: 431 CALORIES, 6GM. FAT, 3GM. SATURATED FAT, 33GM. PROTEIN, 65GM. CARBOHYDRATE, 350MG. CALCIUM

STUFFED PEPPERS

The basic ingredients are like those in the preceding Bean-Cheese Bake, but using the mixture to stuff a vegetable produces a vastly different result. As described in the Notes below, you can match the beans, vegetables, seasonings and cheese to personal taste or an ethnic cuisine of choice.

> 3 cups cooked beans, drained
> 2 to 3 cups diced vegetables of choice, individually or a mixture, including onion, scallion, celery, green or red pepper, hot pepper, tomato, fresh or frozen corn kernels, frozen peas, or precooked white or sweet potatoes, carrots, squash or green beans
> 1½ cups YoChee
> 2 teaspoons seasoning of choice, including oregano, cumin, chili powder, curry powder or fresh dill
> salt
> ½ cup shredded cheddar or other cheese of choice
> 4 medium-large green or red peppers

Preheat the oven to 350°F.

Combine the beans, vegetables, YoChee and seasoning of choice. Season with salt to taste if the beans are not presalted.

Cut the peppers in half through the stem, or leave whole and remove the top. Remove the seeds and any tough ribs. Plunge into a pot of boiling water and cook for 5 minutes. Remove immediately and drain.

Spoon the bean mixture into the prepared peppers. Scatter the shredded cheese on top.

Place the filled peppers in a baking dish. Surround with a little water to keep them moist during cooking. Bake for 20 minutes. At serving time, top with additional YoChee if desired.

Makes 4 servings

Notes: If using canned beans you will need two 1-pound cans. Here are some suggested combinations of beans, vegetables, seasonings and cheese: kidney beans, peppers, onions, corn, tomato, cheddar or Monterey Jack cheese; lentils, celery, sweet potato, scallion, curry powder, Swiss cheese; chickpeas, summer or winter squash, onion, cumin, feta cheese; white beans, peppers, tomato, parsley, oregano, mozzarella and/or Parmesan cheese.

Per serving: 410 calories, 5.5gm. fat, 3gm. saturated fat, 29gm. protein, 66gm. carbohydrate, 415mg. calcium (see YoChievements for comparisons)

CREAMY SPINACH AND CHICKPEAS WITH FETA

Easy and excellent. Serve with cracked wheat pilaf, tomato salad, Greek olives and pita for a delicious meal.

>   2 cups cooked chickpeas, drained
>   ⅓ cup bean cooking liquid
>   1 tablespoon olive oil
>   ¾ pound spinach, chopped (about 8 cups)
>   1 teaspoon cumin
>   1 tablespoon lemon juice
>   ½ cup YoChee
>   4 ounces feta cheese, crumbled (¾ cup)
>   pepper

Combine the chickpeas, cooking liquid, olive oil, spinach and cumin in a large pot. Cover and cook over medium heat for about 10 minutes, until the spinach is tender. Remove from the heat.

While still hot, add the lemon juice, YoChee and feta cheese. Stir until evenly mixed. Season generously with pepper.

Makes 4 servings

> **PER SERVING:** 281 CALORIES, 12 GM. FAT, 5 GM. SATURATED FAT, 16 GM. PROTEIN, 29 GM. CARBOHYDRATE, 320 MG. CALCIUM

Mushroom-Tofu Paprikash

For a hearty meal in less than 30 minutes, serve this creamy paprikash over rice, flat noodles, spirals, bow ties or toast. Complete the menu with broccoli, asparagus or another green vegetable in season, lightly steamed and seasoned with a fresh lemon wedge.

¾ pound mushrooms
1 medium onion, cut in crescents
1 tablespoon soy sauce
¾ pound firm tofu, cut in bite-size cubes (2 cups)
½ cup tomato juice
1 tablespoon paprika
pinch cayenne pepper, optional
½ teaspoon salt
1 cup YoChee

Clean the mushrooms. Cut the stems into small sticks and the caps into halves or quarters, depending on how big they are.

Combine the mushrooms, onion and soy sauce in a saucepan. Cover and cook over medium heat for about 8 minutes, until the mushrooms soften and release their juices.

Add the tofu cubes, tomato juice, paprika, cayenne if desired and salt. Simmer uncovered for 5 minutes.

Remove from the heat and gradually stir in the YoChee until the sauce is creamy. Return to very low heat, if necessary. Do not boil.

Makes 4 servings

Variation: For Mushroom-Chickpea Paprikash, replace the tofu with 2 cups cooked chickpeas.

Per serving: 236 calories, 8gm. fat, 1gm. saturated fat, 22gm. protein, 24gm. carbohydrate, 320mg. calcium (see YoChievements for comparisons)

Soy Sauce Selection

Use a genuine soy sauce, not one doctored with corn syrup and caramel coloring. Real soy sauce is sold in Oriental groceries and natural food stores.

MEXICAN CONFETTI

This colorful stew is ideally prepared using jicama (HEE-kah-mah), a Mexican tuber that has a sweet, nutty flavor (see Note). If you don't like spicy food, the hot pepper can be omitted. On the other hand, heat-lovers can turn it up by adding spicy salsa.

1 jicama about the size of a large softball
1 sweet red or green pepper
1 small onion
1 hot pepper, optional
2 cloves garlic
1 tablespoon olive oil
1 cup fresh or frozen corn kernels
1½ cups cooked kidney, pinto or other pink, brown or red beans
½ teaspoon cumin
¼ teaspoon salt
½ to ¾ cup YoChee

Using a sharp paring knife, remove the brown skin from the jicama. Cut the jicama, sweet pepper and onion into bite-size pieces. Chop the hot pepper if using. Chop the garlic or squeeze it in a garlic press.

Heat the oil in a large skillet. When hot, add the jicama, peppers, onion and garlic. Cook over medium-high heat for about 10 minutes, stirring frequently, until the vegetables are crisp-tender and lightly charred.

Add the corn, beans, cumin and salt. Cook briefly until heated through.

Serve while still hot, with a generous amount of YoChee on top.

Makes 4 ample servings

Note: If you can't find jicama, use potato or 1½ cups diced canned water chestnuts.

Per serving: 266 CALORIES, 5GM. FAT, <1GM. SATURATED FAT, 12GM. PROTEIN, 45GM. CARBOHYDRATE, 150MG. CALCIUM

INDIAN LENTILS WITH CURRIED GREENS

Serve as part of an Indian meal with rice, vegetables, chutney and chapati. The curried greens without the lentils also make an interesting topping for baked potatoes.

> 1 medium onion, chopped
> 2 tablespoons apple juice
> 1 to 2 tablespoons curry powder
> 8 cups coarsely chopped greens, such as spinach, kale, chard or a mixture along with some mustard greens, chicory or other bitter greens (about ½ pound)
> ¾ cup YoChee
> ½ teaspoon salt (reduce if lentils are salted)
> 3 cups cooked lentils, lightly drained
> juice of ½ lemon

Combine the onion and apple juice in a large skillet. Cover and cook over low heat, stirring occasionally, for 5 to 10 minutes, until the onion is translucent.

Stir in the curry powder, adjusting the amount according to the spiciness of the mixture itself, as well as personal taste. Cook, stirring, for 1 minute.

Add the greens and sauté for 5 to 10 minutes, stirring frequently, until tender. The time will vary with the particular greens.

Transfer the cooked greens to a food processor or blender. Add the YoChee and salt. Process until evenly blended.

Put the lentils in a pot and cook until quite hot. Remove from the heat and stir in the creamed greens. Season to taste with lemon juice and additional salt if needed.

Makes 6 servings

> *Per serving*: 192 CALORIES, 1GM. FAT, <1GM. SATURATED FAT, 15GM. PROTEIN, 34GM. CARBOHYDRATE, 200MG. CALCIUM

CREAMY WALNUT YoCHEE PESTO WITH WHITE BEANS AND CARROTS

Beans + a vegetable + a YoChee pesto sauce: This combination takes on vastly different personalities depending on the vegetables and beans you choose. This concept is demonstrated here and in the next recipe.

> **1 cup carrot coins**
> **4 cups cooked white beans or black-eyed peas**
> **¾ cup Creamy Walnut YoChee Pesto (see recipe page 250)**

Steam the carrots or cook them in a small amount of boiling water for 5 to 8 minutes, until just tender. Add the beans and heat through. Remove from the heat.

Just before serving, stir the Creamy Walnut Pesto into the hot vegetables. (If the vegetables have cooled, reheat before adding the YoChee.) Mix gently until the beans and carrots are completely covered with the sauce.

Makes 4 servings

> **PER SERVING:** 336 CALORIES, 6GM. FAT, <1GM. SATURATED FAT, 21GM. PROTEIN, 54GM. CARBOHYDRATE, 270MG. CALCIUM

CREAMY WALNUT YoCHEE PESTO WITH DOUBLE BEANS

> **1 pound green beans**
> **¼ cup dry white wine or water**
> **3 cups cooked chickpeas**
> **¾ cup Creamy Walnut YoChee Pesto (see recipe page 250)**
> **1 large tomato, cut in wedges**

Trim the ends from the green beans and break into 2-inch lengths.

Pour the wine or water into a large skillet. Place over medium heat. When warm, add the green beans, cover and cook for 10 minutes, until tender but still crisp. Add the chickpeas and heat through. Remove from the heat.

Just before serving, stir the Creamy Walnut Pesto into the hot vegetables. (If the vegetables have cooled, reheat before adding the YoChee.) Garnish the completed dish with the tomato wedges.

Makes 4 servings

> **PER SERVING:** 330 CALORIES, 8.5GM. FAT, 1GM. SATURATED FAT, 17GM. PROTEIN, 50GM. CARBOHYDRATE, 205MG. CALCIUM

Barbecue-Style Beans

This is a quick and easy dish that can be made with either canned or home-cooked beans. As an entrée, spoon the beans over baked sweet potato halves, rice, corn bread or even toasted whole grain bread. Add a green salad or cole slaw to complete the menu. Also makes a good choice as part of a Mexican meal instead of refried beans.

1 medium onion, chopped
1 tablespoon chili powder
½ cup catsup (natural unsweetened or fruit-juice-sweetened preferred)
2 teaspoons molasses
⅓ cup orange juice
4 cups cooked black beans, kidney beans or pinto beans, lightly drained
⅓ cup YoChee
hot pepper sauce
salt

Combine the onion, chili powder, catsup, molasses and orange juice in a pot. Bring to a boil. Simmer gently for 5 minutes.

Add the beans and cook 5 minutes longer, or until the beans are quite hot. Remove from the heat.

Stir in the YoChee. Season to taste with hot pepper sauce and salt.

Makes 4 entrée servings; 6 side-dish servings

Per entrée serving: 302 calories, 1gm. fat, <1gm. saturated fat, 18gm. protein, 58gm. carbohydrate, 105mg. calcium (see YoChievements for comparisons)

PASTA DISHES

Mild-flavored soft cheeses such as ricotta, fresh mozzarella and even cottage cheese have long been paired with pasta in traditional dishes. Likewise, rich cream is a common addition to many pasta preparations. As with these foods, YoChee creates a luxurious feel and acts as a medium for various flavoring ingredients, including garlic, herbs and spices. At the same time it elevates the protein, while staying within modest fat boundaries, to produce pasta dishes of main course status.

❧ YoChievements ❧

Pasta Alfredo Style (pg. 157) vs. prepared fettuccini Alfredo
    Similar calories
    86% less fat
    88% less saturated fat
    53% more protein

Creamy Green Linguini with Red Mushroom Sauce (pg. 158) vs. spaghetti with tomato sauce and cheese
    Similar calories
    80% less fat
    50% more protein
    100% more calcium

more…

One-Step Vegetable Lasagna (pg.169) vs. frozen vegetable lasagna
    Similar calories
    50% less fat
    25% less saturated fat
    40% more protein
    64% more calcium

One-Step Spinach Lasagna (pg.170) vs. homemade meatless lasagna
    25% less calories
    70% less fat
    75% less saturated fat
    Similar protein

YoChee Perks for Pasta

Pasta is one of the foods most compatible with YoChee.

YoChee + pasta = a meal with valuable protein.

✔ Stir YoChee into pasta sauces to make them creamy.

✔ Place a bowl of YoChee on the table at pasta meals so everyone can drop YoChee pearls over their pasta.

✔ To liven up the YoChee, season it with garlic, fresh basil, oregano or other favorite herbs.

✔ For a mellow garlic-flavored pasta, top with Roasted Garlic YoChee (page 73).

✔ When dressing pasta with pesto, first mix the pesto with YoChee to taste.

✔ Before putting baked ziti or other pasta casseroles in the oven, drop pearls of YoChee all over the top.

✔ Top pasta in garlic or tomato sauce with a YoChee-olive garnish, for example, Mediterranean Olive Spread (page 75) or Melissa's Olive Spread (page 76).

✔ Instead of tossing pasta with Parmesan cheese, try NoWorry Deluxe Potato Topping (page 249).

CREAMY VEGETABLE PASTA WITH CHEESE

Incredibly simple, yet rich and flavorful.

> 1 pound vegetable or cheese tortellini
> 1 pound asparagus, or cauliflower or broccoli florets
> ¼ cup chopped parsley
> 6 tablespoons YoChee
> ½ cup crumbled feta, blue cheese or goat cheese
> pepper

Bring a large pot of water to a boil for the pasta. Meanwhile, prepare the vegetables of choice, cutting the asparagus into 1-inch lengths or breaking the cauliflower or broccoli into small florets.

Cook the pasta until tender to taste, about 10 minutes or according to package directions. Add the vegetables to the pasta during last 2 minutes of cooking.

Drain the pasta and vegetables. Do not rinse. Transfer immediately to a serving bowl and add the parsley, YoChee and crumbled cheese of choice. Mix to coat the pasta and vegetables with the melting cheeses. Season generously with pepper.

Makes 4 servings

Note: The fresh vegetables can be replaced with 2 cups of frozen green peas. Do not add until the very end of cooking, just long enough to heat through.

PER SERVING: 457 CALORIES, 13GM. FAT, 8GM. SATURATED FAT, 24GM. PROTEIN, 60GM. CARBOHYDRATE, 445MG. CALCIUM

Pasta Cooking Note

When cooking pasta, use plenty of boiling water and let it continue to boil vigorously once the pasta is added. Unless otherwise directed in a recipe, the pasta should be drained as soon is it is done, but not rinsed. The little bit of water and starch that cling to the surface actually contribute to the consistency of the final dish.

NOODLES & YoCHEE

Noodles and cheese is high on the list of comfort foods. This is our new interpretation.

> 1 tablespoon butter
> 2 tablespoons chopped parsley
> ¼ teaspoon salt
> 4 cups cooked noodles, well drained
> ½ cup YoChee
> pepper

Melt the butter in a large pot or skillet. Add the parsley and cook for 1 minute.

Add the salt and the cooked noodles. When hot, turn the heat down low and stir in the YoChee, mixing until it melts and coats the noodles.

Season liberally with pepper.

Makes 2 servings

Note: For the noodles, use leftovers, or cook 6 ounces dry noodles in boiling water until tender. Choose broad noodles, rigatoni, penne, spirals or small shells.

PER SERVING: 442 CALORIES, 7.5GM. FAT, 4GM. SATURATED FAT, 20GM. PROTEIN, 80GM. CARBOHYDRATE, 165MG. CALCIUM

Picking Pasta

Our preference is for whole grain pasta because it is more nutritious. There are many brands available, but we have learned to choose carefully. Some are flavorful and of perfect texture. On the other hand, some taste so strongly of their grain that they dominate the dish, while others either never soften adequately or fall apart if cooking isn't carefully monitored. We suggest you experiment with different varieties and shapes to discover which you prefer.

Grown-up Noodles & YoChee

Comfort food for a sophisticated palate.

½ medium cucumber
1 tablespoon olive oil
2 tablespoons chopped fresh dill, parsley or a combination
1 tablespoon capers, drained
¼ teaspoon salt
4 cups cooked noodles, well drained
½ cup YoChee
pepper
2 tablespoons coarsely chopped walnuts
2 tablespoons crumbled blue cheese, feta, goat cheese, finely diced cheddar, grated Parmesan or other flavorful cheese, optional

Peel the cucumber and cut it in half lengthwise. Scrape out the seeds and discard. Slice each cucumber half lengthwise into very thin strips. Cut the strips into 1½-inch-long segments.

Heat the oil in a 10- to 12-inch skillet. Add the dill, parsley and capers and cook for 1 minute.

Add the cucumbers, salt and cooked noodles. When hot, turn the heat down low and stir in the YoChee, mixing until it melts and coats the noodles.

Season liberally with pepper, sprinkle with the walnuts and top with the optional cheese if desired.

Makes 2 servings

Note: For the noodles, use leftovers, or cook 6 ounces dry noodles in boiling water until tender. Choose broad noodles, rigatoni, penne, spirals or small shells.

Per serving without cheese: 520 calories, 13.5gm. fat, 1.5gm. saturated fat, 22gm. protein, 85gm. carbohydrate, 235mg. calcium

Per serving, including optional cheese: 550 calories, 16gm. fat, 3gm. saturated fat, 24gm. protein, 85gm. carbohydrate, 280mg. calcium

PASTA ALFREDO STYLE

With YoChee you get the sumptuousness of traditional Alfredo with just a fraction of the fat, plus more protein. To dress this up, scatter 2 tablespoons of toasted pine nuts on top.

¾ pound pasta of choice, including ziti, macaroni, linguini or spaghetti
1 medium green pepper, cut in strips
1 medium sweet red pepper, cut in strips
⅔ cup chopped red onion, sweet onion such as Vidalia or Walla Walla, or shallots
up to 2 cups any of the following alone or in combination, optional:
    sliced fresh mushrooms or soaked dried mushrooms
    carrots, cut into matchsticks
    asparagus or green beans, cut into 2-inch sections
    snow peas
    canned artichoke hearts, quartered
1 teaspoon oregano
¼ cup minced fresh parsley
dry wine, cooking sherry or mushroom soaking liquid, if needed
1 cup YoChee
⅓ cup grated Parmesan cheese
pepper
salt

In a large pot, bring water to a boil for cooking the pasta. Cook for about 10 minutes or until cooked to taste.

Meanwhile, combine the vegetables and herbs in a skillet, cover tightly and cook for about 10 minutes, or until just tender. Stir occasionally to promote even cooking. If using canned artichokes, wait until the end to add. If the pan seems dry, add a few tablespoons of dry wine, cooking sherry or mushroom soaking liquid.

Add the cooked, drained pasta to the cooked vegetables and mix well.

Turn the heat very low and add the YoChee and grated cheese. Stir until evenly distributed and the cheese melts.

Season liberally with pepper and salt to taste.

Makes 4 servings

Variation: Replace the Parmesan cheese with crumbled blue cheese, feta or goat cheese.

PER SERVING: 420 CALORIES, 4 GM. FAT, 2 GM. SATURATED FAT, 23 GM. PROTEIN, 78 GM. CARBOHYDRATE, 295 MG. CALCIUM (SEE YOCHIEVEMENTS FOR COMPARISONS)

CREAMY GREEN LINGUINI WITH RED MUSHROOM SAUCE

Spinach pasta is preferred for appearance. However, whole wheat or standard linguini, or even fettuccine can be used in its place.

> 2 cups Italian tomato sauce, homemade or prepared
> 2 cups diced mushrooms (6 ounces)
> ¾ pound spinach linguini
> 1 cup YoChee
> salt
> grated Parmesan cheese, optional

Bring the tomato sauce to a boil in a saucepan. Add the mushrooms and simmer for 10 minutes.

Meanwhile, bring a large pot of water to a boil for cooking the pasta. Cook until done to taste. Drain.

Place the hot pasta in a large serving bowl. Add the YoChee and a pinch of salt. Mix with tongs or two forks until the YoChee coats the pasta. Pour the mushroom-tomato sauce over all.

Serve with Parmesan cheese if desired.

Makes 4 servings

> PER SERVING, WITHOUT OPTIONAL GRATED CHEESE: 325 CALORIES, 2GM. FAT, <1GM. SATURATED FAT, 16GM. PROTEIN, 62GM. CARBOHYDRATE, 200MG. CALCIUM (SEE YOCHIEVEMENTS FOR COMPARISONS)

Choice Cheese

Throughout the book we use Parmesan cheese to encompass a range of hard grating cheeses. Feel free to use Romano, locatelli, sardo or something similar in its place. Fresh grated cheese is preferred for its superior flavor.

Farfalle with Mushrooms, Garlic and Greens

Farfalle is the Italian name for what are commonly known as bow-tie noodles.

    10 ounces farfalle
    2 cups diced mushrooms (6 ounces)
    1 medium onion, chopped
    4 cloves garlic, chopped
    1½ pounds leafy greens, such as Swiss chard, arugula, kale, escarole or
        beet greens, coarsely chopped (16 to 20 cups)
    1½ cups YoChee
    ½ teaspoon salt or to taste
    pepper
    2 tablespoons toasted pine nuts, pumpkin seeds or walnuts, coarsely
        chopped (see Toasty Topping)
    grated Parmesan cheese, optional

Bring a large pot of water to a boil for cooking the pasta. Cook for 10 to 12 minutes or until done to taste. Drain.

While the pasta cooks, combine the mushrooms and onion in a large skillet. Cook for 5 to 8 minutes, stirring occasionally, until the mushrooms soften and release their juices.

Add the garlic and greens and cook over medium-high heat, stirring frequently, until the greens are wilted but still bright green. You will probably have to add the greens in installments as they cook down and there is room in the pot.

Remove the vegetables from the heat and immediately mix in the YoChee, stirring until the sauce is creamy. Season to taste with salt and pepper.

Drain the pasta, add it to the YoChee sauce and mix well. Scatter the toasted nuts on top. If desired, sprinkle with grated Parmesan cheese.

Makes 4 to 6 servings

> *Per serving, based on 4 servings, without optional grated cheese:* 407 calories, 4gm. fat, <1gm. saturated fat, 22gm. protein, 72gm. carbohydrate, 290mg. calcium

Toasty Topping

To toast nuts or seeds, put them in a hot, ungreased frying pan for a few minutes until they are aromatic and just begin to color. For pumpkin seeds, wait until they start popping.

Pasta with Mushrooms, Chickpeas and Peas

Creamy YoChee bonds the pasta to the mushrooms, chickpeas and peas.

> ½ pound penne, macaroni, spirals or small shells
> 1 tablespoon olive oil
> 2 cloves garlic, chopped
> ¾ pound mushrooms, cut in pieces (4 cups)
> 1 teaspoon oregano
> 1 tablespoon cooking sherry or dry wine
> 2 cup cooked chickpeas, drained
> salt
> 1 cup sugar snap peas, cut in pieces, or frozen green peas
> ¾ cup YoChee
> pepper

Bring a large pot of water to a boil for cooking the pasta. Cook for about 10 minutes or until done to taste. Drain.

Meanwhile, heat the oil in a large skillet. Add the garlic and cook for 1 minute. Add the mushrooms, oregano and cooking sherry or wine. Cook for 5 to 8 minutes, stirring occasionally, until the mushrooms soften and release their juices.

Add the chickpeas to the skillet and salt lightly if the beans are unsalted. Cook for 5 minutes longer, or until the beans are heated through and the mushrooms are tender. Add the peas, and cook just long enough to heat through.

Remove the vegetables from the heat, and while still hot, stir in the YoChee. Season liberally with pepper and salt to taste. Stir in the drained, cooked pasta. Serve immediately.

Makes 4 to 6 servings

Per serving, based on 4 servings: 405 calories, 3.5gm. fat, <1gm. saturated fat, 22gm. protein, 76gm. carbohydrate, 185mg. calcium

PASTA WITH GREENS IN PINK SAUCE

The YoChee softens the color as well as the slight sharpness of the sauce.

> ¾ **pound flavorful cooking greens, such as broccoli rabe, arugula, Swiss chard, spinach or escarole**
> **salt**
> **10 ounces short pasta, such as penne, rigatoni, macaroni or spirals**
> **2 cups well-seasoned tomato sauce**
> ⅔ **cup YoChee**
> ⅔ **cup grated Parmesan cheese**
> **pepper**

Wash the greens well. Drain and slice into 1- to 2-inch piecess. You should have 8 to 10 cups.

Bring a large pot of water to a rolling boil. Salt the water and add the greens. When the water returns to a boil, add the pasta. When the pasta is barely cooked but still offers considerable resistance to the tooth, in around three-quarters of the usual cooking time or about 8 minutes, drain the pasta and greens, reserving 1 cup of the cooking water.

In a broad pot or 15-inch skillet, bring the tomato sauce to a gentle boil. Add the drained greens and pasta, along with ½ cup of the reserved cooking water. Turn the heat high and cook, stirring continuously, until the pasta is completely cooked and the sauce coats the pasta. If the sauce becomes dry, add a little more of the reserved cooking water.

Turn off the heat and stir in the YoChee and Parmesan cheese until they melt into the sauce. Season generously with pepper and salt to taste. If it is necessary to reheat the pasta before serving, place over low heat and avoid boiling.

Makes 4 ample servings

Note: For smaller servings, reduce the pasta to 8 ounces but do not alter the other ingredients.

PER SERVING: 410 CALORIES, 6GM. FAT, 3.5GM. SATURATED FAT, 25GM. PROTEIN, 70GM. CARBOHYDRATE, 390MG. CALCIUM

Pasta with Fresh Cheese and Oven-Roasted Vegetables

This is an especially versatile recipe. Despite the lengthy directions, the sauce is easy to make and can be done ahead or while the pasta cooks. Moreover, the vegetables can be chosen according to what you like and what's in season, allowing you to create a somewhat different dish every time.

1½ pounds fresh Italian plum tomatoes
2 tablespoons olive oil
1 teaspoon oregano or rosemary
6 cups vegetables of choice cut into ½-inch pieces, including carrots, eggplant, fennel, asparagus, sweet potato, zucchini, Brussels sprouts, broccoli and cauliflowerets
1 tablespoon chopped garlic
pepper
½ teaspoon salt or to taste
10 ounces pasta of choice
1 cup YoChee
2 tablespoons toasted pumpkin seeds, pine nuts, coarsely chopped walnuts or grated Parmesan cheese, optional

Preheat the oven to 450⁰F.

Dice the tomatoes. You should have 4 to 4½ cups. Mix them with 1 tablespoon of the olive oil and the herb of choice. Place in a nonmetallic 1-quart or 9-inch baking dish.

In a large bowl, combine the vegetable pieces with the remaining tablespoon of olive oil and the garlic. Mix well to coat. Spread the vegetables in a single layer on an oiled baking pan.

Roast the tomatoes and the vegetable pieces in the oven for about 15 minutes, or until the vegetables are tender and the surfaces begin to color. Stir the vegetables a few times during cooking.

Season the roasted tomatoes with a generous amount of pepper and about ½ teaspoon salt or to taste. Combine the oven-roasted vegetables with the tomatoes. Adjust the seasoning if necessary.

Cook the pasta in boiling water until done to taste.

Place the YoChee in the pasta serving bowl. Add a pinch of salt. Beat with a fork until creamy.

If the roasted vegetable sauce has cooled, reheat briefly (see Note). Drain the pasta. Add it to the bowl with the YoChee and mix thoroughly. Add the hot sauce and mix again.

Top the dressed pasta with the nuts or grated cheese if desired. Or serve with grated cheese on the side.

Makes 4 ample servings

Note: If the roasted vegetable sauce is prepared ahead and has cooled down, place it in the oven or on top of the stove for a few minutes so it is hot when added to the pasta.

> *PER SERVING, WITHOUT OPTIONAL NUTS OR CHEESE:* 465 CALORIES, 9 GM. FAT, 1 GM. SATURATED FAT, 20 GM. PROTEIN, 84 GM. CARBOHYDRATE, 200 MG. CALCIUM
>
> *PER SERVING WITH NUTS:* 485 CALORIES, 11 GM. FAT, 1 GM. SATURATED FAT, 21 GM. PROTEIN, 84 GM. CARBOHYDRATE, 200 MG. CALCIUM
>
> *PER SERVING WITH CHEESE:* 480 CALORIES, 11 GM. FAT, 1 GM. SATURATED FAT, 21 GM. PROTEIN, 84 GM. CARBOHYDRATE, 240 MG. CALCIUM

Pasta Measures

When it comes to measuring pasta, a scale is your best bet. However, for those who don't have a kitchen scale or who find it easier to go by volume, here are some pasta conversions to help you gauge properly.

Note: These figures aren't precise since there are differences in volume per weight depending on the grain, brand and shape. The figures here are for such varieties as rigatoni, penne, spirals, macaroni, bow ties and small shells. They also apply to spaghetti, linguini and fettuccine after cooking (or if broken into measurable lengths when dry).

Egg noodles tend to have quite a bit more volume per weight when dry, but do not differ significantly after cooking. You will also find some assistance on package labels.

> 4 ounces dry pasta = 1⅓ to 1½ cups uncooked = 2½ cups cooked
> 6 ounces dry pasta = 2 to 2½ cups uncooked = 3½ to 4 cups cooked
> ½ pound dry pasta = 3 cups uncooked = 5 cooked
> 10 ounces dry pasta = 3½ to 4 cups uncooked = 6 cups cooked
> ¾ pound dry pasta = 4 to 5 cups uncooked = 7 to 7½ cups cooked
> 1 pound dry pasta = 6 cups uncooked = 10 cups cooked
> ½ pound broad egg noodles = 6 cups uncooked = 6 cups cooked

Pasta with Eggplant Sauce

Eggplant and pasta in a smooth pink sauce. At serving time, offer good-quality shaved Romano or Parmesan cheese as a garnish, as well as crushed red pepper flakes for those who like their pasta lively.

> 1 medium eggplant (about 1½ pounds)
> 2 tablespoons olive oil
> 1 large clove garlic, chopped
> 1 large green pepper, cut in strips
> ½ teaspoon salt
> pepper
> 1½ cups canned crushed tomatoes
> 1 medium to large tomato, chopped
> 1 teaspoon oregano
> 1 cup YoChee
> ½ pound pasta of choice

Peel the eggplant and cut it in ¾-inch pieces.

Heat the oil in a large heavy skillet. Cook the garlic until lightly colored.

Add the eggplant, pepper strips, salt and a generous amount of pepper. Cook for about 15 minutes, until the surface of the eggplant starts to color. Stir as needed to prevent sticking and promote even cooking.

When the eggplant is barely brown, cover and cook over low heat for 15 minutes longer to penetrate the interior.

Add the canned and fresh tomatoes and oregano. Cover and cook for 15 minutes, or until the eggplant is very soft.

Remove the pot from the heat. Stir in the YoChee until it completely melts into the sauce. Adjust the salt and pepper to taste.

While the sauce is cooking, cook the pasta. Drain and mix with the sauce.

Makes 4 servings

> **Per serving**: 370 calories, 8.5gm. fat, 1gm. saturated fat, 16gm. protein, 64gm. carbohydrate, 180mg. calcium

PASTA WITH ROASTED EGGPLANT AND RED PEPPER PUREE

The luscious vegetable puree that constitutes the sauce for this dish also makes a good dip for vegetables or pita bread when cooled. The hot pepper can be adjusted to taste by adding it as directed below, omitting it altogether or placing it on the table so everyone can season their meal to taste.

> 1 medium eggplant (about 1¼ pounds)
> 2 medium sweet red peppers (about ¾ pound)
> 2 cloves raw garlic or 4 cloves roasted garlic (see Garlic Notes)
> ½ cup YoChee
> 2 tablespoons lemon juice
> 1 tablespoon olive oil
> ½ teaspoon salt
> ¼ teaspoon crushed red pepper flakes, optional or to taste
> ¾ pound pasta (short type preferred, such as penne, rigatoni or spirals)
> ¼ cup chopped parsley

Preheat the oven to 400°F.

Place the whole eggplant and peppers on a baking sheet. Bake for about 35 minutes, turning the vegetables several times, until the eggplant is soft and the peppers are charred. Remove from the oven. Wrap the peppers in a clean cloth for a few minutes to steam.

When the vegetables are cool enough to handle, remove the peel, seeds and any thick ribs from the peppers. Cut them in pieces and place in a food processor.

Peel the eggplant, cut it in cubes and add them to the food processor along with the peppers. Puree briefly.

Slice the fresh garlic or squeeze the garlic from the roasted cloves and add this to the food processor along with the YoChee, lemon juice, olive oil, salt and crushed red pepper flakes if using. Puree until the mixture is smooth.

Taste and adjust the salt and hot pepper if necessary. The puree can be prepared in advance and refrigerated at this point. Bring the sauce to room temperature before combining it with the pasta.

Bring a large pot of water to a boil for cooking the pasta. Cook the pasta to taste and drain.

Toss the hot pasta with the roasted eggplant and pepper sauce and the parsley. Mix well and serve at once.

Makes 4 generous servings; 3 cups sauce

Per serving: 415 calories, 5gm. fat, 1gm. saturated fat, 18gm. protein, 82gm. carbohydrate, 120mg. calcium

Garlic Notes

This recipe calls for either roasted or raw garlic. Roasted garlic has a mellower flavor than raw garlic, but what you choose is a matter of personal preference.

If you decide on roasted garlic, put the entire head of garlic in the oven while roasting the peppers and eggplant.

Use what you need for this dish. Use the rest as a flavoring elsewhere, for example Roasted Garlic YoChee (page 73).

PASTA WITH SPICY ARTICHOKE SAUCE

This is a particular favorite for its multiple tastes and textures.

> 2 tablespoons olive oil
> ½ teaspoon crushed red pepper flakes
> 2 cloves garlic, chopped
> ¼ cup chopped flat-leaf Italian parsley
> 2 14-ounce cans artichokes hearts, drained
> ¼ cup water or vegetable broth
> 1 cup YoChee
> salt
> ¾ pound spirals or linguini or fettuccine broken into 2- to 3-inch lengths
> ¼ cup walnut pieces or toasted pine nuts

Combine the olive oil, crushed pepper flakes, garlic and parsley in a large skillet. Cook over low heat for a few minutes to infuse the oil with the seasonings. Do not let the garlic brown.

Reserve 2 of the artichoke hearts. Cut the remaining artichoke hearts into small pieces and add them to the skillet along with the water or broth. Cover and cook over moderate heat for 10 minutes, until the artichoke hearts are hot and very soft. Mash to a coarse puree with a potato masher or fork.

Remove the artichoke hearts from the heat. Using a fork or whisk, beat in the YoChee until the sauce is creamy. Season with salt to taste.

Meanwhile, cook the pasta in boiling water until just done. Do not overcook. Drain, reserving about ½ cup of cooking water and leaving some clinging to the strands.

Transfer the pasta to the skillet with the artichoke puree. Stir over low heat, adding a little pasta cooking water as needed to thin the sauce.

Cut the reserved artichoke hearts in pieces. Scatter them over the pasta along with the nuts.

Makes 4 servings

> PER SERVING: 510 CALORIES, 13 GM. FAT, 2 GM. SATURATED FAT, 23 GM. PROTEIN, 80 GM. CARBOHYDRATE, 160 MG. CALCIUM

ONE-STEP VEGETABLE LASAGNA

This is one of our most popular dishes. This easy approach to lasagna uses uncooked noodles, making it much less work than the traditional method in which the pasta is precooked. With this technique the pasta absorbs the tomato sauce as it cooks, imparting a deep, penetrating flavor. For those who prefer a saucier lasagna, additional sauce can be served on the side.

3 cups YoChee
½ teaspoon salt
½ teaspoon nutmeg
4 cups Italian-style tomato sauce
¾ pound lasagna noodles
3 cups lightly cooked sliced or cut-up vegetables, such as carrots, zucchini, yellow squash, eggplant, mushrooms, broccoli, cauliflower, artichoke hearts or others of choice, alone or any combination (see Notes)
2 cups (8 ounces) shredded or thinly sliced mozzarella cheese (see Notes)
⅓ cup grated Parmesan cheese

Preheat the oven to 350°F.

Season the YoChee with the salt and nutmeg.

Spread ¾ cup of the sauce over the bottom of a 9x13-inch baking dish or lasagna pan. Cover with one-third of the noodles. Spread 1½ cups of the seasoned YoChee over the noodles. Arrange half of the vegetables over this. Top with half of the mozzarella cheese. Spread 1 cup of the sauce evenly over all.

Add a second layer of lasagna noodles and layer as above with the remaining YoChee, vegetables, mozzarella, and another cup of sauce. Top with the rest of the noodles and the remaining 1¼ cups of sauce.

Cover the pan tightly with foil and bake for 45 to 60 minutes, or until the noodles are tender. Uncover the pan, sprinkle the Parmesan cheese evenly over the top and bake for 10 to 15 minutes longer.

Let sit at room temperature for at least 15 minutes to set before serving.

Makes 6 servings

Notes: The vegetables can be oven-roasted, braised or lightly steamed. Or use cooked leftovers. The shredded mozzarella can be reduced or omitted for a low-cheese version.

PER SERVING: 515 CALORIES, 11 GM. FAT, 6 GM. SATURATED FAT, 35 GM. PROTEIN, 70 GM. CARBOHYDRATE, 720 MG. CALCIUM (SEE YOCHIEVEMENTS FOR COMPARISONS)

One-Step Spinach Lasagna

As with the preceding lasagna, we forgo the precooking of the noodles, trading less work for a somewhat longer cooking time. Again, you may want to serve additional sauce on the side for those who prefer a saucier lasagna.

½ pound fresh greens such as spinach, kale, Swiss chard or arugula, or 10-ounce package frozen chopped spinach
¼ cup chopped fresh basil and/or parsley
3 cups YoChee
¾ cup shredded mozzarella and/or provolone cheeses, combined in any proportion (see Notes)
½ teaspoon nutmeg
salt
pepper
4 cups Italian-style tomato sauce
¾ pound lasagna noodles
⅓ cup grated Parmesan cheese

Preheat the oven to 350°F.

If using fresh greens, chop them by hand or in a food processor until very fine; you should have about 3 cups.

Place the greens in a strainer and press to remove as much liquid as possible. If using frozen spinach, let it thaw and then press in a similar manner. At the end you should have about 1 cup finely chopped, dry greens.

Combine the greens with the herbs, YoChee, shredded cheese(s), nutmeg and salt and pepper to taste. The amount of salt will vary with the saltiness of the cheeses and may even be unnecessary.

Spread ¾ cup of the sauce over the bottom of a 9x13-inch baking dish or lasagna pan. Cover with one-third of the noodles. Carefully spread half of the YoChee mixture over the noodles. Pour 1 cup of sauce over this, spreading with a spatula or the back of a wooden spoon to cover evenly.

Add a second layer of lasagna noodles and layer as above with the remaining YoChee mixture and another 1 cup of tomato sauce. Top with the rest of the noodles and the remaining 1¼ cups of sauce.

Cover the pan tightly with foil and bake for 45 to 60 minutes, or until the noodles are tender. Uncover the pan, sprinkle the Parmesan cheese evenly over the top and bake for 10 to 15 minutes longer.

Let sit at room temperature for at least 15 minutes to set before serving.

Makes 6 servings

Notes: The shredded cheese can be reduced or even omitted for a low-cheese version. If you are reheating leftovers, you may want to top the lasagna with a little additional sauce to keep it moist.

Per serving: 425 calories, 5 gm. fat, 2.5 gm. saturated fat, 27 gm. protein, 67 gm. carbohydrate, 530 mg. calcium (see YoChievements for comparisons)

Nuttier Nutmeg

Nutmeg is most commonly bought preground. However, for a superior fresh, aromatic flavor, it is better to purchase the whole nutmeg and grind it yourself as needed. Tiny metal nutmeg graters with a compartment to store the nugget are available in housewares stores. Whole nutmeg keeps for years.

FRUIT NOODLE PUDDING

A modestly sweet baked noodle pudding. Popular in Jewish homes at holidays, it is a good choice anytime, especially for entertaining or potluck gatherings, as it can be prepared ahead and is easily multiplied.

- ½ pound broad egg noodles
- 2 cups YoChee
- 2 eggs
- ¼ cup honey or a mixture of honey and maple syrup
- ¼ cup raisins
- 1 cup chopped, peeled apple
- ⅛ teaspoon salt
- ½ teaspoon cinnamon
- 1 tablespoon butter

Preheat the oven to 350°F.

Cook the noodles in boiling water for 6 to 8 minutes, until just tender. Timing will vary with different brands. Drain, rinse with cold water to cool down and stop cooking, and drain thoroughly.

In a large bowl, beat the YoChee with the eggs and sweetener of choice. Stir in the raisins, apple and salt. Add the cooked noodles. Mix thoroughly.

Place the mixture in a deep, greased 2-quart baking dish. Sprinkle the cinnamon on top. Dot with the butter.

Bake for 30 minutes. Let sit at room temperature for at least 15 minutes before serving. Can be eaten warm, at room temperature or chilled.

Makes 6 servings

PER SERVING: 315 CALORIES, 5.5GM. FAT, 2GM. SATURATED FAT, 15GM. PROTEIN, 53GM. CARBOHYDRATE, 185MG. CALCIUM

GRAIN DISHES

Cooked grains and YoChee complement each other well. The slight resistance of grains as you bite into them is perfectly offset by the distinctive creaminess of the YoChee. The dishes in this section can be presented as entrées or accompaniments, depending on what else you are serving and portion sizes.

❧ YoChievements ❧

Broccoli with Brown Rice, Italian Style (pg.176) vs. Rice a Roni®
Broccoli Au Gratin
- 35% less calories
- 75% less fat
- 50% more protein
- 140% more calcium

Mushroom Risotto (pg.178) vs. classic mushroom risotto
- 30% less calories
- 75% less fat
- 70% less saturated fat
- 22% more protein
- 20% more calcium

Cornmeal Cheese Pudding (pg.180) vs. Southern spoon bread
- 12% less calories
- 43% more protein
- 33% less fat
- 42% more calcium

RICE & CHEESE BAKE

This simple, basic dish relies on precooked grains.

3 cups cooked brown rice
⅓ cup chopped parsley
⅔ cup YoChee
¾ cup shredded cheese of choice, such as cheddar, Monterey Jack, Swiss, provolone, Gouda or Edam
salt
hot pepper sauce

Preheat the oven to 350°F.

Combine the rice, parsley, YoChee and ½ cup of the shredded cheese. Season with salt as needed, depending on the cheese and if the rice is preseasoned. Add a dash of hot pepper sauce, according to personal taste.

Place in an oiled 1½-quart or 8- to 9-inch-square baking dish. Scatter the remaining ¼ cup cheese on top.

Bake for 20 minutes.

Makes 4 servings

Variations: Use a combination of cooked brown and wild rice, or replace rice with cooked barley, millet or whole wheat couscous.

PER SERVING: 273 CALORIES, 8GM. FAT, 4GM. SATURATED FAT, 12GM. PROTEIN, 38GM. CARBOHYDRATE, 260MG. CALCIUM

Menu Ideas

Serve Rice & Cheese Bake with a colorful mix of vegetables and chickpeas, kidney beans or white beans.

BAKED RICE WITH BLUE CHEESE

The addition of olives and blue cheese to precooked rice creates a casserole with a robust character.

> **4 cups cooked brown rice**
> **2 tablespoons lemon juice**
> **2 teaspoons prepared mustard**
> **4 scallions, sliced**
> **½ cup sliced green or black olives**
> **1 cup YoChee**
> **4 ounces blue cheese, cut in small cubes (about ½ cup)**

Preheat the oven to 350°F.

Combine all the ingredients, mixing gently so that the cheese remains in chunks.

Place in an oiled 9-inch or 1½-quart baking dish. Cover and bake for 20 minutes, until the rice is hot and the cheese is melted.

Makes 4 servings

> *Per serving*: 345 CALORIES, 8.5GM. FAT, 4GM. SATURATED FAT, 14GM. PROTEIN, 54GM. CARBOHYDRATE, 250MG. CALCIUM

BROCCOLI WITH BROWN RICE, ITALIAN STYLE

Another excellent entrée choice when you have cooked rice on hand.

> 4 cups broccoli cut in bite-size pieces (¾ pound)
> 1 small onion, chopped
> 1 cup sliced mushrooms (3 ounces)
> 2 cups cooked brown rice
> salt
> 1 cup YoChee
> ⅓ cup currants or chopped raisins
> 1 cup Italian-style tomato sauce

Preheat the oven to 350°F.

Steam the broccoli for 8 minutes.

Combine the onion and mushrooms in a skillet and cook, stirring occasionally, for about 5 minutes, until the mushrooms soften and release their liquid.

Combine the onion-mushroom mixture with the rice. Season with salt to taste. Place in an oiled 1½-quart or 8- to 9-inch-square baking pan.

Combine the YoChee with the currants or raisins and half of the broccoli. Place evenly over the rice.

If the tomato sauce is not well-flavored, season to taste with garlic, oregano and basil. Pour the sauce over the casserole. Top with the remaining broccoli.

Bake for about 25 minutes or until everything is quite hot.

Makes 4 servings

PER SERVING: 240 CALORIES, 1.5 GM. FAT, <1 GM. SATURATED FAT, 12 GM. PROTEIN, 48 GM. CARBOHYDRATE, 190 MG. CALCIUM (SEE YOCHIEVEMENTS FOR COMPARISONS)

Rice with Fresh Cheese

This is Italian comfort food to soothe the palate and soul. It can be made with freshly cooked or precooked rice (see Note). For best results, use a good-quality, flavorful olive oil. Although the grated cheese is optional, a little goes a long way towards completing this satisfying dish.

> **1 cup uncooked brown rice**
> **2½ cups water**
> **1 cup YoChee**
> **¼ cup finely chopped flat-leaf Italian parsley**
> **2 tablespoons finely chopped fresh basil**
> **1 teaspoon finely chopped lemon peel, preferably organic**
> **salt**
> **pepper**
> **2 tablespoons extra virgin olive oil**
> **grated Parmesan cheese, optional**

Combine the rice and water in a pot, bring to a boil, cover and simmer for 45 minutes or until the rice is tender and the water is absorbed. It should still be on the moist side.

While the rice cooks, combine the YoChee, herbs and lemon peel in a serving bowl. Season with salt and pepper to taste. If possible, let the mixture rest for 30 minutes or so to allow the flavors to develop.

Add the olive oil to the hot rice and mix well to coat the grains with oil. Add to the YoChee mixture while still hot and mix again.

Serve with grated cheese if desired.

Makes 4 servings

Note: To use leftover rice for this recipe, place 3 cups cooked brown rice in a pot with about ½ cup water. Cover and cook until the rice is hot and has absorbed the water but remains moist.

Per serving, without optional grated cheese: 280 calories, 8.5 gm. fat, 1 gm. saturated fat, 9 gm. protein, 41 gm. carbohydrate, 140 mg. calcium

Mushroom Risotto

This recipe makes a substantial entrée when accompanied by a cooked green vegetable such as asparagus, broccoli or green beans. The risotto can also be used to fill prebaked or steamed peppers. Any leftovers can be stuffed into mushrooms and baked for appetizers.

> ¾ pound cultivated or exotic mushrooms, or a combination
> 2 tablespoons soy sauce
> 2 cups uncooked brown rice
> 4½ cups water or vegetable broth
> ¼ teaspoon nutmeg
> ⅔ cup YoChee
> ⅔ cup grated Parmesan cheese
> salt
> pepper
> ⅔ cup chopped red or sweet onion, sweet red pepper or parsley as garnish

Wash the mushrooms and chop into small pieces. You should have about 4 cups.

Place the mushrooms in a large skillet or broad pot, add the soy sauce and cook over moderate heat, stirring occasionally, for 5 to 8 minutes, or until the mushrooms have begun to soften and release their juices.

Add the rice and 4 cups of the liquid to the mushrooms. Bring to a boil over high heat. Reduce the heat, cover and cook for 45 mintes to an hour, until the rice is tender and surrounded by a rich sauce. Add the nutmeg after half an hour. When the cooking is almost done, stir continuously to incorporate the sauce into the rice. If the rice is dry rather than creamy, add the reserved ½ cup of water or broth.

Remove from the heat and stir in the YoChee and Parmesan cheese. Season to taste with salt and pepper. Spoon onto individual serving plates and top with the garnish of your choice. Serve at once.

Makes 6 entrée servings

Per serving: 315 calories, 5gm. fat, 2.5gm. saturated fat, 14gm. protein, 54gm. carbohydrate, 235mg. calcium (see YoChievements for comparisons)

Reserving Risotto

YoChee risottos can be premade up to the point of adding the YoChee and Parmesan cheese. Reheat before this final step, adding a little more liquid if the rice seems dry.

CREAMY PUMPKIN-FLAVORED RICE

The rich orange hue and delicate flavor of this dish are quite alluring. You can serve it as a first course, side dish, or as an entrée when joined by a cooked vegetable of contrasting color and a mixed green salad.

¾ pound uncooked pumpkin or butternut squash
1 cup uncooked brown rice
3 cups water or vegetable broth
¼ teaspoon nutmeg
⅓ cup YoChee
⅓ cup grated Parmesan cheese
salt
pepper
⅓ cup chopped red or sweet onion, sweet red pepper or parsley as garnish

Cut the pumpkin or squash crosswise into 1-inch-thick slices or from stem to blossom end into wedges or chunks that are no more than 2-inches wide at the broadest point. Discard any seeds. Steam for 10 to 15 minutes, or until a knife just pierces the flesh. The cooking time will vary somewhat with the size of the pieces. Remove the peel and cut the flesh into ¼-inch cubes. You should have about 2¼ cups.

Combine the pumpkin or squash, rice and water in a broad pot or skillet. If desired you can use the liquid left after steaming the vegetable as part of the liquid. Bring to a boil over high heat. Reduce the heat, cover and cook for 45 minutes to an hour, until the rice is tender and surrounded by a rich orange sauce. Add the nutmeg after half an hour. When the cooking is almost done, stir continuously to incorporate the sauce into the rice.

Remove from the heat and stir in the YoChee and Parmesan cheese. Season to taste with salt and pepper. Spoon onto individual serving plates and top with the garnish of your choice. Serve at once.

Makes 4 entrée servings; 6 first-course or side-dish servings

PER ENTRÉE SERVING: 246 CALORIES, 4GM. FAT, 2GM. SATURATED FAT, 9.5GM. PROTEIN, 44GM. CARBOHYDRATE, 185MG. CALCIUM

Cornmeal Cheese Pudding

A cross between baked polenta and a soufflé. In the American South this would be considered an embellished version of traditional spoon bread. An especially good accompaniment for beans.

¾ cup cornmeal
1½ cups water
¼ teaspoon salt
⅛ teaspoon nutmeg
1 teaspoon prepared mustard
½ cup fresh or frozen corn kernels
½ cup shredded cheddar cheese
1 egg, separated
½ cup YoChee

Place the cornmeal in a 1-quart saucepan and gradually add the water, stirring to dissolve any lumps. Cook over moderate heat, stirring continuously, for 8 to 10 minutes, until the cornmeal thickens and comes to a gentle boil. Simmer for 1 minute.

Remove the cornmeal from the heat. Stir in the salt, nutmeg, mustard, corn kernels and shredded cheese to melt. Let cool a few minutes while proceeding with the rest of the recipe.

Preheat the oven to 350⁰F.

In a medium-size bowl, beat the egg yolk into the YoChee. In a separate bowl, beat the egg white until stiff.

Gradually stir the cornmeal-cheese mixture into the YoChee-egg yolk mixture until evenly blended. Gently fold in the egg white.

Spread the batter in a greased, shallow 1-quart casserole or 9-inch-square baking pan. Bake for 40 minutes, until puffed and brown and barely set.

Remove from the oven and let sit for 10 minutes. Spoon onto plates to serve.

Makes 4 servings

Per serving: 198 calories, 7gm. fat, 3.5gm. saturated fat, 10gm. protein, 25gm. carbohydrate, 170mg. calcium (see YoChievements for comparisons)

VEGETABLE SIDE DISHES

One of the most important actions people can take to make a positive impact on their health is to eat as many vegetables as possible. While some people find plain vegetables appealing, most of us are more willing to add them to the menu when they are adorned. This can be a challenge, especially if you don't want to diminish the value of the vegetables with high-calorie fatty or sugary sauces. The recipes in this section prove that YoChee can make vegetables more delicious without detriment.

❧ YoChievements ❦

Sweet Cream Carrots (pg.183) vs. glazed carrots
      50% less calories
      73% less fat
      167% more protein
      50% less carbohydrate
      50% more calcium

Creamy Country-Style Greens (pg.188) vs. frozen creamed spinach
      65% less calories
      98% less fat
      Similar protein

more...

Potato Gratin (pg.195) vs. frozen potatoes au gratin
  Similar calories
  30% less fat
  75% more protein
  60% more calcium

Beautiful Beets (pg.196) vs. canned Harvard beets
  23% less calories
  200% more protein
  32% less carbohydrate
  4 times as much calcium

SWEET CREAM CARROTS

This recipe is very tasty and versatile enough to be a model for a variety of vegetables (see Sweet Cream Options, below).

> **1 pound carrots**
> **1 tablespoon sweet butter**
> **salt**
> **¼ cup apple juice**
> **½ cup YoChee**
> **chopped fresh basil, parsley or mint**
> **pepper**

Peel the carrots and cut on the diagonal into ¼-inch-thick pieces. If the carrots are fat, slice these pieces in half lengthwise. You should have at least 3 cups of vegetable.

Melt the butter in a skillet. Add the carrots and a pinch of salt. Toss the carrots in the butter until they are lightly coated. Add the apple juice, bring to a boil, cover and cook over low heat for 5 to 10 minutes, until the carrots are tender but still firm.

Remove the carrots from the heat. Add the YoChee, stirring until it melts and the sauce becomes creamy. Sprinkle the fresh herb of choice and pepper on top.

Makes 4 servings

Notes: Be sure to let the liquid around the vegetables cool a little before adding the YoChee. It should be hot, but no longer bubbling. If too hot there is a risk that the YoChee will curdle rather than melting into a smooth sauce. If you want to do some of the preparation ahead, stop before adding the YoChee. Just before serving, reheat the vegetables if needed and then proceed. If you need to reheat this once the YoChee is added, keep the heat very low and stir continuously until just warmed through.

PER SERVING: 103 CALORIES, 3GM. FAT, 2GM. SATURATED FAT, 4GM. PROTEIN, 16GM. CARBOHYDRATE, 90MG. CALCIUM (SEE YOCHIEVEMENTS FOR COMPARISONS)

Sweet Cream Options

Replace carrots with 3 cups:

- zucchini cut into 2-inch-long sticks
- cauliflowerets
- a mixture of red, yellow and green pepper strips
- fennel cut into crescents

Crunchy Creamed Corn

This delicious dish is ample for four people as a side dish, but if you have hungry eaters, you may want to double the recipe to feed six. Crunchy Creamed Corn goes nicely with Bean Tostadas. Although designed to be served warm, chilled leftovers are very tasty.

    1 tablespoon orange juice
    1 medium onion, chopped
    ½ cup chopped green pepper
    2 cups fresh or frozen corn kernels
    ½ cup YoChee
    salt
    pepper

Combine the orange juice, onion and green pepper in a skillet. Cook, stirring frequently, for 8 to 10 minutes, until the onion is wilted and translucent.

Add the corn, cover and cook over medium-low heat for 5 minutes, until the corn is quite hot but still crunchy.

Turn the heat very low and stir in the YoChee until it melts around the corn. Season to taste with salt and pepper.

Makes 4 servings

> Per serving: 114 calories, 1gm. fat, <1gm. saturated fat, 6gm. protein, 24gm. carbohydrate, 70mg. calcium

MASHED BROCCOLI

Creamy, coarsely mashed broccoli with a nice bite.

> **2 pounds broccoli**
> **½ cup water**
> **½ teaspoon salt**
> **4 cloves garlic, minced**
> **2 teaspoons curry powder**
> **½ cup YoChee**

Peel the broccoli stems and chop. Divide the tops into tiny florets. You should have about 8 cups total.

Combine the broccoli, water and salt in skillet or saucepan and bring to a boil. Cover and simmer for about 15 minutes, until the broccoli is quite tender.

Add the garlic and curry powder. Continue to cook, uncovered, mashing with a potato masher or fork until the broccoli is reduced to a rough puree. Add more water if needed to keep moist.

Remove from the heat and mash in the YoChee. If need be, return to low heat and cook gently, while stirring, until the puree is hot.

Makes 4 to 6 servings

PER SERVING, BASED ON 4 SERVINGS: 98 CALORIES, 1 GM. FAT, <1 GM. SATURATED FAT, 10.5 GM. PROTEIN, 16 GM. CARBOHYDRATE, 160 MG. CALCIUM

Preparation Pointer

When using YoChee, mashing is often the preferred technique for melding ingredients. A hand potato masher is a handy tool for this job. This inexpensive item is available in most housewares stores.

Richard's Syrian Green Beans

This recipe was inspired by a dish created by the chef at the Blue Mountain Bistro in Saugerties, NY. We are very fond of it and since you can never eat too many vegetables, we always make ample amounts.

½ cup water
1 tablespoon soy sauce
1½ pounds green beans
1 medium red or white onion, coarsely chopped
2 large cloves garlic, sliced
¼ cup chopped dill and/or parsley
1 tablespoon lemon juice
½ cup YoChee
salt
2 tablespoons chopped olives

Combine the water and soy sauce in a broad skillet large enough to hold the green beans. Add the beans, onion, garlic and herbs. Bring to a boil, cover and cook over moderate heat for 12 to 15 minutes or until the beans are cooked to taste. Stir a few times to promote even cooking.

Remove the pan from the heat. Transfer the green beans to a serving dish, leaving the liquid and seasonings in the pan.

Stir the lemon juice into the pan. When the liquid has cooled a little, use a fork to beat in the YoChee until the sauce is creamy. Season to taste with salt.

Pour the sauce over the warm green beans. Garnish with the olives.

Makes 4 to 6 servings

Per serving, based on 4 servings: 105 calories, 1.5gm. fat, <1gm. saturated fat, 6gm. protein, 19gm. carbohydrate, 135mg. calcium

Soy Sauce Selection

Use a genuine soy sauce, not one doctored with corn syrup and caramel coloring. Real soy sauce is sold in Oriental groceries and natural food stores.

CREAMED ITALIAN GREENS

Cooked greens should be on the menu as often as possible. This is an excellent way to present them.

> 1½ pounds leafy greens, such as Swiss chard, kale, arugula, escarole, beet greens, mustard greens or any combination
> 2 large cloves garlic, chopped
> ¼ cup canned crushed tomatoes, tomato puree or tomato juice
> 2 tablespoons capers
> 2 tablespoons balsamic or wine vinegar
> ¾ cup YoChee
> salt

Wash the greens and chop coarsely. You should have 12 to 16 cups loosely packed.

Combine the greens with the garlic and tomatoes in a large heavy skillet. If the volume is too much for the pan, add more greens gradually as they cook down. Cook, uncovered, for about 5 minutes, until all the greens wilt. Stir as needed for even cooking.

Add the capers and vinegar. Cover and cook for 5 to 15 minutes , until the greens are tender. This will vary with the particular greens used.

Remove from the heat. Let cool briefly, then stir in the YoChee until it disappears. Season to taste with salt.

Makes 4 to 6 servings

> **PER SERVING, BASED ON 4 SERVINGS**: 95 CALORIES, 1 GM. FAT, <1 GM. SATURATED FAT, 8.5 GM. PROTEIN, 16.5 GM. CARBOHYDRATE, 250 MG. CALCIUM

CREAMY COUNTRY-STYLE GREENS

Mushrooms meld with greens in a mellow YoChee coating.

> 1½ pounds Swiss chard, collard greens, beet greens, spinach or romaine lettuce
> 6 ounces mushrooms
> ¾ cup coarsely chopped red onion
> 2 tablespoons lemon juice
> ¾ cup YoChee
> salt
> pepper

Wash the greens well, remove any tough stems and cut crosswise into ½-inch wide strips. You should have 12 to 16 cups.

Clean the mushrooms and slice the caps and stems. You should have about 2 cups.

In a pot large enough to hold the greens, cook the mushrooms over moderate heat for 5 to 8 minutes, until they wilt and begin to release their juices. Add the red onion and cook for 2 to 3 minutes.

Add the greens and mix until they begin to wilt and cook down. Cover the pot and cook over low heat for 5 to 15 minutes, depending on the greens, until tender.

Remove from the heat. Stir in the lemon juice and YoChee. Season to taste with salt and pepper.

Makes 4 to 6 servings

> PER SERVING, BASED ON 4 SERVINGS: 98 CALORIES, <1 GM. FAT, <1 GM. SATURATED FAT, 8 GM. PROTEIN, 18 GM. CARBOHYDRATE, 165 MG CALCIUM (SEE YOCHIEVEMENTS FOR COMPARISONS)

Exotic Mushrooms

Using a flavorful variety of mushroom such as cremini or shiitake gives the greens a more earthy taste. But cultivated white mushrooms will do just fine if these aren't available.

GARLIC MASHED POTATOES

Low in fat, but not in flavor.

> 1 small leek, optional
> 1½ pounds potatoes, cut into 2-inch chunks
> 8 cloves garlic, thinly sliced
> ½ cup water
> ½ cup YoChee
> ½ teaspoon salt or to taste
> pepper
> paprika

If using the leek, cut it in half lengthwise, wash well to remove dirt, and chop.

Combine the leek, potatoes and garlic in a pot with the water. Bring to a boil. Cover and cook over low heat for 20 minutes or until the potatoes are very tender. Remove the peel or not, according to personal preference and the thickness of the skins.

Using a potato masher, mash the potatoes along with any liquid remaining in the pot. Then with a fork, whisk or electric mixer, gradually beat in the YoChee until light and fluffy.

Season to taste with salt and pepper. Sprinkle the surface generously with paprika.

Makes 4 servings

> *PER SERVING*: 178 CALORIES, <1GM. FAT, <1GM. SATURATED FAT, 7GM. PROTEIN, 38GM. CARBOHYDRATE, 95MG. CALCIUM

⏰ Pink Potatoes

The color is amusing and the subtle hint of tomato and spiciness is delightful.

> 1½ pounds potatoes, cut into 2-inch chunks
> ½ cup water
> ½ cup YoChee
> 2 scallions, thinly sliced, or 3 tablespoons minced chives
> 1 teaspoon chili powder
> 1½ tablespoons tomato paste
> salt

Combine the potatoes in a pot with the water. Bring to boil, cover and cook over low heat for 20 minutes or until tender. Drain the potatoes. Peel or not according to personal preference and the thickness of the skins.

Add the YoChee, scallions, chili powder and tomato paste. Coarsely mash with a potato masher until uniformly blended.

Season with salt to taste.

Makes 4 servings

Per serving: 165 calories, <1gm. fat, <1gm. saturated fat, 6.5gm. protein, 35gm. carbohydrate, 80mg. calcium

SIMPLE STUFFED BAKED POTATOES

The proportion of ingredients here will vary a little with the size of the potatoes. Exact amounts aren't critical. For convenience, you can make this with freshly baked or prebaked potatoes. Moreover, potatoes can be stuffed and refrigerated up to a day ahead (see Note).

2 baked potatoes (about 8 ounces each)
½ cup YoChee
salt
pepper
paprika

If the potatoes are not already baked, bake them.

Preheat the oven to 350⁰ to 375⁰F.

Cut the potatoes in half lengthwise. If the potatoes are still hot, hold them in a clean kitchen towel while you work with them. Carefully scoop out the insides, leaving the shells intact. A serrated grapefruit spoon or curved grapefruit knife is a handy tool for this job.

Mash the potatoes with a potato masher, rotary or electric beater or by pureeing in a food mill until no lumps remain. Beat in the YoChee until the potatoes are smooth and creamy. Season with salt and pepper to taste.

Mound the potato filling back into the skins. Sprinkle paprika liberally on top. Place the potatoes on a baking pan and put them in the oven for 20 minutes, until very hot and lightly crusted on top.

Makes 4 servings

Note: If the potatoes are stuffed in advance and refrigerated, baking time may need to be extended by 5 to 10 minutes.

Per ½ potato: 145 calories, <1gm. fat, <1gm. saturated fat, 5gm. protein, 31gm. carbohydrate, 70mg. calcium

Baked Potatoes with Whipped Artichoke Filling

Half of one of these stuffed potatoes makes a good side dish. For the focal point of a meal, serve two halves per person. Although prebaked potatoes can be used in this recipe, the directions include baking them along with the garlic cloves.

> 4 medium-size baking potatoes (6 to 8 ounces each)
> 4 large cloves garlic
> ½ cup YoChee
> 6 canned artichoke hearts, drained and chopped
> salt
> pepper
> paprika

Preheat the oven to 400°F.

Scrub the potatoes and prick in several places with a fork. Place the potatoes and unpeeled garlic cloves on a baking sheet. Bake the garlic for 15 to 20 minutes, until soft but barely colored. Remove from the oven and continue baking the potatoes until the insides are completely tender. This will take from 30 to 45 minutes longer.

Remove the potatoes from the oven and reduce the temperature to 350°F.

Hold the hot potatoes in a clean cloth or oven mitt. Cut in half lengthwise and carefully scoop the insides into a mixing bowl, leaving the skins intact. A serrated grapefruit spoon or curved grapefruit knife is a handy tool for this job.

Hold the baked garlic cloves at the root end and squeeze into the bowl with the potatoes. Mash until no lumps remain. Add the YoChee and whip with a fork until creamy. Fold in the artichoke pieces. Season to taste with salt and pepper.

Pack the whipped artichoke-potato filling into the potato shells. Sprinkle the surface of the potatoes liberally with paprika. If desired, the potatoes can be prepared to this point and rebaked later. If they will be held for more than 1 hour, refrigerate.

Return the potatoes to the oven for about 10 minutes, until piping hot. If they have been pre-filled and refrigerated, increase the baking time by 5 to 10 minutes.

Makes 8 side-dish servings; 4 entrée servings

Per ½ potato: 90 calories, <1 gm. fat, <1 gm. saturated fat, 3 gm. protein, 20 gm. carbohydrate, 50 mg. calcium

POTATOES WITH CREAMED KALE

A rustic blend of potatoes and greens that gets a noticeable kick from the hot pepper. Of course, you can leave the hot pepper out if you don't like spicy food. This dish is so satisfying and nourishing that it can even be used as the main feature in a meal.

> 1 pound potatoes, preferably Yukon gold or new potatoes
> 8 cloves garlic, thinly sliced
> 1 fresh hot pepper, minced, or ½ teaspoon crushed red pepper flakes, optional
> ¾ cup water
> ½ teaspoon salt
> ¾ pound kale
> ¾ cup YoChee

Slice the potatoes so they are less than ¼ inch thick. Combine them in a large pot with the garlic, hot pepper, water and salt. Bring to a boil, cover and simmer gently for about 15 minutes, until the potatoes are just becoming tender.

Wash the kale and chop coarsely. You should have 10 to 12 cups loosely packed.

Gradually add the greens to the almost-cooked potatoes, stirring until they wilt and adding more as they cook down and there is room in the pot. When all the greens have been added, cover the pot and cook for 20 minutes or as long as necessary so the greens and potatoes are both completely tender. Stir occasionally during cooking. As the potatoes soften, they will start to break up into small pieces.

Remove the vegetables from the heat and let sit uncovered for a few minutes. While still hot, stir in the YoChee until it is evenly mixed into the vegetables.

Season with additional salt if needed. If you haven't included the hot pepper, you can add hot sauce or pepper to taste.

Makes 4 to 6 servings

PER SERVING, BASED ON 4 SERVINGS: 178 CALORIES, 1 GM. FAT, <1 GM. SATURATED FAT, 10 GM. PROTEIN, 36 GM. CARBOHYDRATE, 225 MG. CALCIUM

Potato Pudding

Serve as an accompaniment to a meal or cut in small squares for an hors d'œuvre.

>   1½ pounds potatoes
>   1 egg
>   1 cup YoChee
>   1 medium onion, cut up
>   1 teaspoon salt
>   ½ cup wheat germ
>   paprika

Preheat the oven to 375°F.

Scrub the potatoes. If the skins are thin you can leave them on. Otherwise peel them. Cut the potatoes into small chunks. You should have 4 to 5 cups.

Combine the potatoes, egg, YoChee and onion in a food processor or blender and puree until the mixture is like thick chunky applesauce. You may have to start and stop the machine and push the mixture around to get it going at first.

Stir the salt and wheat germ into the pureed potatoes.

Place the mixture in a well-oiled shallow 2-quart baking dish. Sprinkle the surface liberally with paprika. Bake for 35 to 45 minutes or until firm and golden on top.

Let stand at room temperature for at least 10 minutes before cutting.

Makes 6 side-dish servings; 24 hors d'œuvre pieces

> **Per side-dish serving:** 175 calories, 2gm. fat, <1gm. saturated fat, 10gm. protein, 30gm carbohydrate, 100mg calcium

> **Per hors d'œuvres piece:** 45 calories, <1gm. fat , <1gm. saturated fat, 2.5gm. protein, 7.5gm. carbohydrate, 25mg. calcium

POTATO GRATIN

This dish is prepared using YoChee cream, rather than YoChee. In addition to the gratin's role as a vegetable side dish, it can serve as the focal point of a vegetable plate entrée, accompanied by a variety of cooked vegetables, along with a fresh tomato, mushroom or green salad.

2 cups YoChee cream (below)
3 large cloves garlic, chopped
¾ teaspoon salt
2 pounds potatoes
¾ cup shredded Emmenthaler or Gruyère cheese
1 teaspoon paprika

Preheat the oven to 425°F. Oil a round 10-inch baking dish or 1½- to 2-quart casserole.

Combine the YoChee cream, garlic and salt. Let sit while preparing the rest of the recipe.

Scrub the potatoes and peel or not according to personal preference and the thickness and condition of the skins. Slice the potatoes so they are no more than ⅛ inch thick.

Layer half the potatoes in the prepared baking dish. Spread ¾ cup of the seasoned YoChee cream over the potatoes. Sprinkle with half of the shredded cheese and ½ teaspoon of the paprika. Top with the remaining potatoes, seasoned YoChee cream, shredded cheese and paprika.

Cover the baking dish and bake for about 50 minutes or until the potatoes are tender. Uncover and bake 10 minutes longer or until the top is golden.

Let cool at least 10 minutes before serving.

Makes 6 side-dish servings; 4 entrée servings

PER SERVING, BASED ON 6 SERVINGS: 235 CALORIES, 4GM. FAT, 2GM. SATURATED FAT, 13GM. PROTEIN, 37GM. CARBOHYDRATE, 300MG. CALCIUM (SEE YOCHIEVEMENTS FOR COMPARISONS)

YoChee Cream

To make YoChee cream, drain yogurt for only about 4 hours.

BEAUTIFUL BEETS

The color alone makes these worth preparing.

> 1 pound beets
> 2 tablespoons honey
> 2 tablespoons cider vinegar
> ½ cup YoChee

Scrub the beets and remove the tops and long roots without cutting into the bulb. Place them on a vegetable steamer and steam until the bulb can be easily pierced with the tip of a sharp knife. This will vary from 30 to 45 minutes, depending on the size and age of the beets.

Remove the beets from the pot. When they are cool enough to handle, remove the skin and cut them into bite-size pieces.

Combine the beets, honey and cider vinegar in a saucepan. Simmer for 5 to 10 minutes, until the honey and vinegar form a glaze around the beets.

Remove from the heat and stir in the YoChee until the sauce is creamy. Serve while still warm.

Makes 4 servings

> PER SERVING: 103 CALORIES, <1GM. FAT, <1GM. SATURATED FAT, 4.5GM. PROTEIN, 22.5GM. CARBOHYDRATE, 75MG. CALCIUM (SEE YOCHIEVEMENTS FOR COMPARISONS)

More Beautiful Beets

Chilled leftovers can served on an antipasto or tapas plate, or set on a lettuce leaf as a salad or attractive garnish. Beets are so good this way, you should really plan on making extra.

Stewed Red Cabbage

This unusual combination of ingredients produces a sensational fusion of flavor and color.

1 pound red cabbage
1 medium onion, thinly sliced
4 cloves garlic, chopped
½ teaspoon salt
½ cup orange juice
2 tablespoons tomato paste
3 tablespoons YoChee

Cut the cabbage into very thin strips. There should be about 5 cups.

In a deep pot, cook the onion over medium heat for about 5 minutes, stirring occasionally, until wilted. You can add a spoonful of the orange juice if needed to keep the onion from sticking. Add the garlic and cook briefly.

Stir in the cabbage and salt. Cook for 3 to 5 minutes, until beginning to wilt.

Add the orange juice and tomato paste and mix well. Cover and cook for about 20 minutes, stirring occasionally, until the cabbage is very tender.

Remove from the heat and add the YoChee, stirring until completely absorbed into the cabbage.

Makes 4 to 6 servings

Per serving, based on 4 servings: 77 calories, <1gm. fat, <1gm. saturated fat, 4gm. protein, 17gm. carbohydrate, 100mg. calcium

SMOTHERED EGGPLANT

Smoky strands of eggplant in a rich, creamy sauce provide a cool vegetable accompaniment. This dish calls for advance planning, as it takes time to prepare and is served at room temperature or chilled. A good choice when you don't want to be in the kitchen at the last minute.

1 large or 2 small eggplants (about 2½ pounds)
2 cloves garlic
1 cup YoChee
3 tablespoons lemon juice
¼ teaspoon salt
1 teaspoon paprika

Broil the eggplant over a gas, wood or charcoal flame until the skin is charred and the inside is quite soft. Turn several times so that all sides cook. This will take from 10 to 20 minutes, depending on the size of the eggplant and the flame.

Let the cooked eggplant sit until it is cool enough to handle. Remove the skin and "string" the eggplant by peeling off sections with your fingers from the stem to the blossom end. Make each "string" the width of a finger or less. Discard any seeds.

In a shallow serving bowl, mash the garlic with a pestle or the back of a spoon. Add a little of the YoChee and mash together. With a fork, beat in the remaining YoChee, lemon juice, salt and paprika.

Stir the stringed eggplant into the seasoned YoChee and mix well. If this will not be eaten within about half an hour, refrigerate.

Serve at room temperature or chilled. Just before serving, sprinkle a little more paprika on top for appearance.

Makes 4 to 6 servings

PER SERVING, BASED ON 4 SERVINGS: 123 CALORIES, 1 GM. FAT, <1 GM. SATURATED FAT, 8 GM. PROTEIN, 24 GM. CARBOHYDRATE, 140 MG. CALCIUM

Fennel in Fresh Tomato Cream Sauce

A grand introduction to this underused, licorice-flavored vegetable. If fennel is not available, this recipe works quite well using other vegetables (see Fresh Tomato Cream Variations, below).

> 1 large bulb fennel (about 1 pound), cut in crescents (4 cups)
> 1 small onion, chopped
> 3 cloves garlic, chopped
> ¼ cup dry wine or water
> 4 Italian plum tomatoes, chopped
> ¼ teaspoon salt
> 8 fresh basil leaves
> ½ cup YoChee
> pepper

Combine the fennel, onion, garlic and wine or water in a skillet. Bring to a boil, cover and cook over low heat for 12 to 15 minutes or until the fennel is just tender but still firm.

Add the tomatoes, salt and 4 of the basil leaves. Cover and continue cooking for 10 minutes.

Remove the pan from the heat. Gently stir in the YoChee. Adjust the salt to taste. Tear up the remaining basil leaves and add along with a generous amount of pepper.

Makes 4 to 6 servings

Per serving, based on 4 servings: 81 calories, <1gm. fat, <1gm. saturated fat, 4.5gm. protein, 14gm. carbohydrate, 115mg. calcium

Fresh Tomato Cream Variations
In place of the fennel, use 1 pound or 4 cups:
- green beans
- flat Italian Romano beans
- thin broccoli "trees" or tops
- cauliflowerets

Creamy Vegetables du Jour au Gratin

When you have leftover cooked vegetables on hand, combine them with YoChee and a breadcrumb topping for an inviting side dish. Of course, you can also steam vegetables expressly for this purpose.

> 3 cups cooked vegetables of choice, including carrots, broccoli, green beans, cauliflower or asparagus
> 1 cup YoChee
> salt
> pepper
> ¼ cup dry bread or cracker crumbs
> 2 tablespoons wheat germ
> 2 teaspoons canola or olive oil

Preheat the oven to 350°F.

Combine the cooked vegetables with the YoChee, stirring well until evenly mixed. If the vegetables are unseasoned, season with salt and pepper to taste. Place in a 1-quart or 8- to 9-inch baking dish.

Combine the bread or cracker crumbs and wheat germ. Season with salt to taste. Mix in the oil until evenly distributed. Sprinkle over the vegetables.

Bake for 15 minutes, until heated through and the crumb topping begins to color.

Makes 4 servings

> *Per serving*: 135 calories, 3.5gm. fat, <1gm. saturated fat, 9gm. protein, 19gm. carbohydrate, 175mg. calcium

Better Bread & Cracker Crumbs

For best nutrition and taste, we recommend making your own crumbs in a blender, using dried whole grain bread or crackers.

The topping can be embellished according to taste by adding fresh or dried herbs or spices to the crumbs, including basil, parsley, oregano, rosemary, cumin, garlic, nutmeg or cinnamon, or a few tablespoons of grated cheese.

BROILED TOMATOES

Broiled Tomatoes make a good appetizer, side dish or salad garnish. Because they are so simple to make and tasty, we often add them to meals that could benefit from a boost of YoChee. If you like, you can assemble them ahead and refrigerate. But wait until mealtime to cook, as they taste best when eaten just after broiling.

> **4 medium to large tomatoes**
> **½ cup YoChee**
> **⅓ to ½ cup goat cheese, feta or blue cheese, crumbled**
> **¼ cup chopped fresh basil or parsley**

Slice the ends off the tomatoes. (You can reserve the ends to rub on grilled bread for flavor.) Cut each trimmed tomato into 3 thick slices. Arrange in a single layer on a baking sheet or shallow roasting pan.

Spread 2 teaspoons of the YoChee on each tomato slice. Top with 1½ to 2 teaspoons of the cheese of choice. Sprinkle with the basil or parsley.

Broil for about 5 minutes, until the topping is melted and lightly browned.

Makes 12 slices, 4 servings

> **PER SLICE:** 40 CALORIES, 2GM. FAT, 1GM. SATURATED FAT, 2.5GM. PROTEIN, 4GM. CARBOHYDRATE, 40MG. CALCIUM

Green-Stuffed Tomatoes

This is a recipe with a lot of leeway as far as ingredients go (see Tomato Tech, opposite). Moreover, everything can be assembled well in advance, giving the cook maximum flexibility. If you set these protein-packed tomatoes on a bed of grains, you might even consider serving them as an entrée.

4 medium tomatoes, 6 to 8 ounces each
1 tablespoon olive oil
4 scallions, chopped
2 cloves garlic, chopped
¼ cup dry breadcrumbs
2 tablespoons chopped fresh basil, parsley or dill, or
   1 teaspoon dried oregano
10-ounce package frozen chopped spinach, thawed and squeezed dry
¼ cup grated Parmesan, Swiss or cheddar cheese, or crumbled feta
   or blue cheese
½ cup YoChee
salt
pepper
nutmeg
cayenne
¼ cup grated Parmesan, Swiss or cheddar cheese

Preheat the oven to 350°F.

Cut a thin slice off the top of each tomato. Using a grapefruit knife and small spoon, hollow out the tomato. Save the pulp and top for another use. Invert the tomatoes on a plate to drain.

In a small pan, heat the oil and sauté the scallions and garlic until soft but not brown. Add the breadcrumbs and herb of choice and cook for 1 minute.

Remove the pan from the heat and mix in the spinach, cheese of choice and YoChee. Season to taste with salt, pepper, nutmeg and a pinch of cayenne. Mix well.

Spoon the mixture into the tomatoes, packing well. Top each with an additional tablespoonful of grated cheese of choice.

The tomatoes can be prepared in advance to this point and refrigerated for as long a two days.

Just before serving, place the tomatoes in a baking dish. Surround with a little water to keep the pan from scorching.

Bake for 15 to 20 minutes, depending on how firm or soft you like your tomatoes. If desired, brown cheese topping briefly under the broiler.

Serve hot or warm.

Makes 4 servings

PER SERVING: 190 CALORIES, 8GM. FAT, 3GM. SATURATED FAT, 12GM. PROTEIN, 20GM. CARBOHYDRATE, 320MG. CALCIUM

Tomato Tech

Green-Stuffed Tomatoes can be adapted to taste.

✔ Choose any of the suggested herbs.

✔ Choose any of the suggested cheeses.

✔ Replace the spinach with 1 cup of chopped, cooked fresh greens, including Swiss chard, collards, kale, mustard greens, arugula or a mixture.

✔ Leave off the cheese topping and garnish the tomatoes with a few toasted pumpkin seeds at serving time.

BAKED TOMATOES WITH WILD RICE STUFFING

These stuffed tomatoes are really quite easy to make yet look so impressive.

> **2 cups Wild Rice Stuffing (recipe follows, or see Note)**
> **4 medium-large tomatoes (about 10 ounces each)**
> **½ cup YoChee**
> **¼ cup chopped parsley**

Prepare Wild Rice Stuffing according to the recipe directions.

Preheat the oven to 350°F.

Slice the tops from the tomatoes and reserve. Scoop out the insides into a bowl. This is most easily done using a curved grapefruit knife and a serrated grapefruit spoon.

Drain the liquid from the scooped-out portion into the bottom of a shallow baking pan large enough to hold the tomatoes in a single layer. Reserve the pulp for another use (see Tomato Tidbits, next page).

Invert the tomato shells on a plate to drain. When done draining, pour this liquid into the baking pan as well.

Mix the YoChee and parsley with the cooked Wild Rice Stuffing. Pack into the hollowed-out tomatoes. Cover with the tomato tops.

Place the tomatoes side by side in the baking pan. Bake for 30 minutes.

Makes 4 servings

Note: If you don't want to prepare the Wild Rice Stuffing, replace it with a well seasoned cooked grain of your choice.

> *Per serving*: 145 calories, 1gm. fat, <1gm. saturated fat, 8gm. protein, 29gm. carbohydrate, 80mg. calcium

WILD RICE STUFFING

1 small onion, chopped
3 ounces exotic or cultivated mushrooms, coarsely chopped (1 cup)
1 tablespoon soy sauce
2 tablespoons water
½ cup wild rice
1¼ cups boiling water

Combine the onion, mushrooms, soy sauce and water in pot. Cover and cook over moderate heat for 5 minutes, or until the onion is tender and the mushroom juices run freely.

Add the wild rice and boiling water. Cover and simmer gently for 50 minutes, until the liquid is absorbed and the rice is tender.

Makes 2 cups

Tomato Tidbits

The reserved tomato pulp can be used in a variety of ways.

✔ Puree, season to taste and simmer for a few minutes to make a delicate sauce for the Baked Tomatoes.

✔ Add to salads or soups.

✔ Use in cooking.

✔ Make a homemade salsa.

Whatever you decide, use within a day.

Sweet Potato Pudding

So sweet and creamy, it's almost like having dessert with the meal. Another attraction is that the pudding can accomodate the cook's schedule, with advance assembly if desired and baking either several hours or just before serving. A favorite at Thanksgiving dinner, but worth preparing more than once a year.

> 3 medium-large sweet potatoes (about 1½ pounds), quartered
> 1 teaspoon grated fresh ginger
> ½ teaspoon cinnamon
> ¼ teaspoon nutmeg
> 1/8 teaspoon salt
> 1 tablespoon minced orange peel, preferably organic
> 2 tablespoons orange juice
> 2 tablespoons molasses
> ¾ cup YoChee
> ¼ cup pecan halves

Preheat the oven to 350⁰F. Lightly oil a 1-quart or 9-inch baking dish.

Steam the sweet potato pieces for about 20 to 25 minutes, until tender. When they are cool enough to handle, remove the skins and mash with a potato masher or fork until completely smooth. Mash in the remaining ingredients except for the pecans.

Turn the mixture into the prepared baking dish. Decorate the top with the pecans.

Bake for 20 to 25 minutes, until the top is lightly browned. If prepared in advance and refrigerated, increase the baking time by 5 to 10 minutes.

Makes 6 servings

Notes: If sweet potatoes are precooked (for example, leftover baked or unsweetened canned), you will need 2 cups mashed. For a crowd at holiday time, double the recipe and bake in a 2-quart or 9x13-inch baking dish.

Per serving: 193 calories, 3.5gm. fat, <1gm. saturated fat, 5gm. protein, 37gm. carbohydrate, 100mg. calcium

Sandwiches, Wraps & Pizzas

Sandwiches and similar bread-based foods, including wraps and pizza, are popular for their simple preparation and easy eating. Moreover, when composed of a whole grain breadstuff with a wholesome filling, these handy meals can be as nourishing and appealing as more work-intensive endeavors.

The recipes in this section employ our star ingredient in a wide range of preparations befitting a variety of tastes and ethnic cuisines. Breadstuffs made with unrefined flours provide a good starting point. Excellent options include whole wheat pita bread and pizza dough, wraps in the form of corn or whole wheat tortillas, chapatis, lavash, "mountain bread" and the like, as well as sliced whole grain breads.

We hope these recipes inspire you to go beyond what you see here. Allow our ideas to serve as a pattern for devising similar dishes on your own, using YoChee in combination with other ingredients on hand.

YoChievements

Portobello Cheddar Burger (pg.211) vs. lean beef patty (3.5 oz. cooked)

33% less calories
70% less fat
57% less saturated fat
32% less protein
50 times as much calcium

more...

Mediterranean Wrap (pg.216) vs. frozen beef and bean burrito
    42% less calories
    98% less fat
    50% more protein
    190% more calcium

Traditional Tomato Pizza (pg.221) vs. Stouffer's® Cheese Pizza
    20% less calories
    33% less fat
    Similar protein
    17% more calcium

YoChee Tip

For sandwiches, wraps and pizzas, YoChee should be very well drained. Allow a minimum of 12 hours and preferably 24 hours, so it is as thick as it can get.

SIMPLE SANDWICHES

You really don't need a recipe to enjoy YoChee on sandwiches. You can simply take a spoonful and spread it on the bread, just as you might apply butter or mayonnaise. The next step is making YoChee an integral part of the filling. For example, you can use it in egg, tuna or chicken salad sandwhich fillings, alone or in combination with mayonnaise.

Here are some additional quick sandwich suggestions.

TOMATO AND CREAMY YOCHEE

Spread your favorite bread generously with YoChee seasoned with a pinch of salt. Top with slices of ripe in-season tomatoes. Sprinkle pepper on top to taste.

OLIVE AND CREAMY YOCHEE

Combine YoChee with chopped green or black olives to taste. Spread on thinly sliced black bread.

VEGETABLE AND CREAMY YOCHEE

Spread bread generously with YoChee seasoned with pepper and, if desired, a pinch of salt. Top with chopped scallions and thinly sliced radishes.

ONION AND CREAMY YOCHEE

Spread bread with YoChee seasoned with pepper and, if desired, a pinch of salt. Top with a slice of raw onion and if desired, a slice of tomato.

CHOPPED WALNUTS AND CREAMY YOCHEE

Spread bread with equal parts cottage cheese and YoChee. Cover with grated walnuts.

THE BIG YOCHEE

Spread bread generously with YoChee. Cover with a slice of your favorite cheese. Top with tomato, sprouts and lettuce.

Open-Face YoCheese Melt

Toast bread lightly. Spread generously with YoChee. Top with mashed avocado seasoned with a pinch of salt and lemon juice. Top with alfalfa sprouts. Cover with a slice of cheddar, Swiss or Monterey Jack cheese. Sprinkle with sesame seeds. Broil or top-brown in a toaster oven until the cheese melts.

White Cloud

Spread a generous layer of YoChee on a toasted English muffin. Pile cottage cheese in a mound on top. Top with a slice of tomato and a heap of alfalfa sprouts. Eat open-face.

YoChee Beans

For each sandwich, mash ¼ cup of cooked beans with ½ tablespoon of ketchup and 1 to 2 tablespoons of YoChee. Spread on rye bread, cornbread or a corn tortilla. If desired, top with a little shredded cheddar, Monterey Jack or other cheese.

Fruit-Nut

Spread YoChee on date-nut or other fruit bread.

Apple Butter and Creamy YoChee

Spread bread generously with YoChee. Spread a layer of apple butter on top. Sprinkle with chopped walnuts.

Fruit and Nuts with Creamy YoChee

Combine YoChee with diced dried figs, prunes, dates or apricots, and sunflower seeds or chopped pecans. Pile on dark bread.

Jam and YoChee-in-the-Middle

Toast 2 slices of bread. Spread each lightly with fruit-juice-sweetened preserves, and put together with a thick layer of YoChee in the middle.

BURGERS

Portobello mushrooms have become a popular burger alternative. Unfortunately, the way they are generally offered may have the savor of a meaty burger but is often lacking the protein. On the other hand, with the help of YoChee, the following two portobello burger recipes compete successfully with meat-based burgers, providing main-dish protein and far less fat.

The directions are per burger.

PORTOBELLO CHEDDAR BURGER

Serve with sliced tomato, onion, sprouts or other favorite burger condiments.

1 large portobello mushroom, 4 to 5 inches across
1 tablespoon catsup or 2 tablespoons prepared tomato sauce
1 clove garlic, finely chopped
¼ cup YoChee
salt
pepper
about 1 ounce thinly sliced cheddar cheese

Preheat the oven to 375⁰F.

Clean the mushroom cap, remove the stem and place gills up in a shallow baking pan. Spread the catsup or tomato sauce over the surface of the mushroom. Sprinkle with the garlic.

Season the YoChee with a pinch of salt and pepper to taste. Spread over the mushroom. Cover with the thinly sliced cheese.

Bake for 20 minutes or until the mushroom is fork-tender.

Makes 1 serving

Note: Burger can be made with Swiss, Monterey Jack or other favorite melting cheese.

PER BURGER: 170 CALORIES, 5GM. FAT, 3GM. SATURATED FAT, 17GM. PROTEIN, 16GM. CARBOHYDRATE, 380MG. CALCIUM (SEE YOCHIEVEMENTS FOR COMPARISONS)

⏰ Portobello Feta Burger

Serve plated or in a pita pocket.

> 1 large portobello mushroom, 4 to 5 inches across
> 1 clove garlic, finely chopped
> ¼ cup YoChee
> salt
> ¼ teaspoon cumin
> ¼ cup crumbled feta cheese
> 2 slices fresh tomato
> freshly ground pepper

Preheat the oven to 375°F.

Clean the mushroom cap, remove the stem and place gills up in a shallow baking pan. Sprinkle with the garlic.

Season the YoChee with a pinch of salt and the cumin. Spread over the surface of the mushroom. Cover with the crumbled feta cheese. Top with the tomato. Season liberally with pepper.

Bake for 20 minutes or until the mushroom is fork-tender.

Makes 1 serving

Variation: For a Portobello Blue Burger, replace the feta with crumbled blue cheese.

Per burger: 180 calories, 8gm. fat, 5.5gm. saturated fat, 15gm. protein, 14gm. carbohydrate, 360mg. calcium

WRAPS

Wraps are versatile in that they can be either eaten like sandwiches or as finger foods. Tortillas and chapatis measuring 8 to 10 inches are ideal for individual wraps, while 12-inch or larger wraps can be halved for serving two or cut in sections for entertaining. As always, our preference is for whole wheat versions.

WARMING

Although it isn't mandatory, warming the wrap before filling improves the flavor. Warming can be done one at a time by cooking the wrap briefly in a dry skillet over medium heat, by holding it over an open flame as on a gas burner, or by placing it on a wire rack over a pan of water and briefly steaming.

Cook the wrap just enough so it is warm, but still soft and pliable. Too much cooking makes the wrap brittle, or in the case of steaming, soggy.

If you are preparing a lot at one time, the unheated wraps can be stacked, wrapped in foil, and warmed in a 350°F. oven for 5 to 10 minutes.

ASSEMBLY

After heating, lay the wrap on a flat surface. Place the filling ingredients in a strip on the lower half, leaving about an inch of wrap showing at each end. Fold the two opposite sides of the wrap over the ends of the filling, as shown in the illustration below. Then roll from the filling end to the top to completely enclose.

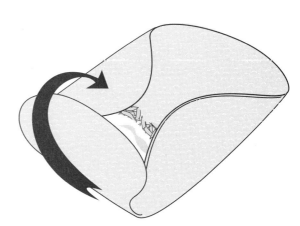

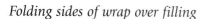
Folding sides of wrap over filling   *Rolling wrap from filling end to top*

Wrap of the Day

This is the basic method for making individual wraps using cooked vegetables—a perfect vehicle for leftovers. With this formula you can make endless varieties in unlimited volume.

1 8- to 10-inch wrap
¼ cup shredded lettuce
½ cup cooked vegetables or vegetable-bean combination
3 to 4 tablespoons YoChee
2 tablespoons shredded cheese of choice, optional

Just before filling, warm the wrap as described on page 213.

Lay the warm wrap on a flat surface. Mound the shredded lettuce on the lower half.

Place the vegetables, YoChee and cheese if using in a strip across the center of the lettuce, leaving about an inch of wrap showing at each end. Fold the wrap over the ends of the filling, then roll from the bottom to the top to completely enclose.

Makes 1 serving

Notes: If using 12-inch wraps or larger, double the filling and cut in halves for 2 servings or in 3-inch segments.

Per wrap, made with cooked mixed vegetables and shredded cheese: 184 calories, 5gm. fat, 3gm. saturated fat, 12gm. protein, 28gm. carbohydrate, 240mg. calcium

Mexican Wrap

To make burritos, add 2 tablespoons guacamole or diced avocado. Season with 1 to 2 tablespoons salsa. Use cheddar or Monterey Jack cheese.

GARDEN RANCH WRAPS

These colorful roll-ups are made with salad vegetables and a piquant dressing. The layout is slightly different than described in the previous recipe. Here the vegetables are arranged in vertical bands, so when the wrap is rolled and sliced, they create a pattern of alternating layers. Feel free to vary the vegetable choices, as long as the proportions stay the same. Note that these wraps can be eaten on the spot or made up to a day in advance.

⅓ cup Ranch Spread (see recipe page 24)
hot pepper sauce or horseradish, optional
2 8- to 10-inch wraps
½ cup shredded romaine, spinach or arugula
½ medium tomato or 1 plum tomato, thinly sliced
½ cup thinly sliced mushrooms
½ cup thinly sliced cucumber
½ cup shredded carrots

Make sure the Ranch Spread is well flavored by adding additional hot pepper sauce or a little horseradish if necessary so that it has a noticeable bite. Spread to cover the entire surface of each wrap.

Starting on the left, lay each vegetable in a narrow band from the top of the wrap to the bottom. Arrange vegetables close together without mixing. Leave a little space at the far end to seal the wrap.

Roll the wrap gently but firmly from left to right. Let sit at least 10 minutes before cutting. If made ahead, wrap in plastic film and refrigerate. Can be stored up to a day.

Cut each wrap in half or segments before serving.

Makes 2 servings

Notes: If made with 12-inch or larger wraps, follow the same procedure, using one wrap. Cut in quarters for 2 servings or slice into smaller segments for an hors d'œuvre.

PER SERVING: 136 CALORIES, 1GM. FAT, <1GM. SATURATED FAT, 7GM. PROTEIN, 32GM. CARBOHYDRATE, 90MG. CALCIUM

Garden Variety

Other vegetable choices include sliced avocado, sweet red or green pepper strips, radishes, sprouts or lightly cooked green beans or asparagus. Mix chopped fresh herbs such as basil, dill, parsley, cilantro or scallions into the greens for flavor.

MEDITERRANEAN WRAPS

This recipe makes enough filling for 8 wraps, but it can be stored for use over several days if you don't need all of it at once.

> 1½ cups dried green or brown lentils
> 3 cups water
> 1 bay leaf
> 2 cloves garlic, chopped
> 1 large stalk celery with leaves, chopped
> 2 medium carrots, chopped
> 1 cup chopped red onion or sweet white onion such as Vidalia, Walla Walla, Maui, Texas sweet
> ¼ teaspoon nutmeg
> 3 tablespoons balsamic vinegar, wine vinegar or lemon juice
> ½ cup chopped sweet red or yellow pepper
> ½ cup chopped parsley
> 1 cup YoChee
> ¼ teaspoon salt or to taste
> 8 8- to 10-inch wraps
> 2 cups shredded lettuce

Combine the lentils, water, bay leaf, garlic, celery, carrots and ½ cup of the onions in a large pot. Bring to a boil, reduce the heat, cover and simmer gently for 20 minutes, until almost cooked. Do not cook too vigorously or the lentils will fall apart.

Add the nutmeg and continue to cook for 10 minutes, until the lentils are tender but still hold their shape and the liquid is just about absorbed.

Remove from the heat and discard the bay leaf. Stir in the vinegar or lemon juice. Season with salt to taste. If you are preparing the lentils ahead of time, stop here and reheat before going on to the next step.

Add the remaining ½ cup of onions, sweet pepper, parsley and YoChee to the warm lentils. Stir until evenly mixed.

Just before serving, warm the wrap as described on page 213.

Scatter ¼ cup of shredded lettuce on the bottom half of each wrap. Place a generous ½ cup of the lentil filling in a strip across the center of the lettuce, leaving about an inch showing at either end.

Fold the ends of the wrap over the filling, then roll from the bottom to the top to completely enclose the filling.

Serve whole, cut in half or, if the wraps are very large, cut in 3-inch segments.

Makes 8 servings; 5 cups filling

Note: These same proportions are adequate for 4 to 6 12-inch or larger wraps.

PER SERVING: 243 CALORIES, 1 GM. FAT, <1 GM. SATURATED FAT, 16.5 GM. PROTEIN, 49 GM. CARBOHYDRATE, 115 MG. CALCIUM (SEE YOCHIEVEMENTS FOR COMPARISONS)

No Need to Wrap
For Mediterranean Stuffed Sandwiches, stuff the lentil filling into pita pockets.

Pizzas

Whether you make a simple pizza built on pita rounds or use a traditional yeast crust, YoChee can make a valuable contribution by adding a flavorful, protein-rich topping.

⏰ White Pita Pizzas

These easy pizzas are made on a base of pita bread. If you have any roasted garlic on hand, squeeze the soft puree from a few cloves on top just before serving.

> **2 2-ounce pita breads**
> **Vegetable Topping of choice (see facing page)**
> **¾ cup YoChee**
> **¼ to ½ cup crumbled feta or grated Parmesan cheese, optional**

Preheat the oven to 400°F.

Use a fork to perforate the circumference of the breads. Separate each into two rounds.

Mix the prepared (and cooled) Vegetable Topping of choice with the YoChee until evenly blended. Add crumbled feta or Parmesan cheese if desired. Spread to cover each pita round completely.

Place on a baking sheet and bake for 15 minutes, until lightly browned at the edges.

Let sit for a few minutes to set filling before serving.

Makes 2 to 4 entrée or accompaniment servings; 4 to 6 appetizer servings

Note: Instead of using pita bread, pizzas can be made using slices of whole grain bread, toasting one side first, piling the filling on the untoasted side, then baking as directed.

> Per round, with broccoli, without optional cheese: 130 calories, 1gm. fat, <1gm. saturated fat, 8.5gm. protein, 24gm. carbohydrate, 115mg. calcium
>
> With feta cheese, for each tablespoon (1 to 2 tablespoons per round) add: 25 calories, 2gm. fat, 2.5gm. protein, 45mg. calcium
>
> With Parmesan cheese, for each tablespoon (1 to 2 tablespoons per round) add: 30 calories, 2gm. fat, 2.5gm. protein, 85mg. calcium

VEGETABLE TOPPINGS

<u>Cooked Greens</u>: Combine ½ pound (5 to 6 cups loosely packed) greens of choice (spinach, beet greens, Swiss chard or a mixture including some radicchio, arugula and endive) in a heavy skillet with 1 tablespoon balsamic vinegar. Cover and cook until tender, about 10 minutes. Chop coarsely. If desired, add ¼ cup minced fresh dill. Cool to lukewarm before mixing with the YoChee and optional cheese.

<u>Broccoli</u>: Chop broccoli florets into very small pieces to make 2 cups. Combine with 1 tablespoon balsamic vinegar and 2 tablespoons water in a heavy skillet. Cover and cook until tender, about 8 to 10 minutes. Season with 1 teaspoon dried oregano. Cool to lukewarm before mixing with the YoChee and optional cheese.

<u>Pepper and Onion</u>: Slice 1 large or 2 medium Spanish, Vidalia or red onion(s) in half lengthwise. Cut each half crosswise into thin half-rings. You should have about 2 cups. Chop green or sweet red pepper to make ½ cup. Combine the vegetables with 1 tablespoon balsamic vinegar in a heavy skillet. Cover and cook over low heat, stirring occasionally, for 20 minutes, until the onions are tender. Cool to lukewarm before mixing with the YoChee and optional cheese. Season lightly with salt if not using feta or Parmesan cheese, and sprinkle liberally with pepper.

Pizza Presentation

As with most pizzas, these can be served as an entrée (2 per person), or 1 round can be used to accompany a meal. You can also cut the pita pizzas into triangles for an hors d'œuvre or as part of an antipasto.

Basic Pizza Crust

It is surprisingly easy to make your own pizza crust. It takes just a few minutes to put the dough together, but it does take planning, as the dough must have at least two hours to rise. The recipe here is for two large or four small pizzas. Each large pizza feeds two to four, while a small pizza is for one or two to share. Once the dough is completed— meaning it has been allowed to rise as directed—it can be refrigerated for a few days or even frozen (see Note).

> 1 tablespoon dry yeast
> 1 cup plus 2 tablespoons very warm water
> 1 teaspoon honey
> 1 teaspoon salt
> 1 tablespoon olive oil
> about 3 cups whole wheat flour

Mix the yeast with 2 tablespoons of the very warm water and the honey in a large bowl. In about 5 minutes, when the yeast is dissolved, add the remaining 1 cup of water, along with the salt, oil and 2 cups of the flour. Beat with a wooden spoon until the flour is incorporated. Gradually add more flour until the dough becomes too difficult to manipulate.

Transfer the dough to a well-floured surface and knead in the remaining flour as needed to make a smooth, elastic dough. Knead for 5 to 10 minutes.

Place the dough in an oiled bowl. Turn so that the entire surface is greased. Cover with a cloth and let rise in a warm spot for a minimum of 2 hours or as long as 10 hours.

When ready to assemble the pizzas, punch down the dough and let it rest for 5 to 10 minutes to make handling easier. Then divide, shape and fill according to the recipe chosen.

Makes dough for 2 large or 4 8-inch pizzas

Variations: For extra protein, add ¼ cup of soy flour and adjust the whole wheat flour accordingly. For a slightly crunchy Cornmeal Crust that is ideal for Tex-Mex Pizza (page 223), substitute up to 1 cup of cornmeal for 1 cup of the flour.

Note: After rising, the dough can be punched down and refrigerated for up to 2 days or frozen. If it is refrigerated, let sit at room temperature for about 30 minutes before shaping. If it is frozen, place in a bowl in a warm spot for several hours until completely thawed and at room temperature. If there is room in the freezer, the dough can be preshaped prior to freezing; in that case, thawing isn't necessary.

Per 8-inch pizza: 350 calories, 5gm. fat, 1gm. saturated fat, 13.5gm. protein, 68gm carbohydrate, 30mg. calcium

TRADITIONAL TOMATO PIZZA

This is a classic pizza, with a layer of YoChee to enhance the taste and nutrition.

> **Dough for 1 large or 2 8-inch pizzas (½ Basic Pizza Crust, opposite)**
> **cornmeal**
> **¾ cup YoChee**
> **⅔ cup shredded mozzarella cheese**
> **1 cup well-seasoned Italian-style tomato sauce**
> **2 tablespoons grated Parmesan cheese**
> **1 tablespoon olive oil**

Preheat the oven to 425°F.

For a large pizza, roll the dough into a thin 12- to 14-inch circle. For individual pizzas, divide the dough into 2 pieces and roll each one into an 8-inch round. Either way, the crust should be about ¼ inch thick. Place the crust(s) on a baking sheet or pizza pan that has been dusted with cornmeal. With your fingers, push the dough out from the center toward the edge to thin the bottom crust a bit and provide a rim around the edge. The pizza is now ready to top and bake.

Spread the YoChee to cover the crust. Scatter the mozzarella cheese on top. Cover with the tomato sauce. If the sauce is not well flavored, add 1 teaspoon oregano and ½ teaspoon dried basil. Top with the Parmesan cheese. Drizzle the olive oil evenly over all.

Bake the pizza for about 20 minutes, until the cheese bubbles a little and the crust is crisp and golden around the edges.

Makes 1 large or 2 8-inch pizzas

PER 8-INCH PIZZA: 642 CALORIES, 20.5 GM. FAT, 7 GM. SATURATED FAT, 35 GM. PROTEIN, 84 GM. CARBOHYDRATE, 555 MG. CALCIUM (SEE YOCHIEVEMENTS FOR COMPARISONS)

Personalizing Pizza

Have fun creating your own pizza variations.

Top the sauce with sliced mushrooms, green peppers, onions, canned artichoke hearts, chopped olives, capers, grilled zucchini or eggplant slices, precooked broccoli florets, slices of fresh garlic or whole cloves of roasted garlic before adding the Parmesan cheese and oil.

Millstream Fresh Tomato Pizza

This pizza is made with fresh tomatoes rather than tomato sauce.

> Dough for 1 large or 2 8-inch pizzas (½ Basic Pizza Crust, page 220)
> cornmeal
> 1 cup YoChee
> ¾ cup shredded mozzarella cheese or a combination with provolone
> 3 medium tomatoes, sliced
> 1 teaspoon oregano
> ½ teaspoon basil
> salt
> pepper
> 2 tablespoons grated Parmesan cheese
> 1 tablespoon olive oil

Preheat the oven to 425°F.

For a large pizza, roll the dough into a thin 12- to 14-inch circle. For individual pizzas, divide the dough into 2 pieces and roll each one into an 8-inch round. Either way, the crust should be about ¼ inch thick. Place the crust(s) on a baking sheet or pizza pan that has been dusted with cornmeal. With your fingers, push the dough out from the center toward the edge to thin the bottom and provide a small rim around the edge. The pizza is now ready to top and bake.

Spread the YoChee to cover the crust. Scatter the shredded cheese on top. Arrange the sliced tomatoes over this. Sprinkle with the oregano, basil, a few pinches of salt and a few turns of the pepper mill. Top with the Parmesan cheese. Drizzle the olive oil evenly over all.

Bake the pizza for about 20 minutes, until the cheese bubbles a little and the crust is crisp and golden around the edges.

Makes 1 large or 2 8-inch pizzas

Note: If desired, place thin slices of raw garlic or whole cloves of roasted garlic on the YoChee layer.

Per 8-inch pizza: 678 calories, 22gm. fat, 7gm. saturated fat, 38gm. protein, 88gm. carbohydrate, 660mg. calcium

TEX-MEX PIZZA

By simply varying the cheese and sauce, you create a completely different pizza.

Dough for 1 large pizza (½ Basic Pizza Crust or Cornmeal Crust variation, page 220)
cornmeal
1 cup YoChee
⅔ cup shredded Monterey Jack cheese
1 cup mild, medium or spicy salsa
¼ cup shredded cheddar cheese
1 tablespoon olive oil

Preheat the oven to 425°F.

Roll the dough into a thin 12- to 14-inch circle about ¼ inch thick. Place the crust on a baking sheet or pizza pan that has been dusted with cornmeal. With your fingers, push the dough out from the center toward the edge to thin the bottom and provide a small rim around the edge. The pizza is now ready to top and bake.

Spread the YoChee to cover the crust. Scatter the Monterey Jack cheese on top. Drop on the salsa by spoonfuls at even intervals. Top with the cheddar cheese. Drizzle the olive oil evenly over all.

Bake the pizza for about 20 minutes, until the cheese bubbles a little and the crust is crisp and golden around the edges.

Makes 1 large pizza

PER LARGE PIZZA: 1465 CALORIES, 58GM. FAT, 24GM. SATURATED FAT, 75GM. PROTEIN, 172GM. CARBOHYDRATE, 1365MG. CALCIUM

ROAST VEGETABLE PIZZA

This is a good choice for parties and entertaining. We make it in the 8-inch size in order to get more of the crisp crust. One 8-inch personal pizza makes a hearty main dish. Cut each pizza in quarters as an appetizer, or into 8 wedges for an hors d'œuvre.

Dough for 2 8-inch pizzas (½ Basic Pizza Crust, page 220)
cornmeal
3 cups sliced raw mixed vegetables of choice, including onion, crookneck squash, zucchini, plum tomato, eggplant, carrot, broccoli florets, sweet red or green pepper, mushrooms, sweet potato, olives and the like
1 cup YoChee
salt
2 cloves garlic, thinly sliced, optional
pepper
1 tablespoon fresh basil, dill or sage
½ teaspoon oregano or rosemary
¼ cup grated Parmesan or other cheese of choice, optional
1 tablespoon olive oil

Preheat the oven to 425°F.

Divide the dough into 2 pieces and roll each one into an 8-inch round about ¼ inch thick. Place the rounds on a baking sheet or pizza pan that has been dusted with cornmeal. With your fingers, push the dough out from the center toward the edge to thin the bottom and provide a rim around the edge. The pizzas are now ready to top and bake.

Prepare the vegetables by cutting them into thin slices, or in the case of broccoli, small florets.

Season the YoChee with a generous pinch of salt. Spread over the bottom of the crusts to cover completely. Distribute the garlic evenly on top, if using. Arrange the vegetables over the YoChee. Season liberally with freshly ground pepper and the herbs of choice. Top with the grated cheese if using. Drizzle the oil evenly over all.

Bake for 15 to 20 minutes or until the crusts are crisp and golden around the edges and the vegetables are cooked.

Makes 2 8-inch pizzas

PER 8-INCH PIZZA WITHOUT CHEESE: 538 CALORIES, 13 GM. FAT, 1.5 GM. SATURATED FAT, 26 GM. PROTEIN, 87 GM. CARBOHYDRATE, 290 MG. CALCIUM

PER 8-INCH PIZZA WITH CHEESE: 595 CALORIES, 17 GM. FAT, 4 GM. SATURATED FAT, 31 GM. PROTEIN, 87 GM. CARBOHYDRATE, 465 MG. CALCIUM

Roast Vegetable Pizza with Pesto

To create a gourmet garlic pizza, omit the salt, garlic and herbs from the Roast Vegetable Pizza recipe. Spread ¼ cup of homemade or store-bought pesto over the YoChee. Top with the vegetables. Leave off the grated cheese. Drizzle lightly with the oil. Bake as directed.

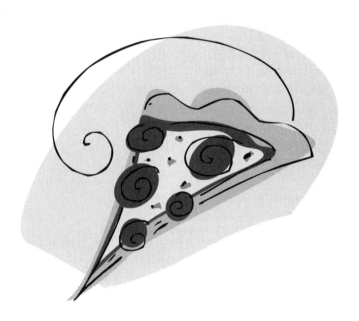

French Olive-Onion Pizza

This is a French Mediterranean-style pizza with an olive-onion topping. It is an excellent choice when entertaining.

> **2 cups sliced red or sweet onion, such as Vidalia, Walla Walla, Maui**
> **1 tablespoon balsamic vinegar**
> **Dough for 2 8-inch pizzas (½ Basic Pizza Crust, page 220)**
> **cornmeal**
> **¾ cup YoChee**
> **salt**
> **¼ cup sliced black olives**
> **¼ cup crumbled feta or goat cheese or grated Parmesan cheese, optional**
> **½ teaspoon dried or 1 tablespoon fresh rosemary**
> **pepper**

Place the onions in a skillet along with the balsamic vinegar. Cover and cook over low heat for 20 minutes, stirring occasionally, until the onions are very tender. If they are cooking too quickly, lower the heat and add a little water to prevent them from sticking or burning.

Prehat the oven to 425°F.

Divide the pizza dough into 2 pieces. Roll each one into an 8-inch round about ¼ inch thick. Place the crusts on a baking sheet or pizza pan that has been dusted with cornmeal. With your fingers, push the dough from the center toward the edge to thin the bottom crust and provide a rim around the edge. The pizzas are now ready to top and bake.

Season the YoChee with a generous pinch of salt. Spread over the bottom of each crust to cover completely. Distribute the onions evenly over the YoChee. Decorate with the olives. Top with the cheese if using. Season with the rosemary and pepper.

Bake for 15 to 20 minutes or until the crusts are crisp and golden around the edges.

Makes 2 8-inch pizzas

> *Per 8-inch pizza without cheese*: 485 calories, 8gm. fat, 1gm. saturated fat, 23gm. protein, 88gm. carbohydrate, 70mg. calcium

> *Per 8-inch pizza with cheese*: 535 calories, 12gm. fat, 4gm. saturated fat, 25.5gm. protein, 89gm. carbohydrate, 350mg. calcium

BAKED GOODS

YoChee functions very much like sour cream in baking, creating a similarly tender product but with a leaner profile. In this section you will find recipes that take advantage of this remarkable capability. The cookies, cakes and pies in "Desserts" are similarly blessed.

✿ YoChievements ✿

Savory Biscuits (pg.228) vs. typical homemade or refrigerated buttermilk biscuits
        Similar calories
        20% less fat
        80% less saturated fat
        75% more protein

YoChee Muffins (pg.231) vs. muffins from a mix
        35% less calories
        43% less fat
        130% more protein
        200% more calcium

Amazing YoChee Piecrust (pg.232) vs. homemade piecrust
        36% less calories
        53% less fat
        87% less saturated fat (when made with oil)
        67% more protein
        16 times as much calcium

Savory Biscuits

Compared to traditional biscuits, these are higher in protein and fiber, with substantially less saturated fat.

1⅓ cups whole wheat flour
⅔ cup cornmeal
¼ cup wheat germ
2 teaspoons baking powder
½ teaspoon baking soda
½ teaspoon salt
¼ cup canola oil
1 tablespoon honey
1 cup YoChee

Preheat the oven to 425°F.

Combine the dry ingredients in a mixing bowl. Stir in the oil and mix with a pastry blender, wire whisk or fork until completely incorporated and crumbly.

Stir in the honey and YoChee. Mix until the ingredients are well blended, kneading gently in the bowl with your hands at the end to form a ball of dough.

Pat or roll the dough gently to form an 8-inch square that is ½ inch thick. Cut into 8 2-inch squares. If desired, you can gently shape them into rounds.

Place the biscuits on an oiled baking sheet, leaving an inch between them for crusty biscuits, or with the sides touching for a tender crust.

Bake for about 15 minutes, until golden.

Makes 8 biscuits

Per biscuit: 208 calories, 8gm. fat, <1gm. saturated fat, 7gm. protein, 29gm. carbohydrate, 150mg. calcium (see YoChievements for comparisons)

TOMATO-CHEESE BISCUITS

A tender biscuit flavored with cheese and tomato.

> 1⅓ cups whole wheat flour
> 1 cup cornmeal
> ¼ cup wheat germ
> 2 teaspoons baking powder
> ½ teaspoon baking soda
> ¼ teaspoon salt
> ½ cup shredded sharp cheddar cheese
> ¼ cup canola or olive oil
> ⅔ cup YoChee
> ½ cup tomato juice

Preheat the oven to 425°F.

Combine the dry ingredients and the shredded cheese in a mixing bowl. Stir in the oil and mix with a pastry blender, wire whisk or fork until completely incorporated and crumbly.

Stir in the YoChee and tomato juice. Mix until the ingredients are well blended, kneading gently in the bowl with your hands at the end to form a ball of dough.

Pat or roll the dough gently to form an 8-inch square that is ½ inch thick. Cut into 8 2-inch squares. If desired, you can shape them by hand into rounds.

Place the biscuits on an oiled baking sheet, leaving an inch between them for crusty biscuits, or with the sides touching for a tender crust.

Bake for about 15 minutes, until golden.

Makes 8 biscuits

> **PER BISCUIT**: 224 CALORIES, 10GM. FAT, 2GM. SATURATED FAT, 8GM. PROTEIN, 27GM. CARBOHYDRATE, 185MG. CALCIUM

Sweet Biscuits

Sweet Biscuits are a slight variation of the Savory Biscuit recipe. Serve them for dessert topped with fresh fruit and your choice of NoWorry Whipped YoChee (see recipes page 301). Or, spread with All-in-One YoChee and Jelly (see recipe page 25).

- 1⅓ cups whole wheat flour
- ⅔ cup cornmeal
- ¼ cup wheat germ
- 2 teaspoons baking powder
- ½ teaspoon baking soda
- ¼ teaspoon salt
- ¼ cup canola oil
- ¼ cup honey or maple syrup
- 1 cup YoChee

Preheat the oven to 425°F.

Combine the dry ingredients in a mixing bowl. Stir in the oil and mix with a pastry blender, wire whisk or fork until completely incorporated and crumbly.

Stir in the sweetener and YoChee. Mix until the ingredients are well blended, kneading gently in the bowl with your hands at the end to form a ball of dough.

Pat or roll the dough gently to form an 8-inch square that it is ½ inch thick. Cut into 8 2-inch squares. If desired, you can gently shape them into rounds.

Place the biscuits on an oiled baking sheet, leaving an inch between them for crusty biscuits, or with the sides touching for a tender crust.

Bake for about 15 minutes, until golden.

Makes 8 biscuits

> **Per biscuit:** 232 calories, 8gm. fat, <1gm. saturated fat, 7gm. protein, 35.5gm. carbohydrate, 150mg. calcium

YoChee Muffins

This basic recipe makes a very tasty, lightly sweetened muffin with a tender inside and crusty top. Muffins Galore (below) offers a cornucopia of flavoring ingredients to create such distinctive muffins as zucchini-walnut, carrot-raisin, apple-date, pear-pecan and so on.

2½ cups whole wheat flour
1 teaspoon baking powder
1 teaspoon baking soda
¼ teaspoon salt
2 tablespoons wheat germ
3 tablespoons oil
¼ cup honey
2 cups YoChee

Preheat the oven to 400°F.

Combine the dry ingredients in a mixing bowl. Make a well in the center and add the remaining ingredients in the order listed. Mix thoroughly with a fork or wooden spoon until the dry ingredients are completely incorporated into the YoChee. The batter will be very thick.

Spoon the batter by ⅓-cupfuls into an oiled or paper-lined muffin tin.

Bake for 20 minutes, until nicely browned.

Makes 12 muffins

PER PLAIN MUFFIN: 169 CALORIES, 4 GM. FAT, <1 GM. SATURATED FAT, 7 GM. PROTEIN, 28 GM. CARBOHYDRATE, 115 MG. CALCIUM (SEE YOCHIEVEMENTS FOR COMPARISONS)

Muffins Galore

Add up to ½ cup of one or more of the following to the dry ingredients. Let your imagination suggest other variations.

✔ raisins
✔ chopped dates or other chopped dried fruit
✔ diced fresh apple or pear
✔ chopped walnuts or pecans
✔ corn kernels
✔ shredded zucchini or carrots, pressed to remove all moisture

AMAZING YoChee Piecrust

This is an excellent all-purpose piecrust. Compare the fat—just 3.6 grams per 3-inch wedge (one-eighth pie), versus traditional crusts ranging from 5 to as much as 10.5 grams of fat per slice. This means dramatically fewer calories, plus a bonus of protein and calcium, rare in piecrusts.

> ¾ cup whole wheat flour
> ¼ teaspoon salt
> ¼ teaspoon baking powder
> 2 tablespoons canola oil, olive oil or butter at room temperature
> 6 tablespoons YoChee

Mix the flour, salt and baking powder in a bowl. Using a pastry blender, wire whisk or fork, cut in the oil or butter until it is thoroughly incorporated.

Work in the YoChee and then gently knead the dough with your hands to form a ball of soft dough. Chill the dough for at least 30 minutes before rolling.

Place the dough on a pastry cloth or waxed-paper-lined surface. Roll into an 11-inch circle. Drape it into a 9-inch pie pan or tart pan, or cut for individual tarts. Press gently into the bottom and up the sides of the pan. Crimp or flute the edges as desired. If there are any tears in the pastry, they can be easily mended by pressing on a thin overlay of the dough.

Bake as directed in recipes.

Makes 1 9-inch shell or 8 to 10 individual tarts

Per 9-inch crust made with oil: 610 CALORIES, 29GM. FAT, 2GM. SATURATED FAT, 20GM. PROTEIN, 73GM. CARBOHYDRATE, 290MG. CALCIUM (SEE YoChievements FOR COMPARISONS)

Per 3-inch wedge or tart: 76 CALORIES, 3.5GM. FAT, <1GM. SATURATED FAT, 2.5GM. PROTEIN, 9GM. CARBOHYDRATE, 35MG. CALCIUM

Per 9-inch crust made with butter: 573 CALORIES, 25GM. FAT, 14GM. SATURATED FAT, 20GM. PROTEIN, 73GM. CARBOHYDRATE, 300MG. CALCIUM

Per 3-inch wedge or tart: 72 CALORIES, 3GM. FAT, 2GM. SATURATED FAT, 2.5GM. PROTEIN, 9GM. CARBOHYDRATE, 35MG. CALCIUM

SALADS & SALAD DRESSINGS

Many people already know how useful plain yogurt can be for making creamy salads and salad dressings. While we agree, in fact there are many applications where YoChee is superior.

There are two principal reasons we prefer YoChee to yogurt: It has a richer, smoother texture and a milder flavor. You will see how well it works in the salads and the salad dressings that follow.

YOUR OWN CREAMY SALADS WITH YOCHEE

Use YoChee to replace up to half the mayonnaise in traditional recipes for egg, macaroni, fish, chicken, tofu and diced vegetable salads and the like. It improves the flavor, texture and value of these dishes.

IMPROVING BOTTLED DRESSINGS

YoChee can be added to almost any prepared salad dressing to make it creamy and more nutritious. The proportion will depend on the consistency of the original dressing, how much you want to mellow the flavor, and the extent of creaminess you desire. The best approach is to beat in a spoonful of YoChee at a time and taste as you go along.

YOCHEE PEARLS

Another favorite way to use YoChee is as salad garnish. Simply spoon several dollops on top of the greens, either before or after they are dressed. These YoChee pearls provide an appealing taste sensation and boost the food value of the salad.

❧ YoChievements ❧

Spicy Orange Coleslaw (pg.235) vs. typical fast-food coleslaw
- 70% less calories
- 67% to 82% less fat
- 62% to 75% less carbohydrate

Russian Coleslaw (pg.235) vs. typical fast-food coleslaw
- 83% less calories
- no fat vs. 10 to 20 grams fat per ½ cup
- 50% to 70% less carbohydrate

Premier Potato Salad (pg.238) vs. typical potato salad
- 57% to 65% less calories
- no fat vs. 14 to 28 grams fat per cup
- 2 to 7 times as much protein
- 110mg. calcium per cup vs. little or no calcium

Classy Carrot Salad (pg.243) vs. typical carrot-raisin salad
- 60% less calories
- no fat vs. 11 grams fat per ½ cup
- 250% more protein
- 100% more calcium

Contemporary Waldorf Salad (pg.244) vs. typical Waldorf salad
- 62% less calories
- 86% less fat
- 80% more calcium

Thick & Creamy Blue Cheese Dressing (pg.246) vs. bottled blue cheese dressing
- 25% less calories
- 33% less fat
- 4 times as much protein
- 4 times as much calcium

Spicy Orange Coleslaw

The name says it all.

⅔ cup Creamy Orange Vinaigrette (see recipe page 245)
hot pepper sauce or cayenne pepper to taste
1 pound cabbage, coarsely shredded (4 to 5 cups)

Season the dressing with hot pepper sauce or cayenne according to personal taste. In a large bowl, combine the cabbage and the dressing. Mix well until the dressing is evenly and thoroughly incorporated. If made ahead, store in the refrigerator.

Makes 1 quart; 6 to 8 servings

Per ½-CUP SERVING: 58 CALORIES, 3.5GM. FAT, <1GM. SATURATED FAT, 1.5GM. PROTEIN, 5GM. CARBOHYDRATE, 45MG. CALCIUM (SEE YoCHIEVEMENTS FOR COMPARISONS)

 ## Russian Coleslaw

In this coleslaw, cabbage is paired with a mildly sweet Russian-style dressing.

6 tablespoons YoChee
6 tablespoons tomato juice
1½ teaspoons honey
2 tablespoons cider vinegar
4 cups finely shredded cabbage (about 1 pound)
salt
pepper

In a large bowl, combine the YoChee, tomato juice, honey and cider vinegar. Mix vigorously until evenly blended. Add the cabbage and mix well. Season to taste with salt and pepper. If made ahead, store in the refrigerator.

Makes 3 cups; 4 to 6 servings

Variations: Add 1 shredded carrot, 2 tablespoons chopped red or green pepper or your favorite relish.

Per ½-CUP SERVING: 30 CALORIES, <1GM. FAT, <1GM. SATURATED FAT, 2GM. PROTEIN, 6GM. CARBOHYDRATE, 50MG. CALCIUM (SEE YoCHIEVEMENTS FOR COMPARISONS)

Caesar Salad

A surprisingly successful Caesar Salad is made using YoChee instead of raw egg, and capers instead of anchovies.

Croutons:
4 ½-inch-thick slices French bread or 2 ½-inch-thick slices larger bread
1 teaspoon olive oil
1 clove garlic, cut in half
Dressing:
½ teaspoon Dijon-style mustard
2 tablespoons YoChee
2 tablespoons olive oil
1 tablespoon lemon juice
1 teaspoon red wine vinegar
½ teaspoon soy sauce
1 tablespoon minced oil-cured or other flavorful black olives
1 tablespoon grated Parmesan cheese
pepper
Salad:
½ pound romaine lettuce (about 10 large leaves)
1½ tablespoons capers
1 tablespoon shaved or grated Parmesan cheese

To prepare the croutons, brush each slice of bread lightly on both sides with some of the olive oil. You can do this with a pastry brush or by pouring the oil into a flat dish and quickly dipping the bread in on each side.

Rub both sides of the bread with the cut garlic. Grill or broil until golden brown on each side. Cut into bite-size pieces.

Mince the garlic that remains and use it for the dressing.

For the dressing, combine the minced garlic, mustard and YoChee in a large salad bowl. Using a fork or wire whisk, beat until smooth. Beat in the olive oil, lemon juice, wine vinegar, soy sauce, black olives and grated Parmesan cheese. Add pepper to taste to make a highly seasoned dressing.

Just before serving, tear the lettuce leaves into 2-inch pieces (you should have about 6 cups). Put them in the bowl with the salad dressing.

Top with the capers, shaved Parmesan cheese and croutons. Mix well and serve at once.

Makes 2 entrée servings; 4 side-dish servings

> *PER ENTRÉE SERVING*: 300 CALORIES, 22 GM. FAT, 4 GM. SATURATED FAT, 9 GM. PROTEIN, 19 GM. CARBOHYDRATE, 185 MG. CALCIUM

> *PER SIDE-DISH SERVING*: 150 CALORIES, 11 GM. FAT, 2 GM. SATURATED FAT, 4.5 GM. PROTEIN, 10 GM. CARBOHYDRATE, 90 MG. CALCIUM

Three Tips

For the croutons, use a good-quality bread. Our preference is always for one made with whole grain flour.

For the dressing, use a genuine soy sauce, not one doctored with corn syrup and caramel coloring. Real soy sauce is sold in Oriental groceries and natural food stores.

The Parmesan cheese should be freshly grated and the best-tasting you can afford. Feel free to use Romano, locatelli, sardo or something similar in its place.

Premier Potato Salad

The flavorful YoChee dressing turns this into a potato salad that is practically fat-free and has a better ratio of protein to carbohydrate than most dishes of this type. If you want a more traditional flavor, just add a little mayonnaise to taste.

1 pound potatoes
¾ cup YoChee
1½ teaspoons prepared mustard
3 tablespoons white wine vinegar or rice wine vinegar
¼ teaspoon salt or to taste
pepper
¼ cup chopped scallions, red onion or sweet onion such as Vidalia or
    Walla Walla
¼ cup chopped sweet red or green pepper
2 tablespoons chopped parsley
¼ teaspoon paprika

Scrub the potatoes, cut them into chunks and steam for 15 to 20 minutes, or until just tender but not breaking apart. The cooking time will vary with the size and type of potato.

Beat the YoChee, mustard and vinegar of choice with a fork to make a smooth dressing. Season with salt and pepper to taste.

When the potatoes are cool enough to handle but still warm, remove the peel and slice or cut into bite-size pieces according to personal preference. Combine them in a bowl with the dressing, scallions or onion, red or green pepper and parsley. Mix gently to coat. Sprinkle liberally with the paprika.

Chill if not served within 1 hour, but remove from the refrigerator at least 15 minutes before serving.

Makes 4 servings; about 1 quart

Note: To prepare this potato salad with leftover cooked potatoes, use about 2½ cups sliced or diced potatoes.

Variations: Replace the parsley and paprika with ¼ cup minced fresh dill. Other additions can include sliced radishes, fresh green peas or cut-up sugar snap peas.

Per 1-cup serving: 114 calories, <1gm. fat, <1gm. saturated fat, 7gm. protein, 25gm. carbohydrate, 110mg. calcium (see YoChievements for comparisons)

SALADE COMPOSÉE (COMPOSED SALAD)

To prepare this French-style salad, start with a bed of greens. Then use what you have on hand to compose a plate with various small portions of raw or cooked seasonal vegetables and other desired garnishes, including Labneh Makbus (YoChee balls). Feel free to expand on the suggestions below.

> lettuce or other fresh salad greens
> several of the following: raw or cooked green beans, sugar peas, asparagus spears or matchsticks of carrots or beets; chickpeas, fava beans, romano beans, cranberry beans, lentils or other cooked legume; shredded raw beets, carrots or zucchini; sliced avocado, cucumber, artichoke hearts or cooked potato; bean sprouts; tomato wedges or bite-size tomatoes; olives; capers
> 2 Labneh Makbus per serving (see recipe page 28)
> olive oil
> pepper
> balsamic or wine vinegar or salad dressing of choice

For each person, cover a flat salad plate with a bed of greens. Arrange separate piles of each chosen ingredient on the greens. Complete each plate with 2 Labneh Makbus.

Drizzle a little olive oil over the Labneh Makbus. Season the salads with pepper.

If desired, dress each salad lightly with additional olive oil and vinegar or a prepared dressing. Or serve the dressing on the side.

Makes 1 salad

> *2 LABNEH MAKBUS*: 21 CALORIES, <1 GM. FAT, <1 GM. SATURATED FAT, 2.5 GM. PROTEIN, 2.5 GM. CARBOHYDRATE, 60 MG. CALCIUM
>
> **NUTRITION FOR THE FINISHED SALAD DEPENDS ON THE VEGETABLES AND DRESSING**

RETRO NUEVO VEGETABLE SALAD

A fresh look at the mayonnaise-based salads popular in the 50s. This recipe is a good vehicle for using leftover cooked vegetables and should be made with a mixture of several. Those that work well include carrots, green peas, green beans, potatoes, sweet potatoes, celery, zucchini, corn, cauliflower, asparagus and even cooked dried beans.

⅓ cup YoChee
2 tablespoons mayonnaise
2 teaspoons prepared mustard
2 tablespoons chopped fresh parsley or dill
1 tablespoon chopped capers
2 cups cooked vegetables cut in ½-inch dice (see Vegetable Tips)

Combine all the ingredients except the vegetables to make a dressing. Mix the vegetables with the dressing until evenly coated. Chill until serving time.

Makes 2 cups; 4 servings

PER ½ CUP SERVING: 145 CALORIES, 6GM. FAT, <1GM. SATURATED FAT, 5.5GM. PROTEIN, 20GM. CARBOHYDRATE, 75MG. CALCIUM

Vegetable Tips

If leftovers aren't available, here are some options:

ꙮ Steam vegetables of choice until tender and dice.

ꙮ Pre-dice the selected vegetables, combine them with a small amount of water or broth in a tightly covered pot, and stew for 8 to 10 minutes or until tender.

ꙮ In either case, you can add any frozen vegetables during the last minute of cooking.

Let the vegetables cool before combining with the dressing.

TSATZIKI

The richness of YoChee is ideal for this time-honored Middle Eastern salad, which traditionally pairs yogurt, garlic, mint and cucumber.

> 1 cup YoChee
> 1 tablespoon lemon juice
> 1 clove garlic, minced
> 1 tablespoon chopped fresh mint or 1 teaspoon crushed dried mint
> ¼ teaspoon salt
> 1 cup thinly sliced or shredded cucumber, conserving any juices

In a serving bowl, use a fork to beat the YoChee, lemon juice, garlic, mint and salt together. Stir in the cucumber and any conserved juices. Mix well.

Makes 4 servings

> PER SERVING: 48 CALORIES, <1GM. FAT, <1GM. SATURATED FAT, 5.5GM. PROTEIN, 6.5GM. CARBOHYDRATE, 125MG. CALCIUM

INDIAN TOMATO & CUCUMBER SALAD

A refreshing accompaniment to Indian dinners.

> 1 cup YoChee
> 2 tablespoons lemon juice
> 1 to 2 teaspoons curry powder
> ½ teaspoon cumin
> ¼ teaspoon salt
> 1 cup chopped tomato, conserving any juices
> 1 cup chopped cucumber, conserving any juices
> ¼ cup chopped onion (preferably a sweet variety such as Vidalia, Texas sweet, Walla Walla)

In a serving bowl, use a fork to beat the YoChee, lemon juice and seasonings together to make a smooth dressing. Use the lesser amount of curry powder for a milder dressing, increasing according to potency and taste. Let the dressing sit for 5 minutes for flavors to meld. Adjust curry if necessary.

Add the tomato, cucumber, onion and any conserved juices. Mix the salad well.

Makes 4 to 6 servings

> PER SERVING, *BASED ON 4 SERVINGS*: 55 CALORIES, <1GM. FAT, <1GM. SATURATED FAT, 6GM. PROTEIN, 8GM. CARBOHYDRATE, 130MG. CALCIUM

Greek YoChee Squash

This somewhat unusual salad, prepared with YoChee cream rather than YoChee, is a good accompaniment to grains and beans.

> **2 cups shredded unpeeled zucchini (from an about 10-ounce squash)**
> ½ **teaspoon salt**
> ½ **teaspoon cumin seeds**
> ¾ **cup YoChee cream (see Quick YoChee Cream, below)**
> ½ **cup minced green pepper**
> ½ **tablespoon lemon juice**
> **olive oil, optional**

Mix the shredded zucchini with the salt. Place in a colander or strainer and drain for about 30 minutes. Squeeze to extract as much moisture as possible.

Meanwhile, toast the cumin seeds in a dry skillet until lightly colored and aromatic. Cool and grind with a mortar and pestle or pound with a rolling pin until fine.

In a serving bowl, combine the YoChee cream, drained squash, green pepper, lemon juice and ½ teaspoon of the freshly ground cumin. Sprinkle with the remaining cumin and chill until ready to serve. If desired, a little olive oil can be drizzled over the surface of the salad just before serving.

Makes 4 servings

Notes: Servings are relatively small, as this is rich-tasting and meant to be one of several dishes on the menu. Double the recipe for 6 larger servings.

Per serving: 52 calories, <1gm. fat, <1gm. saturated fat, 5gm. protein, 8.5gm. carbohydrate, 105mg. calcium

Quick YoChee Cream

YoChee cream is made by draining yogurt for only 4 hours. For this recipe, if you haven't already made the YoChee cream, you can place 1 cup of yogurt in your draining device and let it sit for 30 minutes while preparing the rest of the dish.

⏰ CLASSY CARROT SALAD

Those who are fond of sweet carrot salads will be impressed by this version.

- ½ cup YoChee
- 1 teaspoon honey
- 1 tablespoon lemon juice
- ¼ teaspoon cinnamon
- ⅓ cup crushed pineapple canned in unsweetened pineapple juice, lightly drained
- 3 tablespoons currants
- 2 cups shredded carrots (4 medium)

Combine the YoChee, honey, lemon juice and cinnamon. Stir in the drained crushed pineapple and currants. Add the carrots and mix well. Chill for at least 15 minutes for the flavors to marry.

Makes 2½ cups; 4 to 6 servings

PER SERVING, BASED ON 4 SERVINGS: 80 CALORIES, <1GM. FAT, <1GM. SATURATED FAT, 3.5GM. PROTEIN, 17GM. CARBOHYDRATE, 85MG. CALCIUM (SEE YOCHIEVEMENTS FOR COMPARISONS)

GINGER-BEET SALAD

Use freshly cooked or leftover beets for this slightly sweet and piquant salad.

- 2 cups sliced or diced cooked beets
- ¼ cup Creamy Ginger-Soy Dressing (see recipe page 246)
- 1 tablespoon toasted pumpkin seeds, pine nuts or walnuts, optional

Combine the beets with the dressing. Serve at once or refrigerate until needed. Just before serving, garnish with the toasted seeds or nuts if desired.

Makes 4 servings

PER SERVING: 95 CALORIES, 6GM. FAT, <1GM SATURATED FAT, 2GM. PROTEIN, 10GM. CARBOHYDRATE, 35MG. CALCIUM

Contemporary Waldorf Salad

This gently sweetened apple-celery-nut salad is an improvement on the original version in every way. Try to prepare it at least 15 minutes in advance for the flavors to marry. It can be prepared several hours ahead and refrigerated.

> 2 medium apples
> 1 tablespoon lemon juice
> 1/3 cup orange juice
> 2 stalks celery, chopped (¾ cup)
> ¼ cup chopped dates
> ¼ cup chopped pecans
> 1 teaspoon honey
> ½ cup YoChee

Peel the apples or not according to personal preference. Core and chop.

Combine the apples with the lemon juice and 1 tablespoon of the orange juice. Mix well to prevent browning. Add the celery, dates and pecans.

Beat the remaining orange juice and honey into the YoChee to make a smooth dressing. Pour over the salad ingredients. Mix well, cover and let sit for 15 minutes.

If made more than half an hour before serving, refrigerate.

Makes 4 cups; 4 generous servings

> PER 1-CUP SERVING: 160 CALORIES, 5.5GM. FAT, <1GM. SATURATED FAT, 4GM. PROTEIN, 27GM. CARBOHYDRATE, 80MG. CALCIUM (SEE YoCHIEVEMENTS FOR COMPARISONS)

CREAMY ORANGE VINAIGRETTE

This salad dressing doubles as a sauce for tempeh, tofu or fish. It is also the choice for Spicy Orange Coleslaw.

⅓ cup fresh orange juice
2 tablespoons balsamic or red wine vinegar
1 teaspoon finely minced orange peel, preferably organic
⅛ teaspoon salt
¼ cup YoChee
2 tablespoons flavorful oil, such as extra virgin olive, walnut, toasted pumpkin seed, hemp or flaxseed
cayenne, white or black pepper, optional

Combine the orange juice, vinegar, orange peel and salt in a bowl. Using a fork or wire whisk, beat in the YoChee until smooth. Gradually beat in the oil until the dressing is emulsified. Season to taste with a pinch of cayenne, white or black pepper.

Makes ⅔ cup

PER TABLESPOON: 35 CALORIES, 3GM. FAT, <1GM. SATURATED FAT, <1GM. PROTEIN, 2GM. CARBOHYDRATE, 15MG. CALCIUM

Dressing in Advance

For convenience, all of our dressings can be made ahead. In general, these and other dressings made with YoChee keep well in the refrigerator for about 5 days.

Thick & Creamy Blue Cheese Dressing

A luxurious dressing for green salads or for binding macaroni in cold pasta salads. It can also double as a dip.

½ cup YoChee
2 tablespoons mayonnaise
1 teaspoon prepared mustard
3 tablespoons lemon juice
2 tablespoons olive or canola oil
¼ cup crumbled blue cheese

Place the YoChee in a bowl. Using a fork or wire whisk, beat in the mayonnaise, mustard and lemon juice. When smooth, beat in the oil. Fold in the blue cheese.

Makes ⅔ cup

> Per tablespoon: 64 calories, 6 gm. fat, 1 gm. saturated fat, 2 gm. protein, 1 gm. carbohydrate, 40 mg. calcium (see YoChievements for comparisons)

 ### Creamy Ginger-Soy Dressing

Use on a salad of sturdy greens, such as coarsely chopped romaine, radicchio or endive.

¼ cup extra-virgin olive oil, alone or mixed with another flavorful oil such as walnut, hazelnut, toasted pumpkin seed or toasted sesame seed
¼ cup YoChee
2 tablespoons balsamic vinegar, raspberry vinegar, rice wine vinegar or another flavorful but gentle vinegar
⅓ cup water
1 teaspoon soy sauce
¼ teaspoon grated fresh ginger
1 teaspoon fruit-juice-sweetened orange marmalade

Using a fork or wire whisk, beat the oil into the YoChee. Gradually beat in the remaining ingredients until the dressing is creamy and emulsified.

Makes ⅔ cup

> Per tablespoon: 55 calories, 5.5 gm. fat, <1 gm. saturated fat, <1 gm. protein, 1 gm. carbohydrate, 15 mg. calcium

NoWorry
Savory Sauces & Toppings

Imagine no-fat or low-fat creamy sauces!

A flavorful sauce is a traditional culinary approach to turning simple foods into something memorable. Sauces, however, are frequently laden with fat, thereby spoiling an otherwise healthful dish. Consequently, this is a place where YoChee can really shine. It provides the basis for a sensible sauce or topping that complements foods nutritionally, as well as esthetically, as shown below in YoChievements.

No Worry

In general, one cup of sauce is enough for dressing four cups of food, or four to six servings. As a topping, two tablespoons are usually sufficient. However, some of these sauces and toppings are so modest in terms of calories and fat that you can comfortably exceed these recommendations.

Cooking Advantage

An exceptional quality of YoChee is that unlike yogurt, it doesn't curdle easily in a hot medium. This is a great asset when it comes to preparing cooked sauces.

Note than when cooking YoChee sauces, it is important to keep the heat very low and stir continuously. These sauces take only a few minutes to cook but require your constant attention.

More Sauce Options

In addition to the recipes here, you will find some quick topping ideas in "Starting Out with YoChee" (pages 21-25).

∾ YoChievements ∾

NoWorry Deluxe Potato Topping (pg.249) vs. sour cream
    45% less calories
    80% less fat
    3.5 times as much protein
    4.5 times as much calcium

NoWorry Creamy Mustard Dill Sauce (pg.249) vs. tartar sauce
    84% less calories
    no fat vs. 32 grams fat per ¼ cup
    5.5 grams protein vs. no protein per ¼ cup
    125 mg. calcium vs. no calcium per ¼ cup

Yo-Cheese Pesto (pg.250) vs. commercial pesto sauce
    40% less calories
    50% less fat
    Similar protein

Artichoke Cheese Sauce (pg.255) vs. standard cheese sauce recipe
    40% less calories
    70 % less fat
    35% more protein

NoWorry Deluxe Potato Topping

Mash this topping into a baked potato for superlative taste and excellent protein value.

> 1 cup YoChee
> ¼ cup grated Parmesan cheese
> 3 tablespoons minced scallions or chives
> salt
> pepper

Combine all ingredients, seasoning with salt and pepper to taste.

Makes 1 cup

> *Per ¼ cup*: 68 calories, 2gm. fat, 1gm. saturated fat, 7gm. protein, 5gm. carbohydrate, 185mg. calcium (see YoChievements for comparisons)

 ## NoWorry Creamy Mustard Dill Sauce

An excellent choice for topping such vegetables as carrots, broccoli, cauliflower, snow peas and green beans, as well as fish. Keep in mind that the character of the sauce has a lot to do with the caliber of the mustard used.

> 1 cup YoChee
> 2 tablespoons prepared mustard
> 1 tablespoon lemon juice
> 2 tablespoons fresh dill
> salt

Mix all the ingredients together, adding a touch of salt only if necessary.

Makes 1 generous cup

Note: This sauce can be used on hot or cold food, but it should not be heated.

> *Per ¼ cup*: 48 calories, <1gm. fat, <1gm. saturated fat, 5.5gm. protein, 6gm. carbohydrate, 125mg. calcium (see YoChievements for comparisons)

Serving and Storing

YoChee sauces and toppings that don't require cooking can be used at once, held at room temperature for about 1 hour or stored in the refrigerator for about 5 days. If they are refrigerated, take out long enough before serving to remove the chill.

Yo-Cheese Pesto

By using YoChee to replace some of the olive oil typically used to make pesto, you cut the fat in half and the calories by 40 percent without sacrificing protein or taste.

½ cup grated Parmesan cheese (2 ounces)
¼ cup pine nuts or pumpkin seeds
2 cups lightly packed fresh basil leaves or a mixture of basil and parsley
2 cloves garlic, chopped
¼ teaspoon salt
2 tablespoons olive oil
¼ cup YoChee

If the cheese is not grated, grate it in a food processor. Add the nuts and continue to process until finely ground. Add the herbs, garlic and salt. Process to a thick paste.

With the machine running, gradually add the oil and then the YoChee until the sauce is evenly blended and creamy.

Makes 1 cup

Per ¼ cup: 185 calories, 15gm. fat, 4gm. saturated fat, 9gm. protein, 4gm. carbohydrate, 240mg. calcium (see YoChievements for comparisons)

Creamy Walnut YoChee Pesto

Unlike classic pesto, which is drenched with oil, the only fat in this pesto comes from the walnuts.

¼ cup walnuts
2 cups lightly packed herbs or greens of choice, such as basil, parsley, arugula and spinach, individually or in combination
2 cloves garlic, chopped
¼ teaspoon salt
1 tablespoon light miso
¼ cup YoChee

Grind the walnuts in a food processor. Add the herbs or greens, garlic and salt. Puree to a thick paste. Add the miso and YoChee. Process once more to make a smooth, thick sauce.

Makes ¾ cup

Per 2 tablespoons: 104 calories, 8gm. fat, <1gm. saturated fat, 5gm. protein, 6gm. carbohydrate, 100mg. calcium

NoWorry Spicy Chickpea YoChee Pesto

This is the leanest of all our pesto recipes, and it packs a lot of protein for the calories.

2 tablespoons almonds
½ cup cooked chickpeas, drained
2 cups lightly packed fresh basil leaves or a mixture of basil and parsley
2 cloves garlic, chopped
¼ cup YoChee
½ teaspoon salt or to taste
¼ teaspoon hot pepper sauce or to taste

Toast the almonds in a dry skillet for a few minutes, until aromatic and lightly colored. This intensifies the flavor of the pesto, but can be omitted if you are in a hurry.

Grind the almonds to a fine meal in a food processor. Add the chickpeas and process until ground. Add the herbs and garlic. Puree to a thick paste. Add the YoChee and process until the pesto is evenly blended.

Season with salt and hot pepper sauce to make a highly seasoned sauce, keeping in mind that the flavor will be diluted when it is spread over other foods.

Makes 1 cup

Per ¼ cup: 78 calories, 3gm. fat, <1gm. saturated fat, 5gm. protein, 9gm. carbohydrate, 90mg. calcium

Pesto isn't Just for Pasta

Serve YoChee pestos in the following ways:

✔ Combine with pasta in the traditional manner.
✔ Mix into hot steamed vegetables or warm beans.
✔ Serve as a sauce on grilled vegetables.
✔ Use as a baked potato topping.
✔ Add a few spoonfuls to flavor soup.
✔ Spread on crackers or sandwiches.
✔ Spoon into raw mushroom caps.
✔ Garnish slices of tomato, cucumber or raw zucchini rounds.

Note: One cup of pesto is enough to dress 1½ to 2 pounds of pasta or vegetables, or 3 to 4 cups of beans. This will serve 4 as an entrée, or 6 as an accompaniment.

NoWorry Creamy Tomato Salsa

This fresh salsa is perfect for chips and dips or spicing up guacamole, beans, tacos, burritos, enchiladas, chile rellenos or other Mexican specialties. You may need to adjust the spiciness according to taste and the strength of your chili powder.

> 1 tablespoon olive oil
> 1 small onion, finely chopped
> 2 cloves garlic, finely chopped
> 2 tablespoons chili powder
> ½ teaspoon ground cumin
> 1 cup diced fresh or canned tomatoes
> ½ cup YoChee
> salt

Heat the oil in a small pot or skillet. Sauté the onion and garlic for 2 to 3 minutes, until wilted. Add the chili powder and cumin and cook briefly. Add the tomatoes, bring to a boil and simmer for 5 to 8 minutes to make a thick sauce.

Transfer the sauce to a bowl. Using a fork, beat in the YoChee.

Season with salt to taste.

Makes 1½ cups

Note: This salsa can be served immediately, while still warm. If made ahead, handle it like you would an uncooked YoChee sauce, following the instructions for Serving and Storing on page 249.

PER ¼ CUP: 55 CALORIES, 2.5GM. FAT, <1GM. SATURATED FAT, 2GM. PROTEIN, 5.5GM. CARBOHYDRATE, 50MG. CALCIUM

NoWorry Creamy Tomato Topping

An ideal topping for beans. Sprinkle a little chopped fresh parsley, cilantro or basil over all for appearance.

- ½ cup YoChee
- ¼ cup canned crushed tomatoes
- ¼ cup finely chopped rehydrated sun-dried tomatoes
- hot pepper sauce to taste

Combine the YoChee and tomatoes in a bowl. Mix until evenly blended. Add hot pepper sauce to taste.

Makes about ¾ cup

Note: To rehydrate sun-dried tomatoes, run quickly under cold water, then let sit for about 5 minutes to soften before chopping.

Per 2 tablespoons: 21 calories, <1 gm. fat, <1 gm. saturated fat, 2 gm. protein, 3 gm. carbohydrate, 45 mg. calcium

 ## NoWorry Tomato-Ginger Cream

A dollop completes any soup, especially one with a tomato or carrot base. This "cream" is also tasty on cooked asparagus, broccoli, carrots, cauliflower, fennel, black or white beans or other simply prepared vegetables.

- 6 tablespoons YoChee
- 2 tablespoons tomato juice
- 1 teaspoon orange juice
- 1 teaspoon grated fresh ginger or ¼ teaspoon ground dried ginger

Combine all the ingredients, beating with a fork until smooth.

Makes ½ cup

Per 2 tablespoons: 18 calories, <1 gm. fat, <1 gm. saturated fat, 2 gm. protein, 2.5 gm. carbohydrate, 45 mg. calcium

NoWorry Curry Topping

A flavorful topping for beans, grains, baked potatoes or steamed vegetables that is made with YoChee cream rather than YoChee.

1 teaspoon curry powder
½ cup YoChee cream (drain 4 hours or see Quick YoChee Cream, page 242)

Mix ½ teaspoon curry powder into the YoChee cream and let sit for 5 minutes. Taste. If not flavorful enough, add the remaining ½ teaspoon curry powder, mix and let sit at least 5 minutes longer before serving. If not used immediately, refrigerate.

Makes ½ cup

> **Per 2 tablespoons:** 23 calories, <1gm. fat, <1gm. saturated fat, 2.5gm. protein, 2.5gm. carbohydrate, 60mg. calcium

YoChee Aioli

This recipe is inspired by a French garlic-mayonnaise sauce called aioli. Perfect on broccoli, asparagus, green beans, carrots, potatoes, chickpeas or fish, or as dipping sauce for artichokes.

¼ cup lemon juice
2 cloves garlic, minced
1 cup YoChee
¼ cup vegetable broth or bean cooking liquid
1 tablespoon olive oil
¼ teaspoon salt or to taste

Combine the lemon juice and garlic in a small saucepan. Bring to a boil and cook for 3 to 5 minutes, until just 2 tablespoons remain. Remove from the heat and, using a wire whisk, beat in 1 tablespoon of the YoChee until it melts. Repeat with a second tablespoon of YoChee.

Return the pot to the lowest heat possible. Continue to add the YoChee, one tablespoon at a time, beating well after each addition until it melts.

When all the YoChee has been added and the sauce is warm, beat in the broth and olive oil. Add salt according to the saltiness of the liquid used and personal taste.

Serve while sauce is still warm

Makes 1 cup

> **Per ¼ cup:** 82 calories, 3.5gm. fat, <1gm. saturated fat, 5gm. protein, 7gm. carbohydrate, 120mg. calcium

Artichoke Cheese Sauce

A thick cream sauce meant to just coat the surface of hot pasta or vegetables. It can turn plain pasta into a gourmet dish, and is equally excellent over steamed cauliflower, broccoli, potatoes or even chickpeas.

> 14-ounce can artichoke hearts in water
> 1 cup YoChee
> ½ cup grated cheese of choice, such as Parmesan, provolone, cheddar, Monterey Jack, Swiss or other natural cheese, individually or mixed
> 2 tablespoons sun-dried tomatoes
> ⅛ teaspoon hot pepper sauce
> ¼ cup chopped parsley

Drain the artichoke hearts, reserving the liquid. Chop them into small pieces.

In a saucepan, combine the artichoke hearts with the remaining ingredients except for the parsley. Stir in 3 tablespoons of the reserved liquid. Place over the lowest heat your stove allows and cook, stirring continuously, for about 5 minutes, until the cheese melts and the sauce is hot. If needed, gradually stir in another tablespoon of the reserved liquid or water to create a sauce that is quite thick but not stiff. Do not boil.

When the sauce is hot and creamy, remove it from the heat and stir in the parsley.

To serve, combine the warm sauce with hot pasta or freshly steamed vegetables and mix gently until the sauce is evenly distributed.

Makes 2¼ cups

Note: The amount here is enough for 4 servings when combined with ¾ pound of pasta or a good size-head of cauliflower or 4 cups of cooked vegetables and/or chickpeas.

> Per generous ½ cup: 148 calories, 5gm. fat, 3gm. saturated fat, 11.5gm. protein, 13.5gm. carbohydrate, 225mg. calcium (See YoCheivements for comparisons)

YoChee Sauce Warning

When preparing cooked YoChee sauces, be sure to keep the heat very low and stir continuously. These sauces take only a few minutes to cook but require your constant attention.

NoWorry Roasted Red Pepper Sauce

Another sauce with enormous potential. We originally conceived this as a topping for grilled or roasted vegetables such as zucchini, eggplant, carrots, sweet potatoes, beets and portobello mushrooms. But we found it was also appealing on chickpeas, black beans, white beans and lentils. It would be tantalizing on simply prepared fish, too.

1 medium red pepper (4 to 6 ounces)
1 large clove raw garlic or 2 large cloves roasted garlic
2 tablespoons orange juice
¾ cup YoChee
¼ teaspoon salt
dash hot pepper sauce

Roast the red pepper over an open flame or in a 450° F. oven for about 30 minutes or until it is charred on all sides. When the skin is completely blistered, wrap the pepper in a clean kitchen towel to steam for a few minutes. When cool, peel off the skin using a small paring knife. Cut the pepper open and remove the seeds and any thick ribs. Cut into several pieces.

Combine the roasted pepper with the remaining ingredients in a blender or food processor. Puree until smooth and creamy. Adjust hot pepper sauce to taste.

Makes about 1 cup

Per ¼ cup: 46 calories, <1gm. fat, <1gm. saturated fat, 4gm. protein, 7gm. carbohydrate, 95mg. calcium

Service with Style

Spoon NoWorry Roasted Red Pepper Sauce over vegetables, beans or fish. Garnish with chopped parsley and walnut halves.

DESSERTS

     It is no secret that many desserts rely on butter, shortening, heavy cream, cream cheese and sour cream. The recipes in this chapter demonstrate the remarkable ability of YoChee to replace these typical high-fat ingredients.

     When used in frozen desserts and puddings, YoChee imparts a rich, smooth texture. In baked goods, it creates a tender crumb. In all cases, it adds notable protein and calcium.

     Our recipes are further enhanced by combining the YoChee with other wholesome ingredients, including whole grains and unrefined sweeteners.

✻ YoChievements ✻

Chocolate Mousse (pg.262) vs. conventional chocolate mousse
- 46% less calories
- 62% less fat
- 67% less saturated fat
- Similar protein
- 20% less calcium

Banana Pudding (pg.264) vs. banana pudding from boxed mix (using 2% milk)
- Similar calories
- 80% less fat
- 100% more protein
- 20% more calcium

more…

Fruit & Nut Fudge (pg.276) vs. typical chocolate-nut fudge
  25% less calories
  33% less fat
  35% less carbohydrate
  3 grams protein per 1-ounce vs. no significant protein
  100% more calcium

Creamy YoChee Brownies (pg.278) vs. typical cream cheese brownies
  33% less calories
  20% less fat

Custardy YoCheesecake (pg.289) vs. New York-style cheesecake
  60% less calories
  99% less fat
  Similar protein
  Similar carbohydrate
  100% more calcium

Frozen Whipped Strawberry Cream Pie (pg.294) vs. commercial "thaw and serve" pie
  47% less calories
  85% less fat
  200% more protein
  25% less carbohydrate
  200% more calcium

POACHED PEARS AND CREAM

Poached fruit in a delicate cream sauce is delicious served either warm or chilled. Peaches, as well as pears, are excellent prepared this way.

6 firm but ripe pears
1½ cups water
½ cup maple syrup
1 teaspoon vanilla extract
¾ cup YoChee
⅓ cup sliced toasted almonds

Quarter the pears from stem to blossom end and cut away the core. Slice each quarter lengthwise into 2 or 3 wedges, depending on size.

Combine the water, maple syrup and vanilla in a 2- to 3-quart pot or skillet large enough to hold the fruit. Bring to a boil. Add the pears and simmer gently for 20 minutes. If the pears are not completely covered with the syrup, turn them over. Continue to cook for 10 to 20 minutes longer or until the pears are spoon-tender. This will vary with the variety and ripeness.

Turn off the heat and transfer the fruit to a serving dish. Let the syrup cool for about 5 minutes.

Place the YoChee in a bowl. While the syrup is still warm, use a fork or wire whisk to gradually beat it into the YoChee until creamy .

Pour the sauce over the pears. Serve warm or chill. Garnish with the almonds just before serving.

Makes 6 to 8 servings

Variation: For Poached Peaches and Cream, use 8 peaches. Peel and slice into wedges. Simmer 15 to 20 minutes or until the peaches are tender but still hold their shape. Transfer the fruit to a serving dish. Continue to boil the syrup for 10 minutes or until slightly thickened and somewhat reduced. Proceed as above.

PER SERVING, BASED ON 6 SERVINGS: 223 CALORIES, 3.5 GM. FAT, <1 GM. SATURATED FAT, 4 GM. PROTEIN, 46.5 GM. CARBOHYDRATE, 110 MG. CALCIUM

Fresh Fruit with Raspberry Swirl

This dessert is as glamorous to behold as it is to eat.

> **12-ounce package frozen unsweetened raspberries**
> **3 to 4 tablespoons plus 1 teaspoon honey**
> **½ cup YoChee**
> **½ teaspoon vanilla extract**
> **6 large ripe peaches or nectarines or 2 ripe mangoes, peeled and sliced**
> **½ cup fresh blueberries**

In a food processor, combine the frozen raspberries with 3 tablespoons of the honey and process until completely pulverized. Taste and if not sweet enough, add another tablespoon of honey and process again.

Let the raspberry mixture sit until it is the consistency of a semi-frozen puree. If not assembling at once, refrigerate.

Combine the YoChee, the remaining teaspoon of honey and the vanilla in a bowl. Whip with a fork. If not assembling at once, refrigerate.

To prepare for service, reserve ¼ cup of the raspberry puree. Divide the remainder evenly among 6 dessert plates or shallow bowls. Dividing evenly, place 2 or 3 dollops of the sweetened YoChee on top of each portion of raspberry puree. Using a knife, swirl the YoChee into a decorative pattern.

Place an equal amount of the sliced fruit and blueberries on top of each dish of raspberry swirl. Top with a dollop of the remaining raspberry puree. Serve at once or refrigerate for later.

Makes 6 servings

> **Per serving**: 155 calories, <1gm. fat, <1gm. saturated fat, 3.5gm. protein, 37.5gm. carbohydrate, 60mg. calcium

SWEET MAPLE CREAM WITH BERRIES

A lovely fresh cream dessert that we like to serve in long-stemmed wine glasses to accentuate its elegance. Servings are intentionally small, as the combination is rich and it doesn't take much to satisfy. This is best made at least an hour ahead so it has a chance to set, and can be held a day or two in the refrigerator.

> 1 cup YoChee
> ½ cup sour cream
> 2 tablespoons maple syrup
> 2 teaspoons vanilla extract
> ¾ cup blueberries, raspberries, blackberries or sliced strawberries
> 2 tablespoons fruit-juice-sweetened berry preserves

In a bowl, combine the YoChee, sour cream, maple syrup and vanilla. Mix until creamy and completely blended.

Spoon into wine glasses or small custard cups. Refrigerate for at least 30 minutes before topping with fruit.

Mix the berries with the preserves until evenly combined. Let sit at least 5 minutes.

Spoon fruit on top of fresh cream mixture. Return to the refrigerator for at least 30 minutes before serving.

Makes 6 servings

> *PER SERVING*: 198 CALORIES, 3.5 GM. FAT, 2.5 GM. SATURATED FAT, 4 GM. PROTEIN, 13 GM. CARBOHYDRATE, 105 MG. CALCIUM

Sweet Maple Cream Variations

The fruit topping can be altered by replacing the berries with either orange sections, diced peaches or mango mixed with a complementary preserve.

Chocolate Mousse

Rich and elegant. The better the quality of the chocolate, the better the flavor of the dessert.

> **4 ounces semisweet chocolate (see Note)**
> **1 cup YoChee**
> **2 tablespoons orange juice**
> **1 teaspoon minced orange peel, preferably organic**

Melt the chocolate by cooking it in a double boiler or in a small heatproof bowl set in a pan of gently simmering water. Be careful not to let any water come in contact with the chocolate. If your stove has a very low heat setting, you can melt the chocolate directly over the heat, but be very careful not to scorch it.

When the chocolate is melted, transfer it to a bowl with the YoChee, using a rubber spatula to get all of it. Beat with a rotary or electric mixer or a wire whisk until the mixture is light and fluffy. Beat in the orange juice and the peel.

Spoon the mousse into small individual dishes. Eat at once or chill.

Makes 6 ¼-cup servings

Note: If you want to use semisweet chocolate chips for this recipe, you will need ½ cup plus 1 tablespoon.

> *Per serving*: 119 calories, 6gm. fat, 3gm. saturated fat, 4gm. protein, 15.5gm. carbohydrate, 80mg. calcium (see YoChievements for comparisons)

🕐 TORTONI

Tortoni is a frozen Italian dessert that is typically served in small paper cups.

> **2 cups YoChee**
> **⅓ cup honey**
> **1½ teaspoons almond extract**
> **2 tablespoons finely ground almonds**

Whip the YoChee, honey and almond extract together with a rotary or electric mixer until light and fluffy.

Line a muffin tin with 8 paper muffin cups. Spoon the YoChee mixture into the muffin cups. Sprinkle each with about 1 teaspoon of the ground almonds. Freeze.

When frozen, remove the tortoni-filled paper cups from the muffin tin and wrap in freezer proof wrapping. Return to the freezer.

To serve, remove from the freezer and let soften for 15 to 25 minutes at room temperature. At 15 minutes the tortoni will still be icy, becoming creamier as it sits. It is a matter of personal preference and, of course, if you eat it slowly you can have it both ways.

Makes 8 servings

> **PER SERVING**: 92 CALORIES, 1 GM. FAT, <1 GM. SATURATED FAT, 5.5 GM. PROTEIN, 17 GM. CARBOHYDRATE, 120 MG. CALCIUM

 BANANA PUDDING

The rich silkiness of the pudding is nicely contrasted by a garnish of either chopped walnuts, slivered toasted almonds or unsweetened shredded coconut.

> 2 ripe bananas
> 2 tablespoons orange juice
> 2 tablespoons honey
> 1 teaspoon vanilla extract
> 1½ cups YoChee
> chopped walnuts, slivered almonds or unsweetened shredded coconut, optional

Peel the bananas and break them into pieces. Puree in a blender or food processor with the orange juice, honey and vanilla. When smooth, add the YoChee and process until smooth and light.

Spoon into serving dishes. Eat at once or put in the refrigerator for later.

If desired, just before serving sprinkle some chopped walnuts, slivered almonds or unsweetened shredded coconut on each dish.

Makes 2 cups; 4 to 6 servings

Note: Although ½-cup servings are the usual portion, because of its richness, smaller servings may be adequate for some people.

Variation: For Mango Pudding, replace bananas with 1½ cups peeled diced mango, along with any pulp and juice you can scrape from the pit. Omit the orange juice.

PER ½ CUP SERVING, WITHOUT GARNISH: 157 CALORIES, <1GM. FAT, <1GM. SATURATED FAT, 8.5GM. PROTEIN, 31GM. CARBOHYDRATE, 180MG. CALCIUM (SEE YOCHIEVEMENTS FOR COMPARISONS)

SOFT-SERVE BANANA YOCHEE

This dessert involves preparing a simple fruit and YoChee base, which is frozen and later whipped in a food processor. It tastes best if you process it just before serving, producing a smooth and creamy soft-serve consistency.

> 2 ripe bananas
> 3 tablespoons orange juice
> 3 tablespoons honey
> 2 teaspoons almond extract
> 1½ cups YoChee

Peel the bananas and break them into pieces. Puree in a food processor or blender with the orange juice, honey and almond extract. When smooth, add the YoChee and process until smooth and light.

Transfer the mixture to shallow metal pan. Cover with foil. Freeze.

Just before serving, remove the frozen mixture from the pan and break it into chunks. Place in the food processor and process to the consistency of soft-serve ice cream.

Serve at once. Follow directions below for storing any uneaten portions.

Makes 2-plus cups; 4 to 6 servings

Variation: For Soft-Serve Mango YoChee, replace bananas with 1½ cups peeled diced mango, along with any pulp and juice you can scrape from the pit. Omit the orange juice and almond extract..

PER SERVING, BASED ON 4 SERVINGS: 170 CALORIES, <1GM. FAT, <1GM. SATURATED FAT, 8.5GM. PROTEIN, 35.5GM. CARBOHYDRATE, 180MG CALCIUM

Storing Soft-Serve YoChee

After the final processing, uneaten Sott-Serve YoChee can be packed into a container and frozen for future service.

✔ If frozen solid, let it stand at room temperature for about 10 minutes before serving to soften slightly. This mode of service will not be as creamy.

✔ If desired, you can break up the frozen portion and reprocess it just before serving to replicate the original consistency.

STRAWBERRY MAPLE FREEZE

The blending of YoChee with fruit produces a variety of flavorful frozen desserts. Using the formula below, try your hand with other fruits as well.

2 cups fresh strawberries
3 tablespoons fruit-juice-sweetened berry preserves
1 cup YoChee
½ teaspoon vanilla extract
1 to 2 tablespoons maple syrup

Combine the berries and preserves in a blender or food processor and puree.

Pour into a bowl and beat in the YoChee, vanilla and maple syrup until evenly combined. The amount of maple syrup needed will depend on the sweetness of the berries and individual taste; begin with 1 tablespoon and taste and adjust if needed.

Transfer the mixture to a shallow metal pan or freezer container. Cover with foil. Freeze for 2 to 3 hours, until firm.

Break the mixture into chunks and return it to the food processor. Process until smooth. This may require a little stopping and scraping the sides until the frozen YoChee begins to soften. Continue until the mixture is the consistency of soft-serve ice cream.

At this point you can eat the frozen YoChee or return it to a freezer container and freeze solid. If frozen, let sit at room temperature for 10 to 15 minutes before serving to soften slightly.

Makes 1 pint

Per ½ cup: 110 CALORIES, <1 GM. FAT, <1 GM. SATURATED FAT, 5.5 GM. PROTEIN, 21 GM. CARBOHYDRATE, 155 MG. CALCIUM

PINEAPPLE-ORANGE SHERBET

Very cool and refreshing. Plan ahead by freezing the pineapple at least 3 hours in advance. However, the pineapple can be stored in the freezer for as long as 3 months, so you can conveniently keep the makings of this quick dessert on hand.

> **20-ounce can crushed pineapple in unsweetened pineapple juice**
> **¼ cup frozen unsweetened orange juice concentrate**
> **¼-inch by 2-inch strip orange peel, preferably organic**
> **¾ cup YoChee**
> **1 tablespoon maple syrup or honey**

Remove the undrained pineapple from the can and transfer to a 1-pint freezer container (see Pineapple Pointer). Freeze until solid.

Shortly before serving, remove the frozen pineapple from the container. Using a cleaver or similarly heavy knife, cut it into large chunks.

Place the frozen pineapple chunks in the food processor. Add the orange juice concentrate, orange peel and YoChee. Process until the mixture is of sherbet consistency, stopping and scraping with a rubber spatula as needed. Add the sweetener and process to incorporate.

Serve at once.

Makes 3 cups; 6 servings

> PER ½ CUP: 97 CALORIES, <1GM. FAT, <1GM. SATURATED FAT, 4GM. PROTEIN, 20.5GM. CARBOHYDRATE, 80MG. CALCIUM

Pineapple Pointer

If there is too much pineapple for the container, reserve some of the fruit to make Classy Carrot Salad, page 243.

Apricot Almond Biscotti

Don't be put-off by the lengthy directions. Biscotti, which are double-baked lightly sweetened cookies, are easy to prepare once you have the knack of shaping and slicing the dough. They keep well, and their characteristic hard texture makes them perfect for dunking.

½ cup almonds (2½ ounces)
2 cups whole wheat flour
½ teaspoon baking powder
½ teaspoon baking soda
⅛ teaspoon salt
½ teaspoon ground ginger
½ cup dried apricots, cut in tiny pieces (3 ounces)
⅔ cup YoChee
⅔ cup honey
½ teaspoon almond extract

Preheat the oven to 350°F. Roast the almonds in a shallow pan in the oven for 5 to 8 minutes, until lightly colored. Shake the pan a few times during baking, being careful not to overcook. Remove from the oven, and when cool enough to handle, chop or slice.

Reduce the oven to 325°F. and position the rack so it is in the center. Cover a cookie sheet with aluminum foil, shiny side up.

In a large bowl, combine the flour, baking powder, baking soda, salt and ginger. Stir in the apricot pieces and chopped almonds.

In a separate bowl, beat together the YoChee, honey and almond extract. Add the YoChee mixture to the flour mixture and stir until the dry ingredients are completely moistened. When you can no longer mix it with a spoon or rubber spatula, knead gently with moist hands to form a ball of dough that holds together. Divide the dough in half.

Cover a work surface with waxed paper. Place one ball of dough on this surface. With moist hands, press the dough into a log that is 2½ inches wide, ½ inch high and 9 inches long. Make the ends of the log rounded.

Transfer the log of dough to the prepared cookie sheet and repeat the process with the remaining dough. Space the logs about 3 inches apart on the cookie sheet.

Bake for 30 minutes, until golden in color and firm to the touch. Remove the baked logs from the oven and reduce the heat to 275°F.

Immediately slide the foil onto a cutting board and carefully peel away from the baked logs. While they are still hot, cut the logs on the diagonal and at a slight angle into slices less than ½ inch thick. Do this using a serrated knife with a gentle sawing motion, holding the log in place with a clean dishtowel or potholder. This is a little tricky until you get used to it.

Lay the slices on a cut side, close together, on an unlined cookie sheet. If you need to use more than one cookie sheet, adjust the oven racks to divide the oven into thirds.

Return the cookies to the oven and bake them for 10 to 15 minutes, until the bottoms are just golden. Turn the cookies and put them back in the oven, reversing the cookie sheets if using more than one. Bake for 10 to 15 minutes longer, until both sides are lightly toasted. Do not overbake; the cookies will continue to harden as they cool. The timing will vary with the thickness of the cookies, the quality of the cookie sheet and whether there is more than one tray in the oven at a time.

Transfer the finished biscotti to a wire rack to cool completely before storing.

Makes about 30 cookies (yield may vary depending on how you slice the logs)

PER BISCOTTI: 75 CALORIES, 1 GM. FAT, <1 GM. SATURATED FAT, 2 GM. PROTEIN, 15 GM. CARBOHYDRATE, 20 MG. CALCIUM

Cutting Dried Fruit

A kitchen scissors is a handy tool for cutting dried fruit into small pieces.

Orange Walnut Biscotti

Similar to the previous biscotti recipe, this time flavored with orange and walnuts.

½ cup walnuts (2 ounces)
1¼ cups whole wheat flour
¾ cup cornmeal
½ teaspoon baking powder
½ teaspoon baking soda
⅛ teaspoon salt
2 tablespoons minced orange peel, preferably organic (see Orange Tips)
½ cup YoChee
¼ cup honey
¼ cup maple syrup
¼ cup orange juice

Preheat the oven to 350⁰F. Roast the walnuts in a shallow pan in the oven for about 5 minutes, until lightly colored. Shake the pan a few times during baking, being careful not to overcook. Remove from the oven and chop coarsely.

Reduce the oven to 325⁰F. and position the rack so it is in the center. Cover a cookie sheet with aluminum foil, shiny side up.

In a large bowl, combine the flour, cornmeal, baking powder, baking soda and salt. Stir in the orange peel and chopped walnuts.

In a separate bowl, beat together the YoChee, honey and orange juice. Add the YoChee mixture to the flour mixture and stir until the dry ingredients are completely moistened. If you cannot mix it thoroughly with a spoon or rubber spatula, knead gently with moist hands to form a ball of dough that holds together. Divide the dough in half.

Cover a work surface with waxed paper. Place half of the dough on this surface. With moist hands, press the dough into a log that is 2½ inches wide, ½ inch high and 9 inches long. Make the ends of the log rounded.

Transfer the log of dough to the prepared cookie sheet and repeat the process with the remaining dough. Space the logs about 3 inches apart on the cookie sheet.

Bake for 35 minutes, until golden in color and firm to the touch. Remove the baked logs from the oven and reduce the heat to 275⁰F.

Immediately slide the foil off the cookie sheet and carefully peel away from the baked logs. While they are still hot, cut the logs on the diagonal and at a slight angle into slices less than ½ inch thick. Do this using a serrated knife with a gentle sawing motion, holding the log in place with a clean dishtowel or potholder. This is a little tricky until you get used to it.

Lay the slices on a cut side, close together, on an unlined cookie sheet. If you need to use more than one cookie sheet, adjust the oven racks to divide the oven into thirds. Return the cookies to the oven and bake them for about 15 minutes, until the bottoms are just golden. Turn the cookies and put them back in the oven, reversing the cookie sheets if using more than one. Bake 10 to 15 minutes longer, until both sides are lightly toasted. Do not overbake; the cookies will continue to harden as they cool. The timing will vary with the thickness of the cookies, the quality of the cookie sheet and whether there is more than one tray in the oven at a time.

Transfer the finished biscotti to a wire rack to cool completely before storing.

Makes 32 cookies (yield may vary somewhat depending on how you slice the logs)

PER BISCOTTI: 63 CALORIES, 1 GM. FAT, <1 GM. SATURATED FAT, 1.5 GM. PROTEIN, 12.5 GM. CARBOHYDRATE, 15 MG. CALCIUM

Orange Tips

For the orange peel, take 1 large organic orange and use a vegetable peeler to remove a thin layer of peel. Mince. You should have about 2 tablespoons. Juice the orange and use ¼ cup for the recipe.

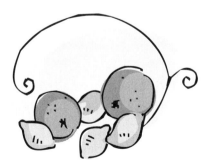

Orange Walnut Drops

These chewy drop cookies use the same ingredients as the preceding biscotti recipe but take less time to make and bake.

> 1¼ cups whole wheat flour
> ¾ cup cornmeal
> ½ teaspoon baking powder
> ½ teaspoon baking soda
> ⅛ teaspoon salt
> 2 tablespoons minced orange peel, preferably organic (see Orange Tips, preceding page)
> ½ cup coarsely chopped walnuts
> ½ cup YoChee
> ¼ cup honey
> ¼ cup maple syrup
> ¼ cup orange juice

Preheat the oven to 375°F.

In a large bowl, combine the flour, cornmeal, baking powder, baking soda and salt. Stir in the orange peel and chopped walnuts.

In a separate bowl, beat together the YoChee, honey, maple syrup and orange juice. Add to the flour mixture and stir until the dry ingredients are completely moistened.

Form the dough into 1½-inch balls, using about 1 tablespoon for each. Place on an oiled cookie sheet. Flatten each ball using the tines of a fork.

Bake for 12 to 15 minutes, until lightly colored. Transfer the cookies to a cooling rack as soon as they emerge from the oven.

Makes 32 cookies

> **Per cookie:** 63 calories, 1gm. fat, <1gm. saturated fat, 1.5gm. protein, 12.5gm. carbohydrate, 15mg. calcium

NUTTY YoCHEESECAKE BARS

A custardlike topping on a nut-crumb base. Best when chilled.

½ cup whole wheat flour
2 tablespoons ground flaxseeds
¼ teaspoon nutmeg
1 tablespoon maple syrup
2 tablespoons chopped walnuts or pecans
2 tablespoons chopped sunflower seeds
1 cup YoChee
1 egg
3 tablespoons honey
1 tablespoon orange or apple juice

Preheat the oven to 350⁰F. Oil an 8-inch-square baking pan.

In a mixing bowl, combine the flour, ground flaxseeds and nutmeg. Stir in the maple syrup and work together with your hands until crumbly. Add the chopped nuts and seeds. Press the mixture into the bottom of the prepared pan. Bake for 12 minutes.

Meanwhile, beat together the YoChee, egg, honey and juice.

Remove the pan from the oven. Use a rubber spatula to spread the YoChee mixture evenly over the partially baked crust. Return to the oven for 30 minutes, until the surface is just set.

Cool to room temperature, then chill for at least half an hour before serving.

To serve, cut into 12 bars, each 1 inch wide and 4 inches long. Store in the refrigerator.

Makes 12 1x4-inch bars

PER BAR: 82 CALORIES, 2.5 GM. FAT, <1 GM. SATURATED FAT, 3.5 GM. PROTEIN, 12 GM. CARBOHYDRATE, 50 MG. CALCIUM

Nutmeg Note

For a superior fresh flavor, purchase whole nutmeg and grate it yourself. Nutmeg graters with a compartment to store the nugget are available in housewares stores.

Rugelach

Rugelach are classic Eastern European cookies made by rolling pastry dough around a sweet filling. Two typical versions are presented here, one with a raisin-nut filling, the other flavored with fruit preserves.

> *Dough:*
> 1½ cups whole wheat pastry flour
> ½ teaspoon salt
> 2 teaspoons baking powder
> 2 tablespoons butter
> 2 tablespoons canola oil
> ⅓ cup honey
> ½ cup YoChee
> *Raisin-Nut Filling:*
> ⅓ cup chopped walnuts
> ½ cup chopped raisins
> 2 tablespoons wheat germ
> ¾ teaspoon cinnamon
> *Jam Filling:*
> 9 tablespoons high-quality fruit preserves
> *To Finish:*
> cinnamon

Combine the flour, salt and baking powder in a bowl. Cut in the butter with a pastry blender or wire whisk. When completely incorporated, do the same with the oil.

Stir the honey and YoChee into the flour. Mix as much as possible with a wooden spoon, then use your hands to knead the dough gently in the bowl to form a ball that holds together. Cover the bowl and refrigerate the dough for at least one hour.

Preheat the oven to 400°F.

Divide the dough into 3 balls. Working with one at a time, on a floured surface roll the dough from the center out to form a thin 9-inch round. Follow the directions below for filling.

For Raisin-Nut Rugelach: Cut each circle of dough into 8 wedges. Combine the filling ingredients and sprinkle some on each wedge. Roll up from the broad end to the tip to enclose the filling.

For Jam Rugelach: Spread 3 tablespoons of the preserves to cover each round of dough. Cut into 8 wedges. Roll up from the broad end to the tip to enclose the filling.

Place the filled rugelach on an ungreased baking sheet. Dust with cinnamon.

Bake for 12 to 15 minutes, until lightly browned. Transfer to a wire rack to cool.

Makes 24 rugelach

> **PER RAISIN-NUT RUGELACH**: 78 CALORIES, 3 GM. FAT, 1 GM. SATURATED FAT, 2 GM. PROTEIN, 11.5 GM. CARBOHYDRATE, 15 MG. CALCIUM
>
> **PER JAM RUGELACH**: 65 CALORIES, 2 GM. FAT, <1 GM. SATURATED FAT, 1 GM. PROTEIN, 11 GM. CARBOHYDRATE, 25 MG. CALCIUM

FRUIT & NUT FUDGE

A delicious, rich confection.

> ½ cup YoChee
> ¼ cup natural unsweetened, unsalted peanut butter (creamy or crunchy)
> ¼ cup honey
> 2 tablespoons unsweetened cocoa powder, carob powder or a mixture
> ½ teaspoon vanilla extract
> 1 to 1½ cups oats
> ¼ cup chopped dates
> 2 tablespoons chopped nuts

Mix the YoChee, peanut butter, honey, cocoa or carob powder and vanilla until evenly blended. Fold in 1 cup of the oats along with the dates and nuts. Add additional oats if needed to form a fairly stiff mixture.

Shape into a 4x8-inch rectangle on a waxed-paper- or foil-lined surface. Chill.

Cut into 1-inch pieces to serve. For keeping, wrap and store in the refrigerator.

Makes 16 1-inch pieces

Notes: Due to differences in the stiffness of YoChees and peanut butters, the amount of oats needed may vary. When shaping the fudge, wet your hands to make handling easier.

PER 1-INCH PIECE: 90 CALORIES, 3GM. FAT, <1GM. SATURATED FAT, 3GM. PROTEIN, 13GM. CARBOHYDRATE, 25MG. CALCIUM (SEE YOCHIEVEMENTS FOR COMPARISONS)

🕐 COCOA CHUNKS

Frozen snack cubes that you can pop in your mouth when the mood hits.

- **1 very ripe banana**
- **3 tablespoons YoChee**
- **1 tablespoon unsweetened cocoa or carob powder**
- **½ cup sunflower seeds**
- **2 tablespoons shredded unsweetened coconut**
- **1 cup crispy brown rice cereal**

Mash the banana with a potato masher or fork. Add the YoChee and mix until smooth. Add the cocoa or carob powder and stir until evenly distributed. Add the remaining ingredients and mix well.

Spoon the mixture into an ice cube tray or other small pan and place in the freezer for several hours to harden. Serve "ice cubes," or cut into squares when ready to eat.

Makes 14 to 18 cubes

PER CUBE, BASED ON 14 CUBES: 48 CALORIES, 2.5 GM. FAT, <1 GM. SATURATED FAT, 2 GM. PROTEIN, 5 GM. CARBOHYDRATE, 10 MG. CALCIUM

Creamy YoChee Brownies

YoChee does an excellent job of making brownies fudgy.

¾ cup whole wheat flour
¼ cup unsweetened cocoa powder
½ teaspoon baking powder
⅛ teaspoon baking soda
¼ teaspoon salt
½ cup chopped walnuts
⅔ cup YoChee
2 tablespoons canola oil
¼ cup maple syrup
¼ cup honey
1 teaspoon vanilla extract

Preheat the oven to 350°F. Oil an 8-inch-square baking pan.

Combine the flour, cocoa powder, baking powder, baking soda, salt and nuts in a bowl. Mix well.

Combine the YoChee, oil, maple syrup, honey and vanilla in a separate bowl. Beat until smooth.

Stir the YoChee mixture into the flour mixture until they are completely blended and no dry spots remain. Spread the batter into the prepared pan.

Bake for 20 to 25 minutes, until the brownies are still slightly soft in the center but a toothpick comes out clean. Do not overbake.

Let cool in the pan for 15 minutes before cutting.

Makes 16 small or 8 2-inch brownies

Per 2-inch brownie: 197 calories, 9gm. fat, 1gm. saturated fat, 5gm. protein, 28gm. carbohydrate, 80mg. calcium (see YoChievements for comparisons)

Double Chocolate Zucchini Cake with Variations

An especially tender and tasty cake. The zucchini version was eaten enthusiastically by an 11-year-old.

- 1¼ cups whole wheat pastry flour
- ⅓ cup unsweetened cocoa powder
- ½ teaspoon baking powder
- ½ teaspoon baking soda
- ¼ teaspoon salt
- 1¼ cups lightly packed shredded zucchini (from an about 6- ounce squash)
- ¼ cup canola oil
- ½ cup honey
- ½ cup YoChee
- ½ teaspoon vanilla extract
- ⅓ cup semisweet chocolate chips

Preheat the oven to 350°F. Oil an 8-inch-square baking pan.

Combine the dry ingredients in a mixing bowl. Stir in the zucchini.

In a separate bowl, beat together the oil, honey, YoChee and vanilla. Using a rubber spatula, fold this into the dry ingredients, mixing gently but thoroughly until the batter is evenly blended and there are no visible dry spots. The batter will be thick and resemble chocolate frosting.

Spread the batter into the prepared pan. Wet the rubber spatula to smooth the surface. Scatter the chips evenly over the top.

Bake for 30 minutes or until a toothpick inserted into the center of the cake comes out clean. Cool completely before serving.

Makes 8 servings

Per serving: 228 calories, 10gm. fat, 2gm. saturated fat, 4.5gm protein, 36gm. carbohydrate, 70mg. calcium

Variations on the Theme

For Double Carob Zucchini Cake, replace the cocoa powder with carob powder, or use a mixture. Use carob chips instead of chocolate chips.

For Double Chocolate Carrot Cake, replace the zucchini with 1¼ cups shredded carrots.

EASIER THAN PIE

This baked apple-pear pudding is "easier than pie" and just as tasty, but with far less fat and fewer calories. The proportion of pears and apples can be altered, so long as you have about 2¼ pounds total, or 6 cups thinly sliced. For best flavor, use some of each. As with pie, serve this warm or at room temperature, plain or with one of our NoWorry Whipped YoChees (see recipes page 301). Chill any leftovers and eat cold, or bring back to room temperature.

> 4 medium apples, peeled and thinly sliced
> 2 medium pears, peeled and thinly sliced
> ½ cup chopped walnuts
> 1 cup fresh whole wheat breadcrumbs
> 1 teaspoon cinnamon
> ¼ teaspoon nutmeg
> 1 cup YoChee
> 1 tablespoon lemon juice
> ⅓ cup honey
> 2 tablespoons maple syrup

Preheat the oven to 350°F. Oil a shallow 1½-quart baking dish or deep 10-inch pie pan.

In a large bowl, combine the apples, pears, walnuts, breadcrumbs, ¾ teaspoon of the cinnamon and the nutmeg.

Put the YoChee in a separate bowl and beat in the lemon juice, honey and maple syrup. Fold this into the fruit. Transfer the mixture to the prepared baking dish and sprinkle with the remaining ¼ teaspoon cinnamon.

Bake for 30 to 40 minutes or until the fruit is tender and the top is lightly colored.

Makes 6 to 8 servings

PER SERVING, BASED ON 6 SERVINGS: 285 CALORIES, 7.5GM. FAT, 1GM. SATURATED FAT, 7GM. PROTEIN, 53GM. CARBOHYDRATE, 115MG. CALCIUM

Easy Homemade Breadcrumbs

To make fresh breadcrumbs, take a slice of good-quality whole grain bread. Remove any thick, tough crust. Grate in a blender or food processor.

SKILLET PEAR COBBLER

A good brunch choice. If possible, serve while still warm, topped with NoWorry Whipped Almond YoChee (see recipe page 301). But even at room temperature, this is a tasty treat.

> 3 tablespoons canola oil
> 2 tablespoons maple syrup
> 2 tablespoons coarsely chopped walnuts or pecans
> 2 firm but ripe pears, peeled and thinly sliced
> 2 tablespoons honey
> ⅓ cup YoChee
> ¼ cup orange juice
> ⅔ cup whole wheat flour
> ⅓ cup cornmeal
> 2 tablespoons wheat germ
> 1 teaspoon baking powder
> ¼ teaspoon baking soda
> ⅛ teaspoon salt

Preheat the oven to 425°F.

Heat 1 tablespoon of the oil in a 10-inch ovenproof skillet or omelet pan. Add the maple syrup and cook for 1 minute, until the syrup is just warm. Remove from the heat. Scatter the nuts in the pan, then arrange the pears in a somewhat circular pattern, overlapping as needed to cover the bottom of the pan. Set aside.

Combine the honey, YoChee and orange juice.

In a separate bowl, combine the dry ingredients. Stir in the remaining 2 tablespoons oil and mix with a pastry blender, wire whisk or fork until completely incorporated and crumbly. Make a well in the center, pour in the YoChee mixture and stir gently until combined and no dry spots remain.

Drop the dough evenly by spoonfuls over the entire surface of the pears. Place the pan on a baking sheet and bake for 20 minutes, until the top is brown and a toothpick inserted into the center comes out clean.

Let cool on a rack for a few minutes, then run a knife around the edge of the pan and invert the cake onto a plate. Cut into wedges and serve will still warm.

Makes 6 to 8 servings

PER SERVING, BASED ON 6 SERVINGS: 240 CALORIES, 9.5GM. FAT, 1GM. SATURATED FAT, 5GM. PROTEIN, 37.5GM. CARBOHYDRATE, 100MG. CALCIUM

Very Berry Shortcakes

Each component of these fruit-topped cakes can be made either ahead of time or just prior to serving. The biscuit base can be served warm or at room temperature, or even put together and kept in the refrigerator for last-minute baking. If made in advance, both the fruit and topping should be refrigerated until just before assembly.

Sweet Biscuit Base:
⅔ cup whole wheat flour
⅓ cup cornmeal
2 tablespoons wheat germ
1 teaspoon baking powder
¼ teaspoon baking soda
2 tablespoons canola oil
2 tablespoons maple syrup or honey
½ cup YoChee
Fruit:
2½ cups sliced strawberries (about 1 pound or 1 dry pint)
¼ cup orange juice
1 tablespoon maple syrup or honey
1½ cups blueberries (about ½ pound or a little less than 1 dry pint)
Topping:
1 cup NoWorry Whipped YoChee or Orange YoChee (see recipes page 301)

Preheat the oven to 425°F.

For the biscuit base, combine the dry ingredients in a mixing bowl. Mix in the oil with a pastry blender, wire whisk or fork until completely incorporated.

Add the sweetener and YoChee. Mix until the ingredients are well blended, kneading gently with your hands at the end to form a ball of dough.

Oil a baking sheet or the removable bottom of a 9-inch tart pan. Pat the dough into an 8- to 9-inch circle, ¼ inch high. Using the tines of a fork, divide the dough into 6 pie-shaped wedges. Do not separate.

Bake for 15 minutes, until golden.

The fruit topping can be prepared while the biscuit base bakes or ahead of time. Combine 2 cups of the strawberries, the orange juice and sweetener in a blender or food processor. Process quickly to a coarse puree. Transfer to a bowl and stir in the blueberries and remaining ½ cup sliced strawberries. If prepared in advance, chill until serving time.

To serve, separate the big biscuit into 6 wedges. Split each wedge horizontally by piercing through the center with a fork. Lay soft side up on individual serving plates. Top with the fruit and a big dollop of the topping of choice.

Makes 6 servings

> *Per serving*: 246 calories, 6gm. fat, <1gm. saturated fat, 9gm. protein, 42gm. carbohydrate, 200mg. calcium

Maple-Pecan Apple Cake

Tender and flavorful. Top with NoWorry Whipped Almond YoChee or Whisky Cream Sauce (see recipes pages 301-302).

> ²⁄₃ cup YoChee
> 1 egg
> 2 tablespoons canola or walnut oil
> ¹⁄₃ cup plus 2 tablespoons maple syrup
> 2 medium apples
> 1½ cups whole wheat pastry flour
> 1 teaspoon baking powder
> ½ teaspoon baking soda
> ¼ teaspoon salt
> ¼ teaspoon nutmeg
> ¹⁄₃ cup chopped pecans

Preheat the oven to 350⁰F. Lightly oil an 8-inch-square or 9-inch-round baking pan.

Put the YoChee in a large bowl. Beat in the egg, oil and ¹⁄₃ cup of the maple syrup.

Peel the apples. Shred on a box grater or in a food processor; you should have about 1½ cups. Stir into the YoChee mixture.

Combine the flour, baking powder, baking soda, salt and nutmeg in a bowl. Add to the YoChee mixture. Stir gently but thoroughly until completely combined and no dry spots remain.

With a rubber spatula, scrape the batter into the prepared pan, spreading evenly. Sprinkle the pecans over the top. Drizzle evenly with the remaining 2 tablespoons maple syrup.

Bake for 40 to 45 minutes or until the cake is firm and a toothpick inserted into the center comes out clean. Serve warm or at room temperature.

Makes 6 to 8 servings

> *Per serving, based on 6 servings*: 280 calories, 10.5gm. fat, 1gm. saturated fat, 7gm. protein, 43gm. carbohydrate, 145mg. calcium

Fresh Fruit Coffeecake

A simple cake that takes advantage of seasonal fruit.

      1 cup YoChee
      2 tablespoons canola oil
      ⅓ cup honey
      1¼ cup whole wheat flour
      1 teaspoon baking powder
      ½ teaspoon baking soda
      ¼ teaspoon salt
      2 cups blueberries, or peeled sliced apples, pears, peaches or bananas
      ¼ teaspoon cinnamon
      2 tablespoons sliced almonds, Brazil nuts or hazelnuts
      3 tablespoons maple syrup
      1 tablespoon butter

Preheat the oven to 375°F. Oil an 8-inch-square baking pan.

In a large bowl, beat the YoChee with the oil and honey. Add the flour, baking powder, baking soda and salt. Mix gently but thoroughly to form a soft dough.

Pat the dough into the prepared pan. Arrange the fruit, overlapping slightly, on top of the dough. Sprinkle evenly with the cinnamon, scatter with the nuts, and drizzle the maple syrup over all. Dot with tiny pieces of the butter.

Bake for 45 minutes or until a toothpick inserted into the center comes out clean. Cool in the pan before cutting.

Makes 8 to 9 pieces

Per serving, based on 8 pieces: 219 calories, 6gm. fat, 1gm. saturated fat, 6gm. protein, 38gm. carbohydrate, 120mg. calcium

Cinnamon Streusel Coffeecake

This is truly the kind of dessert experience that the word "coffeecake" evokes, with its flavorful cinnamon-nut filling and sweet crunchy topping.

Cake:
1½ cups YoChee
3 tablespoons canola oil
6 tablespoons honey
2 cups whole wheat flour
2 teaspoons baking powder
½ teaspoon baking soda
Filling:
¼ cup raisins
⅓ cup chopped walnuts
2 tablespoons wheat germ
¼ teaspoon cinnamon
2 tablespoons maple syrup
Topping:
3 tablespoons maple syrup
2 tablespoons wheat germ
½ teaspoon cinnamon
1 tablespoon butter

Preheat the oven to 375°F. Oil an 8- or 9-inch-square baking pan.

In a large bowl, beat the YoChee with the oil and honey. Add the flour, baking powder and baking soda. Mix gently but thoroughly to form a soft dough. Pat half of the dough into the prepared pan.

For the filling, sprinkle the raisins, nuts, 2 tablespoons of wheat germ and ¼ teaspoon of cinnamon evenly over the dough. Drizzle with 2 tablespoons of maple syrup. Pat the remaining dough over the raisin-nut filling, spreading to cover. It may be easiest to do this using your fingers. Top the cake with the remaining 3 tablespoons of maple syrup, 2 tablespoons of wheat germ and ½ teaspoon of cinnamon. Dot with tiny pieces of the butter.

Bake for about minutes or until a toothpick inserted into the center comes out clean. Cool in the pan before cutting.

Makes 9 to 12 pieces

Per serving, *based on 9 servings*: 296 calories, 9.5gm. fat, 1.5gm. saturated fat, 9gm. protein, 48gm. carbohydrate, 180mg. calcium

BANANA CAKE

Cakes such as this, made without added shortening, tend to have a spongy texture that is a bit unusual. This rendition has a very nice flavor—silky banana with undertones of spices.

> 2 cups whole wheat pastry flour
> 1 teaspoon baking soda
> ¾ teaspoon baking powder
> ¼ teaspoon salt
> 1 teaspoon cinnamon
> ½ teaspoon nutmeg
> 2 eggs
> 2 medium bananas, mashed (1 cup)
> ¾ cup honey
> ¼ cup orange juice
> ½ cup YoChee
> 1 teaspoon vanilla extract

Preheat the oven to 350°F. Oil and flour a 9-inch tube pan.

Combine the dry ingredients in a mixing bowl.

In a separate bowl, using a wire whisk or rotary beater, beat the eggs. Then beat in the banana, honey, orange juice, YoChee and vanilla in that order, until smooth.

Pour the YoChee-banana mixture into the dry ingredients. Mix gently but thoroughly until the batter is evenly blended and there are no visible dry spots.

Pour the batter into the prepared pan. Bake for 45 minutes or until a toothpick inserted into the center of the cake comes out clean.

Let cool for 10 minutes. Remove from the pan and cool completely on a wire rack.

Makes 10 to 12 servings

PER SERVING, BASED ON *10* SERVINGS: 188 CALORIES, 1.5 GM. FAT, <1 GM. SATURATED FAT, 5 GM. PROTEIN, 42 GM. CARBOHYDRATE, 70 MG. CALCIUM

ZUCCHINI CAKE

Like the preceding Banana Cake, this too has no added shortening. The dense, wet, honey-cake consistency is different from traditional cakes, but people seem to enjoy it nonetheless.

2 cups whole wheat pastry flour
1 teaspoon baking soda
¾ teaspoon baking powder
¼ teaspoon salt
1 teaspoon cinnamon
½ teaspoon nutmeg
10 ounces zucchini, shredded (1½ cups)
2 eggs
1 cup honey
¼ cup orange juice
½ cup YoChee
1 teaspoon vanilla extract

Preheat the oven to 350°F. Oil and flour a 9-inch tube pan.

Combine the dry ingredients in a mixing bowl. Stir in the shredded zucchini.

In a separate bowl, using a wire whisk or rotary beater, beat the eggs. Then beat in the honey, orange juice, YoChee and vanilla in that order, until smooth.

Pour the YoChee mixture into the dry ingredients. Mix gently but thoroughly until the batter is evenly blended and there are no visible dry spots.

Pour the batter into the prepared pan. Bake for 45 minutes or until a toothpick inserted into the center of the cake comes out clean.

Let cool for 10 minutes. Remove from the pan and cool completely on a wire rack.

Makes 10 to 12 servings

PER SERVING, BASED ON 10 SERVINGS: 216 CALORIES, 1.5 GM. FAT, <1 GM. SATURATED FAT, 5 GM. PROTEIN, 49 GM. CARBOHYDRATE, 65 MG. CALCIUM

⏰ Custardy YoCheesecake

The texture of this easy-to-make dessert is a cross between cheesecake and baked custard. It has a very good flavor and a very professional appearance. Leave enough time to chill the cake for several hours before serving.

3 cups YoChee
3 eggs, separated
⅔ cup honey
2 tablespoons arrowroot or cornstarch
1 teaspoon vanilla extract

Preheat the oven to 325°F. Prepare a 9-inch springform or 9x1½-inch deep tart pan with a removable bottom by rubbing it with butter and dusting it with flour. If the pan has a tendency to leak, as many do, wrap the outside of the pan with foil.

Place the YoChee in a mixing bowl. With a rotary or electric beater, beat in the egg yolks, one at a time. Beat in the honey, starch and vanilla.

In a separate bowl, use a clean beater to beat the egg whites until they form soft peaks. Gently fold the beaten egg whites into the YoChee mixture until evenly blended.

Pour the batter into the prepared pan. Place the pan in the center of the oven.

Bake for 60 to 70 minutes, until the center is set and the surface is nicely colored. Turn the oven off, open the door and leave the cheesecake inside to cool slowly for 30 minutes. Remove the cake from the oven, cool to room temperature, then refrigerate for several hours, until well chilled.

Makes 8 to 10 servings

PER SERVING, BASED ON *10* SERVINGS: 187 CALORIES, 2 GM. FAT, <1 GM. SATURATED FAT, 10 GM. PROTEIN, 33 GM. CARBOHYDRATE, 185 MG. CALCIUM (SEE YOCHIEVEMENTS FOR COMPARISONS)

Berry Vanilla YoCheesecake

Drop small dollops of fruit-juice-sweetened cherry, raspberry, strawberry, boysenberry or similar preserves (about ¼ cup total) evenly over the top of the cheesecake before baking.

🕐 Pumpkin Pie

A cross between classic pumpkin pie and cheesecake. Serve plain or top with a NoWorry Whipped YoChee (see recipes page 301).

> 1 prebaked Ginger Snap Crust (opposite) or other 9-inch crust of choice
> 15-ounce can pumpkin puree (about 1¾ cups)
> ⅛ teaspoon salt
> 1 cup YoChee
> 1 egg
> ½ cup molasses
> 2 tablespoons maple syrup or honey
> 1 teaspoon cinnamon
> ½ teaspoon nutmeg
> ¼ teaspoon ginger
> ½ teaspoon vanilla extract

Preheat the oven to 350⁰F. (Of course, this will not be necessary if you are baking the crust while you prepare the filling.)

Place the pumpkin in a large bowl. With a fork or wire whisk, beat in the remaining ingredients in the order listed.

Pour the filling into the prebaked crust. Bake for 40 to 45 minutes, or until the filling is just set. Note that as the pie cools, the filling will become firmer.

Cool to room temperature before serving. If you prepare the pie more than several hours before eating, refrigerate once it has cooled.

Makes 8 servings

> PER SERVING: 226 CALORIES, 4GM. FAT, 1GM. SATURATED FAT, 6GM. PROTEIN, 52GM. CARBOHYDRATE, 145MG. CALCIUM

GINGER SNAP CRUST

1½ cups cookie crumbs made from ginger snaps (see below)
¼ cup wheat germ
4 to 5 tablespoons orange juice, apple juice or other pure fruit juice

Preheat the oven to 350°F.

Combine the cookie crumbs with the wheat germ. Stir in enough juice to keep the mixture together when pressed between your fingers.

Moisten your fingers with water and press the crumbs over the bottom and up the sides of a deep 9-inch pie pan. Bake for 10 minutes.

Remove from the oven and let cool for a few minutes before filling.

Makes 1 9-inch crust

> PER 9-INCH CRUST: 1155 CALORIES, 24GM. FAT, 5GM. SATURATED FAT, 17GM. PROTEIN, 207GM. CARBOHYDRATE, 190MG. CALCIUM

Snappy Ginger Crust Crumbs

We suggest using ginger snaps that don't contain hydrogenated shortening or artificial ingredients.

Prepare the crumbs by grinding about 34 cookies in a blender or food processor.

Fresh Fruit Tart with YoChee Filling

This elegant tart tastes as impressive as it looks. Be sure to begin well in advance, since it needs to chill for several hours. Assembly can take place as much as a day ahead.

Crust:
½ cup whole wheat flour
⅓ cup cornmeal
1 tablespoon ground flaxseeds
½ teaspoon baking powder
¼ teaspoon baking soda
2 tablespoons canola oil
¼ cup yogurt
1 tablespoon honey

YoChee Filling:
1½ cups YoChee
2 tablespoons honey
1 teaspoon vanilla extract

Fruit Glaze:
3 cups peeledsliced peaches or nectarines, strawberry halves, blueberries
   or raspberries, or a combination
2 tablespoons honey
1 tablespoon cornstarch or arrowroot
2 tablespoons lemon juice

To prepare the crust, preheat the oven to 425°F.

In a mixing bowl, combine the dry ingredients. Stir in the oil and mix with a pastry blender, wire whisk or fork until completely incorporated and crumbly. Stir in the yogurt and honey. Mix until all the ingredients are well-blended, kneading gently in the bowl with your hands at the end to form a ball of dough.

Oil a 9-inch tart pan or pie pan with a removable bottom. Press the dough over the bottom and up the sides of the pan to make a thin shell. Prick the surface liberally with a fork. Bake for 10 minutes, until golden. Cool before filling.

For the filling, use a fork to beat together the YoChee, honey and vanilla. Refrigerate if not used right away.

For the fruit glaze, place 1 cup of the fruit in a small saucepan and mash with a potato masher or fork. Add the honey, cornstarch or arrowroot and lemon juice. Set over low heat and cook, stirring continuously, until the mixture is thick and translucent and no longer has a milky appearance. Remove from the heat and let cool for a few minutes.

When the crust is at room temperature, fill it with the sweetened YoChee. Arrange the remaining 2 cups of fruit on top. Using a spoon, gently spread the glaze over the fruit to completely cover.

Chill for several hours before serving.

Makes 8 to 10 servings

> *PER SERVING, BASED ON 8 SERVINGS*: 188 CALORIES, 4GM. FAT, <1GM. SATURATED FAT, 6.5GM. PROTEIN, 33GM. CARBOHYDRATE, 135MG. CALCIUM

Frozen Whipped Strawberry Cream Pie

This frozen cream pie is nice to have on hand in the freezer for unexpected company. Note that it needs some time to defrost before serving. Some people like it at the partially frozen stage, in which case it needs to stand about 30 minutes at room temperature. Allow an hour for the pie to defrost to a soft, creamy texture. The pie can also be left in the refrigerator for a few hours to soften.

> 1 pint strawberries
> 2 tablespoons orange juice
> ¼ cup honey
> 1½ cups YoChee
> 1 baked 9-inch Chocolate Crumb Crust (opposite)

Wash the strawberries, remove the hulls and cut in quarters. Puree 1½ cups of the strawberries in a blender or food processor. Add the orange juice, honey and YoChee. Process until smooth and creamy. Taste for sweetening and adjust to taste; the amount of honey needed may vary with the sweetness of the berries.

Cut the remaining strawberries into small pieces. Fold them into the whipped strawberry YoChee. Spread this mixture into the baked crust. Cover with foil and freeze until firm, at least 2 to 3 hours.

To serve, let the pie stand at room temperature to soften to taste.

Makes 8 servings

Note: When the pie is completely frozen, overwrap in another layer of foil or a freezer bag. The taste is best when eaten within a month, but it can be held in the freezer for as long as 3 months.

Variation: For Frozen Whipped Banana Cream Pie, replace the strawberries with 2 bananas, pureeing them both for the filling and reducing the honey to 3 tablespoons.

Per serving: 175 calories, 2.5 gm. fat, <1 gm. saturated fat, 6.5 gm. protein, 33 gm. carbohydrate, 100 mg. calcium (see YoChievements for comparisons)

CHOCOLATE CRUMB CRUST

1¼ cups chocolate graham cracker crumbs (see Crumb Counsel)
¼ cup wheat germ
4 to 5 tablespoons orange juice

Preheat the oven to 350°F.

Combine the cookie crumbs with the wheat germ. Stir in just enough orange juice to keep the mixture together when pressed between your fingers.

Press the crumbs over the bottom and up the sides of a 9-inch pie pan. Bake for 10 minutes.

Remove from the oven and let cool to room temperature before filling.

Makes 1 9-inch crust

PER 9-INCH CRUST: 770 CALORIES, 18GM. FAT, 4GM. SATURATED FAT, 19GM. PROTEIN, 135GM. CARBOHYDRATE, 55MG. CALCIUM

Crumb Counsel

We suggest using a brand of cookies that doesn't contain any hydrogenated shortening or artificial ingredients.

To prepare the crumbs, grind about 9 full graham crackers (double squares) in a blender or food processor.

Cheese Danish

In the old-world tradition. Because this is made with a yeast dough that needs to rise, be sure to allow enough time.

Dough:
2¼ teaspoons active dry yeast
½ cup warm water
1 egg
¼ teaspoon salt
3 tablespoons honey
2 tablespoons oil
¼ cup nonfat dry milk powder
about 2 cups whole wheat flour
Filling:
¾ cup pot cheese or farmer cheese
½ cup YoChee
¼ cup honey
½ teaspoon vanilla extract
2 tablespoons chopped raisins
1 egg, separated
2 tablespoons slivered almonds

To prepare the dough, sprinkle the yeast over ¼ cup of the warm water and let it stand for 5 to 10 minutes until frothy. Stir to dissolve completely.

In a large bowl, beat the egg with the salt, 3 tablespoons of honey and the oil. Add the dissolved yeast, remaining warm water, milk powder and enough whole wheat flour to make a dough you can knead. Turn onto a floured surface and knead for about 10 minutes.

Place the dough in an oiled bowl, cover and let it rise in a warm spot for 1 to 1½ hours, until doubled.

Punch the dough down and roll it into an 8x16-inch rectangle. Cut into it into 8 4-inch squares.

Prepare the filling by combining the pot cheese or farmer cheese, YoChee, ¼ cup honey, vanilla, raisins and egg yolk. Mash together with a fork until evenly blended.

Place about 2 tablespoons of the filling in the center of each square of dough. Press or pull the dough gently with your hands to enlarge it a little as you work to cover the filling.

Bring the corners of the dough to the center of the filling. Where the edges come together, lift and pinch to seal (see illustration below). Leave a small opening in the center, but pinch the outside corners tightly to prevent leaking.

Shaping Danish

Place the danish on an oiled cookie sheet. Cover with a cloth and let rise in a warm spot for 30 to 40 minutes, until light.

Preheat the oven to 425°F.

If the edges of the dough have separated during rising, stretch and press them together again. As the dough rises in the oven, the danish will open, but if sealed beforehand, the filling will not leak out.

Beat the remaining egg white with a teaspoonful of water to loosen. Use this to paint the tops of the danish, including the exposed cheese center. Sprinkle the almonds over the open centers.

Bake for 12 to 15 minutes, until golden. Cool completely before serving.

Makes 8 danish

PER DANISH: 330 CALORIES, 13GM. FAT, 5.5GM. SATURATED FAT, 13.5GM. PROTEIN, 43GM. CARBOHYDRATE, 240MG. CALCIUM

NoWorry

Whipped YoChee & Dessert Toppings

With our NoWorry recipes there is little need to hold back when it comes to dessert toppings. Instead of high-fat whipped cream or chemical imitations, just top fruit or baked goods with one of these YoChee miracles.

In general, one-fourth cup is the suggested serving size. However, feel free to be more extravagant, since compared to conventional toppings, you get a good return of protein and calcium from a modest calorie investment, as shown in YoChievements.

You may want to adjust the sweetening in these recipes a little according to taste and use: On plain cakes, baked apples or tart fruit, a sweeter taste may be desired. For sweet pies and fruit desserts, a subdued topping makes a better contrast.

The other dessert toppings in this chapter, while a bit more caloric, still offer all the benefits of YoChee.

‷ YoChievements ‷

NoWorry Whipped YoChee (pg. 301) vs. lightly sweetened
    whipped cream
        50% less calories
        99% less fat
        5 times as much protein
        6 times as much calcium

more...

Chocolate Fudge Frosting and Filling (pg.303) vs. canned
chocolate fudge frosting
10% less calories
Similar fat
9 times as much protein
20% less carbohydrate
12 times as much calcium

Handling YoChee Toppings

All the toppings in this chapter can be used immediately after
preparation. But if not served within half an hour, refrigerate.

If the topping thickens on storage, beat it with a fork to lighten.

NoWorry Whipped YoChee

1 cup YoChee
1 tablespoon honey or maple syrup
1 teaspoon vanilla extract

Using a fork or wire whisk, beat the ingredients together until creamy.

Makes 1 cup

Per ¼ cup: 62 calories, <1gm. fat, <1gm. saturated fat, 5gm. protein, 9.5gm. carbohydrate, 120mg. calcium (see YoChievements for comparisons)

 ## NoWorry Whipped Almond YoChee

1 cup YoChee
1 tablespoon maple syrup
1 teaspoon almond extract

Using a fork or wire whisk, beat the ingredients together until creamy.

Makes 1 cup

Per ¼ cup: 55 calories, <1gm. fat, <1gm. saturated fat, 5gm. protein, 8gm. carbohydrate, 120mg. calcium

 ## NoWorry Whipped Orange YoChee

1 cup YoChee
2 tablespoons orange juice
2 to 3 teaspoons honey
½ teaspoon grated orange rind, preferably organic

Using a fork or wire whisk, beat the ingredients together until creamy.

Makes 1 cup

Per ¼ cup: 57 calories, <1gm. fat, <1gm. saturated fat, 5gm. protein, 9gm. carbohydrate, 120mg. calcium

WHISKEY CREAM SAUCE

A simple but impressive way to glamorize plain cakes or fruit pies. Note that because of the alcohol, the calorie content is a bit higher.

> **1 cup YoChee**
> **2 tablespoons Irish whiskey**
> **1 tablespoon honey**

Using a fork or wire whisk, beat the ingredients together until creamy.

Makes 1 cup

Variations: Replace the whisky with rum, cognac or Calvados

> *PER ¼ CUP:* 75 CALORIES, <1GM. FAT, <1GM. SATURATED FAT, 5GM. PROTEIN, 9GM. CARBOHYDRATE, 120MG. CALCIUM

COINTREAU CREAM

More genteel than the preceding hard-liquor version.

> **2 tablespoons cointreau**
> **1 cup YoChee**
> **½ to 1 tablespoon honey or maple syrup**

Using a fork or wire whisk, beat the liqueur into the YoChee until creamy. Add the sweetener according to personal taste and intended use.

Makes 1 cup

Variation: Replace the cointreau with amaretto, Grand Marnier, Kahlua or other sweet dessert liqueur.

> *PER ¼ CUP:* 79 CALORIES, <1GM. FAT, <1GM. SATURATED FAT, 5GM. PROTEIN, 11GM. CARBOHYDRATE, 120MG. CALCIUM

Cappuccino Spread/Dip/Filling

Use this spread on plain cake, cookies or biscotti, or as a dessert dip for strawberries, apple or pear slices or chunks of peaches or nectarines. It can also be used as the filling in a layered cake. Prepare in advance and refrigerate, if possible, to give the flavors a chance to blend.

> 1 cup YoChee
> 1 rounded tablespoon honey
> 1 tablespoon finely ground French roast or espresso coffee
> 2 teaspoons finely chopped semisweet chocolate
> ¼ teaspoon cinnamon
> pinch nutmeg

Mix all the ingredients together in a bowl. Best if chilled for at least 15 minutes before using.

Makes 1 cup

> PER 2 TABLESPOONS: 36 CALORIES, <1GM. FAT, <1GM. SATURATED FAT, 2.5GM. PROTEIN, 3GM. CARBOHYDRATE, 60MG. CALCIUM

Chocolate Fudge Frosting and Filling

Use to fill or frost plain cakes or cupcakes. Once frosted, be sure to refrigerate.

> ½ cup YoChee
> ¼ cup natural unsweetened, unsalted peanut butter (creamy or crunchy)
> ¼ cup honey
> 2 tablespoons unsweetened cocoa powder
> ½ teaspoon vanilla extract

Using a fork, beat all the ingredients together until evenly blended.

Makes ¾ cup

> PER 2 TABLESPOONS: 125 CALORIES, 5.5GM. FAT, 1GM. SATURATED FAT, 4.5GM. PROTEIN, 16.5GM. CARBOHYDRATE, 50MG. CALCIUM (SEE YOCHIEVEMENTS FOR COMPARISONS)

Index

YoChee Funnel This reusable and durable funnel sits comfortably on a glass or empty yogurt container. When done, the YoChee slides right out. Makes 1 cup YoChee from 2 cups yogurt. Dishwasher safe. *Material*: Polypropylene *Size*: 6½" high (funnel only)

Deluxe YoChee Maker This self-contained unit has a reservoir to hold drained liquid and a lid to provide a clean, sealed environment. Holds about 1 quart yogurt to make 2 cups YoChee. Dishwasher safe. *Material*: Plastic/Stainless steel mesh *Size*: 5x5x5"

THE ABC'S of FRUITS & VEGETABLES & BEYOND by Steve Charney & David Goldbeck. 112-page, full-color illustrated children's book introduces the alphabet via fun-filled poems, then moves beyond as children grow, with recipes, food facts, riddles, lore and more, all featuring fruits and vegetables.

AMERICAN WHOLEFOODS CUISINE: Over 1300 Meatless, Wholesome Recipes from Short Order to Gourmet by Nikki & David Goldbeck. A classic of contemporary vegetarian cooking, plus 100 pages of valuable kitchen information. 580 pages. More than 250,000 in print.

THE GOOD BREAKFAST BOOK by Nikki & David Goldbeck. 485 recipes to jumpstart the day. Quick weekday getaways to elegant brunches. Great for families.

HEALTHY HIGHWAYS: The Traveler's Guide to Healthy Eating by Nikki & David Goldbeck. State maps and local directions to 1,900 healthy eateries and natural food stores throughout the U.S. Bookbuyers have exclusive access to free online updates so listings are always current.

................ORDER VIA THE WEB, MAIL, FAX OR PHONE................

___ **Eat Well The YoChee Way** /Paper $18.95 .... $ _____

___ **The ABC's of Fruits & Vegetables & Beyond** /Paper $16.95 .... $ _____

___ **American Wholefoods Cuisine** /Paper $21.95/Hardcover, rare 1st ed, $100..... $ _____

___ **The Good Breakfast Book** /Paper $9.95 .... $ _____

___ **Healthy Highways**/Paper $18.95.. $ _____

___ **Deluxe YoChee Maker** $15.95 .... $ _____

___ **YoChee Funnel** $11 .... $ _____

 MERCHANDISE TOTAL .... $ _____

SHIPPING: First item $4.75, each additional item $2.25; Canada $8.25, plus $3.25 $ _____

NY SALES TAX (NY residents add local sales tax to merchandise AND shipping)........... $ _____

TOTAL ENCLOSED .... $ _____

Name _____ Address _____

State _____ Zip_____ Phone _____ Email _____

VISA/Mastercharge/American Express

Card # _____ — _____ — _____ —__ _____ Expires _____

Signature _____ Print Name _____

Orders must be accompanied by payment in U.S. funds or charged. Faxed credit card orders accepted. Checks payable to Ceres Press. **Questions?** Email CEM620@aol.com. For more books, free recipes, information, and online discounts, visit us on the web at **www.HealthyHighways.com**

CERES PRESS • PO Box 87 • Dept Y2 • Woodstock, NY 12498 • Phone/FAX 888-804-8848